Srimad Bhagavad Gita
Demystified!

Congratulations! I am absolutely thrilled! It's wonderful that "Bhaga-vad Gita Demystified" will finally be out for the public to read and enjoy. The demystification of Bhagavad Gita needed the insight of a scientist to draw the parallels between natural law and the Supreme Being. This is the underlying beauty of this translation. It is a very valuable insight and I feel privileged to have been a part of both the beginning and conclusion of this work.

Sheila Good M.A

"There are several commentaries by various authors on Bhagavad Gita out there but what sets Dr. Sankar Chakrabarti's volume apart from those is his explanation of Shlokas on the basis of well-estab-lished scientific principles. Dr. Chakrabharti is basically a scientist by training and spiritualist by desire. He is very well qualified in 'demystifying' Bhagavad Gita, both for a lay person and scientifically minded individual".

Dr. Bal Krishen Bhat

I just finished reading the five chapters you sent me. They are elegant with lucid commentary and beautiful poetry. I am privileged to be able to read them first and honored to write a foreword to this unique contribution by you to humanity.

Professor Subba Rao

"With his Scientific analytical background and an excellent under-standing of Sanskrit language it is no wonder that Dr. Sankar would come up with a beautiful demystified explanation of this ancient and yet eternally living scripture. The logic and science behind Sankar's arguments are clear and understandable. The poem in it is simple and lucid. It is no exaggeration that through this demystified narra-tion we all can clearly see the applicability of this scripture to our own Kurukshetras. "

E. B.Bhaskar
Engineering Manager, Hewlett Packard Co.

This book has filled a void in the lives of busy people who are in-trigued by the divinity of Krishna and provided classical interpreta-tions of the divine messages of in English literature. I, personally, enjoyed reading the book "Bhagavad Gita Demystified" and sincerely recommend this book to everyone to add positive mental energy to their purpose of life.

Avtar Krishan Handa, PhD
Professor of Molecular Genetics
Purdue University, West Lafayette. Indiana, USA

Srimad Bhagavad Gita

Demystified!

A Blueprint for a Life of Bliss

By Dr. Sankar Chakrabarti, Ph. D.

Hawkspring Publishing
Corvallis, Oregon USA

Hawkspring Publishing
Publisher since 2022
Corvallis, OR USA

Cover art by Ashis Mondal.

ISBN 978-1-958778-03-6 Print Version

Library of Congress Control Number: 2023901229

HSPub 2203-2023031013

In Memory Of

My Parents
Shanti and Madhusudan Chakrabarti

and

My In-Laws
Sushila and Vasudev Kombrabail

Contents

BOOK 1

Arjuna Vishada Yoga

Hero Swimming in Grief and Confusion

1

BOOK 2

Samkhya Yoga

Path to Bliss by Understanding Reality

9

BOOK 3

Karma Yoga

Work – A Path to Liberation

25

BOOK 4

Jnana Yoga

Path of Knowledge and Wisdom

33

BOOK 5

Karma-Sannyasa Yoga

Path of work-renunciation

43

BOOK 6

Abhyasa Yoga

Path of Practice

53

BOOK 7

Jnana-Vijnana Yoga

Path of Knowledge and Rational Discrimination

63

i

Foreward
*by Dr. Subbarao Bondada**

It is a great honor to write this foreword to a unique interpretation and beautiful poetic translation of the *Bhagavad Gita* by my dear friend, Dr. Sankarlal Chakrabarti. I first met Dr. Chakrabarti when he was my senior and a uniquely talented molecular biology researcher in graduate school at the Tata Institute of Fundamental Research, Mumbai, India. At that time, I knew him to be a philosopher and a man of intellect, but I was not aware of his mastery of the Sanskrit language and Hindu classics. This was revealed to me when he visited us in Lexington, Kentucky about a decade ago when he participated in our Sadhana group's reading of the *Bhagavad Gita*. We were learning the verse

> *"sarvasya chāhaṁ hṛidi sanniviṣṭo*
> *mattaḥ smṛitir jñānam apohanaṁ cha*
> *vedaiśh cha sarvair aham eva vedyo*
> *vedānta-kṛid veda-vid eva chāham"*

which is the 15th verse of the 15th chapter of the *Bhagavad Gita*.

Sankar explained to us how both memory and its loss can come from the divine. Later I learned that Sankar was inspired and decided to undertake this particular project of trying to put the *Bhagavad Gita's* message in the context of the "laws of nature" for the benefit of present and future generations. He also decided to translate each verse of Bhagavad Gita into English as well as Bengali, his native language. Thus arose the present work, *Srimad Bhagavad Gita, Demystified*.

The readers of this work may already be aware that Bhagavad Gita is probably the most well-known Hindu religious text in the world. It has been translated into many languages and commented upon by many scholars through the millennia. The Bhagavad Gita, along with the Upanishads and Brahma Sutras, is one of the three texts of Hinduism called Prasthanatrayam. The Upanishads provide the philosophical basis of Atman (individual consciousness), Brahman (universal consciousness or divine) and reincarnation, the three tenets of Hinduism. The Brahma Sutras provide explanations of the upanishadic philosophy, also known as Vedanta.

The *Bhagavad Gita* provides the essence of *Upanishads* in the context of day-to-day life, especially how one can live a peaceful life while performing daily duties and attain salvation. It is provided in the context

---

* Dr. Subbarao Bondada is a Professor in the Department of Microbiology, Immunology and Molecular Genetics at the University Of Kentucky Medical Center, Lexington, KY.

of the dilemma of Arjuna, the hero of *The Mahabharata*, the great epic, to fight or not against his teachers and close relatives in a fratricidal war. The advice to Arjuna is given by none other than the divine incarnation, Lord Krishna, in the battlefield called Kurukshetra. He was to lead the Pandava army against the armies of the Kauravas, his cousins. Arjuna becomes overcome with grief at the thought of killing his elders and relatives, drops his bow and sits down in the chariot asking for guidance from Lord Krishna. The Bhagavad Gita is presented as Lord Krishna's answers to several questions by Arjuna which could have been asked by anyone who wants to know how to respond in difficult situations and how to live a life of fulfilment.

Just as a song can be sung beautifully in different tunes, the song of God, has had many poetic renderings. Sankar's poetic translation of Bhagavad Gita gives a unique context and perspective. My comments will be limited to the English version as I am not familiar with the Bengali language.

The beauty of the Bhagavad Gita is that many different scholars have been able to interpret its context to support diverse philosophies. The three great Acharyas of India are Sri Sankara, Sri Ramanuja and Sri Madhva, respectively the founders of three distinct schools of Hindu philosophy, Advaita (identity of Atman and Brahman), Visishtadvaita (dual nature of Atman and Brahman with merging of Atman into Brahman upon enlightenment) and Dvaita (permanent duality of Atman and Brahman). Each wrote their own commentaries on the Bhagavad Gita and were able to find strong support for their diverse philosophies in the Bhagavad Gita. Sankar's poetic translation of the *Bhagavad Gita* adds to this rich tradition with a different context.

An understanding of the Bhagavad Gita involves understanding the divinity of Lord Krishna as He explains the nature of Brahman, diversity in human beings, and how to conduct oneself in life. In the religious context Lord Krishna is perceived as the ultimate God/Divine, while in certain philosophies He is considered the Brahman or universal Consciousness. In this unique interpretation, *Bhagavad Gita Demystified*, Sankar explains the divine as natural laws which have no beginning or end and have to be discovered by humanity. For example, the force of gravity has been present since the beginning of the universe with no end in sight but understood only after Sir Isaac Newton's discoveries. All life forms come to being through natural laws which remain even after the death of those same beings. Sankar interprets the *Bhagavad Gita*'s teachings as the idea that performing actions according to natural laws is one and the same as actions done for the grace of the ultimate God. He emphasizes the idea of karma yoga, which is action without seeking the fruits of those actions, much like many sages and seers including Swami Vivekananda, the great philosopher who brought Hinduism to Western world.

In Sankar's interpretation of the *Bhagavad Gita*, human beings are divided into four types (varnas) according to their "gunas" (translated by Sankar as mental propensities or attitudes) but not according to their birth, a point also made by many modern commentators of the *Bhagavad Gita*. Individual's behaviors are divided into three types of gunas: *satva* (equanimity, goodness, self-less), *rajas* (passionate activity with deep interest in the results), and *tamas* (dullness, ignorance). Every individual is thought to have these three gunas in different proportions. Sankar's commentary nicely elucidates how these three gunas lead to four kinds of people labelled as brahmins (intellectual class), kshatriyas (warrior and ruling class), vysyas (agriculture and trading class) and sudras (work to support others), who together further the broader interests of society. He makes the point that the same four archetypes are present in all societies working for the welfare of the society as a whole, though they may not have the same names as in India. Sankar emphasizes that *Bhagavad Gita* does not propose classification of varnas by birth but by the combinations of the three gunas in each individual.

Sankar's special insight into *Bhagavad Gita* is also revealed in his commentary of Chapter 11, Vishwa-roopa-darshana Yoga, which is normally translated as a vision of the form of the universe. For an ordinary person, it is difficult to imagine the divine form described in this chapter, and indeed, Lord Krishna gives divine eyes to Arjuna to have this vision. Sankar titles this chapter "Path to the Divine Realizing the Big Picture View of the World." He surmises that "understanding of the big picture makes a person more and more aware of the fundamental truths about reality, which brings the individual closer to the Divine, who is the Truth in reality." According to him it is the intellectual eye (jnana nethra) that provides the big picture view to people.

Sankar's wisdom and exclusive perspective of equating faith in God with faith in the natural law is nowhere more evident than in his translation of the most beautiful verse of *Bhagavad Gita*, verse 66 in the 18th chapter. Lord Krishna says:

*"sarva-dharmān parityajya mām ekaṁ śharaṇaṁ vraja
ahaṁ tvāṁ sarva-pāpebhyo mokṣhayiṣhyāmi mā śhuchaḥ"*

for which Sankar provides a wonderful translation in a poetic form.

*Abandoning all other "dharma";
Take shelter in Me, in Me alone;
I shall cause you to be released;
From all sins, you ought never mourn; ||*

Sankar explains that the release of a person from anxiety and unhappiness is possible through complete faith in "Me (Lord Krishna)", equating "Me" with the laws of the universe.

Bhagavad Gita, Demystified and its unique intellectual interpretation will stand alone among the myriad commentaries and translations of this central text of Hinduism, and enhances our understanding of the relationship between the divine and the nature. It is my sincere belief that present and future generations will benefit from its guidance.

Foreward by Jaidev Dasgupta, Ph.D.*

Man has always been intrigued by the question of how to live. "*What is the best way of living?*" And life, being a sequence of actions, gives rise to questions: "how do I act?", "what is right action?", and "what is my purpose? Through theological and philosophical reasonings different traditions reach different solutions to these questions. The *Bhagavad Gita*, or the *Gita*, as it is usually referred to in India, is one of those few books in the world that imparts that knowledge. It is the quintessential wisdom of Hinduism that has evolved from the ancient Brahminic religion.

Set in the context of an impending war between two sets of cousins for the kingdom of Kurukshetra, the *Bhagavad Gita* is a poem of 700 verses. It deliberates on whether to kill or not, and under what conditions such a heinous act is justifiable or even advisable. And through this deliberation – a dialogue between Arjuna and his friend god Krishna – answers surface to address the age-old questions: "Where do I come from?", "Who am I?" and "Where am I going?"

Right before the battle, the mighty warrior Arjuna - one of the five Pandava brothers facing an array of equally powerful fighters in support of their cousins, the Kauravas - is dejected and having second thoughts like "Why fight?" "Why kill kinsmen, elders and teachers who deserve love and respect?" "Will such an act not create disorder and chaos in society?" It is for Krishna to lift the clouds of doubt that have descended on his warrior friend at this crucial moment, and prepare him for the battle. Krishna says: A person is an embodied self. This self never dies, is unborn, cannot be killed or destroyed. What exists cannot cease to exist, and what is nonexistent cannot come into existence. This self is eternal, immovable, all-pervading and unmanifest. Creatures are unmanifest before birth, manifest out of it and abide in it during life, and, finally, dissolve back into it. The self persists forever. Hence, the impressions of someone killing someone or someone being killed by someone are wrong. Thus, Arjuna should perform his sacred duty by fighting with strong resolve and mind detached from the dualities of life and death, victory and defeat, pleasure and pain. Since the cycle of birth and death is inevitable, there is no reason to grieve the loss of others. The goal is to perform actions with a mind impartial to the fruits of action. Relinquishing attachment to results of

---

* Jaidev Dasgupta has been a scientist, entrepreneur, and a social-worker. He writes on Indian culture, history and philosophy. Jaidev authored the book In Search of Immortality: An Introduction to Indic World-Views.

action creates a disciplined mind with equanimity. Content with the self within himself, suffering does not disturb such a man, nor does he crave pleasure. Attachment, fear and anger leave him. Self-control beyond hatred and attraction brings serenity, peace and joy. Renunciation of all desires and acts without craving, possessiveness and personality frees man from delusion and brings him to the infinite spirit with pure calm and bliss.

Seeking bliss and liberation from the *samsara* – the perpetual cycle of birth and death – is the goal of life in traditional Indian thought. Toward this end, certain schools of thought believe in renouncing the world that ties man into action and the *samsara*. Digressing from all such views, the *Bhagavad Gita* asks man not to renounce action, but to renounce *attachment* to the fruits of action. It offers three paths – one of knowledge, one of action and one of devotion – to discipline the mind for dispassionate action.

On the battlefield, Krishna assumes the role of a teacher, patiently answering question after question raised by Arjuna. To remove all doubts from his friend's mind and assure him of the veracity of the knowledge imparted, Krishna grants Arjuna divine eyes to see the ultimate reality and reveals his own eternal cosmic form, the *vishvarupa*. Thus consoled, instructed, enlightened and convinced, armed with knowledge and discipline, Arjuna decides to fight the enemy. The *Gita* thus establishes that the truth about life can be reached through rational means; there is no room for blind faith. Even God can be questioned!

Many scholars, thinkers, theologians and philosophers have translated, interpreted and written commentaries on the *Bhagavad Gita*. Where Dr. Sankar Chakrabarti's *Bhagavad Gita Demystified* stands apart from such efforts is his approach to understanding this deep and condensed book of knowledge. He posits that the *Gita* isn't about religious doctrine. Rather, it has a scientific basis by knowing which one can build a happy, fulfilling and successful life free of stress or anxiety – which he considers is the divine life. All it takes is to understand the true nature of reality. By not understanding or by defying reality one cannot expect to be happy. In this sense, the message of the *Bhagavad Gita* is universal: it is relevant to all in every age and culture.

The most striking departure Chakrabarti makes from other efforts to understand the *Gita* is his interpretation of *purusha* as natural laws, rather than a soul or the seat of consciousness. According to the Samkhya, a dualistic Indic philosophy, *prakriti* (matter) and *purusha* (soul) are the two building blocks of the world. Being fundamentally different substances, these two do not interact physically. Only when *prakriti* is in the vicinity of *purusha*, does it evolve into 23 different categories such as intellect, mind, ego, and so on. As matter and the laws, it follows are not two separate entities, with *purusha* as natural laws the *Bhagavad Gita Demystified* collapses the matter-soul dualism of Samkhya into a monism in which matter alone (with inherent natural laws) is the underlying reality of the world. At the same time, it retains the three mental qualities – *sattva* (placid, pure), *rajas* (active, aggressive), and *tamas* (dark inertia, destructive) – as part of the material matrix. *Prakriti*, in the Samkhya, is not exactly what we moderns understand by matter; it consists of mental dispositions that are necessary to understand the true nature of reality. This material reality is eternal, has no beginning or end, is indestructible, and hence is supreme and divine. God, according to Chakrabarti, is the deification of this reality beyond which nothing exists.

In other words, personal gods are only a construct: Vishnu, Shiva, Devi and other gods and goddesses are individual masks through which specific aspects of ultimate reality are exposed and act as interfaces between humans and this reality. Krishna himself is one such mask which becomes abundantly clear upon revealing his cosmic form to Arjuna. Therein also lies the need for a personal god and the root of bhakti or devotion to that form: Arjuna, though exhilarated by the vision of the cosmic form of Krishna, is unable to bear the sight for long and begs Krishna to revert back to his pleasant personal form of the friend to whom he can relate.

Through his lens of fundamental reality in the *Gita*, Chakrabarti takes a fresh look at Krishna's teachings to Arjuna on the battlefield. He goes behind the verses in Sanskrit and the symbols which originate in ancient Indian culture, to reveal their meaning and significance in simple English. He patiently describes and explains the discourse between Arjuna and Krishna to the modern reader, who may be secular in belief or may not be acquainted with Indian religious philosophy.

The *Bhagavad Gita* is a deceptively simple book. Even a casual reader may get the sense of understanding it. However, since it presents Indic thoughts of a few millennia in a concise form, set in the context of the Hindu view of life, returning to the *Gita* multiple times becomes necessary to grasp it in totality. The concepts of infinite spirit, atman, karma, nishkam, renunciation, sthitaprajna, and many others require full understanding to appreciate the message of the epic poem. This is where *Bhagavad Gita Demystified* expends significant effort to elucidate these concepts, preparing the modern mind to receive the ancient message. Reading the commentaries, not only the translated verses, is of utmost importance to understand the author's views.

At times, readers may find themselves questioning Chakrabarti's views – for example, that modern science and western philosophy in the "Age of Enlightenment" are really a recapture and restatement of the philosophy enunciated in the *Bhagavad Gita*. To enjoy and absorb the wisdom of this book, one may benefit from suspending these reservations, allowing some leeway to the author who has spent years reading, contemplating, translating and interpreting the *Gita*, and hence is thoroughly imbued with its narrative.

Bhagavad Gita Demystified, in addition to being a new interpretation, offers masterful rendering of the Sanskrit verses in English, maintaining their original poetic beauty. This too is a mark of originality of Sankar Chakrabarti. Many good translations of the *Gita* are available, but to achieve translation, and maintaining lucidity while keeping many original phrases – which bring the reader closer to the *Bhagavad Gita* in Sanskrit – is rare. Here is verse 11.6, for example:

> *Pashyādityānvasunrudrānashvino marutastathā I*
> *Bahunyadrshtpurvānni pashyāshcharyānṇi bhārata II   (Bhagavad Gita)*
>
> *See the Adityas, the Basu-s, the Rudra-s;*
> *see the Asvins as well as all the Maruta-s |*
>
> *Many wonders not seen by any one in past-a;*
> *behold them too, Oh the prince of Bharatha || (Bhagavad Gita Demystified)*

The terms and names such as Aditya, Basu, Rudra, Maruta, Asvins, Purushottam, Sri Hari, Vasudeva, Maha-baho, Kaunteya are all explained in a glossary.

Thus, *Bhagavad Gita Demystified* not only engages its readers through beautiful translation but also enriches the experience through the glossary, commentaries, and "Looking Aheads" which lay out in advance what to expect in the next part.

Translating and interpreting an ancient text – that has been widely read in many languages and interpreted multiple times over the centuries – and making it relevant to modern times is a daunting task. Chakrabarti, with his in-depth knowledge of the content and the language of the text, his understanding of the Hindu world-view, and a clear idea of what he wishes to accomplish, has successfully achieved the goal. To be benefited fully from this effort, I urge the readers to go through the book attentively.

Finally, as the narrative is set against the backdrop of an imminent war, it would be wrong to assume that the *Gita* is a wartime philosophy, applicable only in times of emergency. That context is a metaphor for the sense of immediacy in life. We can't postpone living, put aside our life and decide to take care of it when we are back from vacation, because even on vacation life continues; it requires alertness, awareness, mindfulness, and discipline of mind. The *Bhagavad Gita* is about life and taking charge of it with a deep sense of responsibility and duty toward oneself and the world. Nothing is more gratifying and fulfilling than engaging and working with one's own life, creating meaning and purpose, evolving in oneself and thus also changing the world. How to accomplish this is what Chakrabarti is conveying to the audience through *Bhagavad Gita Demystified*.

August 7, 2022 Jaidev Dasgupta, Ph.D.

Editor's Note

Sankar and I worked together for many years in the tech industry. I found him to be one of the most pleasant and insightful people that I've ever worked with. After he retired, he and I would meet regularly at Starbucks just to stay in touch and often to engage in philosophical conversations that spun out of the current news or events in our lives. I credit him with teaching me the notion of detachment, which has proven to be useful during trying times.

Sankar made several passes at translating and commenting on the Bhagavad Gita. He would distribute these via an email list for comment. I was privileged to be on that list. It was where I began to understand where his personal philosophy came from. After a bit of arm-twisting, several of us convinced him that this work should be published. After my retirement I created a small publishing business. Sankar was gracious enough to let me present his work to you.

For this version, Sankar gave himself the challenge of translating the Gita into English while maintaining the Sanskrit poetic style. There are several rhythmic and poetic enhancements in these verses that help with this. His intention was that these verses be read aloud, which I was able to get him to do once or twice.

For me, this work is refreshing. So many religious texts get bogged down in mysticism and subservience to some deity. It becomes easy to lose the wisdom and insight of its original authors. The exercise of reading them becomes mindless, just a ritual and not a practical education. This work is different. Sankar points out that the "deity" to be subservient to is the set of natural laws of the universe. Arguing with these leads to natural consequences. This is a description of how the universe works. That's useful!

Sadly, particularly sadly for me since he was a good friend, Sankar passed away late in the publishing process. Fortunately, the book was nearly finished, just needing a round of two of copy editing. Any faults you may find in this text are my own.

It was difficult finishing it up without Sankar's guiding hand. There are so many questions that I wish I could ask him, but this book will have to do. I believe it will serve us well. I know that I plan on giving copies of it to my children and grandchildren.

Lonnie Mandigo
Hawkspring Publishing
January, 2023

Prelude

What is in "Srimad Bhagavad Gita - Demystified"?

"Srimad Bhagavad Gita" is a blueprint to build a productive, happy, successful life.

Bhagavad Gita is an ancient scripture from India, perhaps more than 3000 years old. Technically it is a very small section of the great Indian epic "Mahabharat". The epic itself spans over a hundred thousand verses; Bhagavad Gita is only seven hundred verses long. Though it is small in size, for ages Bhagavad Gita has been regarded as the pinnacle of ancient Indian philosophical thinking.

Written in the Sanskrit language, unfamiliar to most people in the west as also in modern India, and seeped in deep spiritual symbolism, Bhagavad Gita (BG) by itself is a difficult book to comprehend. BG is widely regarded as a religious text. However, when the spiritual language and symbolism is peeled off, one finds that the book is hardly a book of religious doctrine. Rather it is a blueprint to construct a happy, blissful life based on the true nature of reality. The views, the logic, and the action plans presented in Bhagavad Gita are true for the whole of mankind in all ages. This realization spawned this current work aiming to bring the message of Bhagavad Gita to all of the non-Sanskrit knowing population by making it simpler to read and understand. "Bhagavad Gita - Demystified" is an English translation of The Bhagavad Gita with notes added in each chapter to demystify the spiritual language and symbolism. Also, to make the content more lucid and easily understandable the original Sanskrit verses have been translated into rhyming English verses. Original structure and content of the Bhagavad Gita has been maintained in this demystified work. BG contains eighteen chapters called "Yoga"s. Like the original text, the demystified translation has eighteen different chapters or Books. Each Book is a faithful English translation of the Sanskrit verses of the corresponding Yoga in the original text along with some demystifying explanation.

BG is basically a didactic, not a sermon. It is a dialog between a wise teacher and a curious student bound by the love of friendship. In each yoga, BG describes some aspect of reality and implies practices which a seeker could do to get rid of his malady, melancholy, lethargy, anxiety, and agitation. The underlying theory of BG is that the root cause of man's misery and grief is his defective knowledge of the nature of reality; that is, spiritually speaking his delusions about the nature of reality. In each chapter, BG describes some aspect of the true nature of reality, understanding that a man can dispel his own delusions and thus liberate himself from states of misery and grief and finally attain a state of bliss.

In many yogas BG deliberates on the nature of reality itself. Though thousands of years old, BG's view of reality is surprisingly the same as the view of the world held by modern Physics. In fact, in many ways, views of modern physics seem to be restatements of reality described in this ancient text. BG maintains the world is composed of matter (Prakriti) and natural laws (Purusha); and that every change in the world, life, death, evolution, is controlled by the Purusha. BG maintains that the world is permeated by the Purusha everywhere and in every direction; implying that the world is controlled, bound by natural laws. By implication it asserts that nothing occurs at random in the world. And that the notion of God or some Supreme Divine is really the deification of natural laws, the Purusha in BG's vocabulary. This equation demystifies the content of BG.

Purusha, that is natural law, is not partial to anyone; nor is the Supreme Divine. Neither can it be bribed for one's own good nor can it be persuaded to cause harm to anyone else. Thoughts of influencing the natural laws, that is, the Purusha are simply delusional. Such delusions are often the root cause of misery in the deluded ones.

How should a person get rid of his delusions? BG encourages a very activist path. A man must be actively engaged in his world through his efforts and action. Man should continue to perform his karma, to burn away his delusions to attain happiness and bliss. Man must work sincerely but not remain stuck to his expectation of the result is BG's recommended motivation. To believe that the result of an action is produced by the doer of the action is a delusion, since the result of any action is determined by the natural laws and not by the desire of the doer. BG's recommended path is really the path followed by scientists who must toil and experiment on and on and recognize the errors in their thinking (that is, their delusions) till the underlying truth of nature is revealed to them.

BG's recommended path is the path of karma or action, of rational intelligence, of wisdom and faith in the natural laws, (the Divine). Avoiding karma, absconding duty does not bring happiness or success. All these are spelt out in only seven hundred verses. BG is not enthusiastic about other postulated paths to construct a happy fulfilling life.

In a deep dive of the human mind, BG analyzes the structure of mental propensity which in BG's term is called "Guna". BG theorizes that there are only three fundamental Gunas. The myriads of different propensities displayed by people are actually various combinations of the three elemental gunas. It shows how the type of mental propensity dominating a person ultimately affects the quality of life of that person; and by understanding the overall landscape, what a man should practice to modify his mental propensity to attain a happier life. Analyzing the mental propensity (Guna) farther, BG shows how stratification in every society is a natural expression of mental propensities of the members of the society.

In some chapters, BG also elaborates its views on what is good and what is bad, suggesting what behaviors man should adopt and practice and which type of behavior a man should abhor.

Though widely regarded as a religious text, BG is thus in essence a blueprint for building a happy successful life; building a life of bliss in every age no matter what his religious persuasion is. By developing a true understanding of reality, by understanding his own internal world, the world of his mind, a man can himself chart out a path of blissful life.

BG is not a sermon. It is a conversation between two loving friends. The tone of deliberation throughout this book is NOT that "Thou Shall do this … "; rather it is that "Thou should know this …". There is no threat or promise of punishment in any after world to seek converts. It merely spells out the knowledge of reality and the gunas. The choice of following the path and acting on the knowledge is left to the individual. BG provides the blueprint to guide a man to change himself and achieve success, happiness, and bliss; not depending on any mythical god or supernatural being. Man can and should reconfigure himself to be on the path of bliss if he so chooses.

BOOK 1
Arjuna Vishada Yoga

Hero Swimming in Grief and Confusion

Arjuna = Name of a hero in the epic Mahabharata.
"Vishada" = State of mind of deep sadness, despondency.
"Yoga" = A path of focused, disciplined effort to reach a goal.
BG = Srimad Bhagavad Gita.

What is in Book 1 - Arjuna-Vishada-Yoga

Bhagavad Gita, BG for short, is a distillation of ancient Hindu philosophy, dealing with the nature of reality, nature of life and death; on how to live in dharma and how to understand one's own self and others. Though BG is widely regarded as religious scripture, when one peels off the shell of mysticism and they find that BG is actually a user manual for a man to construct a happy, productive, successful life. In short it is a user manual for a man to attain a divine life.

BG is a very small portion, less than one-percent, of the great Indian Epic Mahabharat. BG is written in Sanskrit as superbly beautiful poetry. This work is an attempt to translate BG to an English poem of rhyming verses in the style of Sanskrit "Shloka" and a style of Bengali poetry known as "Payaar". Hopefully this translation will make it easier for English speakers to understand the advice espoused in BG. Along with the translation of the verses, in the beginning of every chapter short explanatory notes have been added to demystify the contents so that a reader can "see" the practical advice rendered in BG. Hopefully it will become clear that BG is actually a poem describing the true nature of reality based on material foundation. Following the Samkhya Darshana, BG's axiom is that only by understanding the true un-deluded view of reality can a man attain a divine life. So, by understanding BG, a person may construct a happy successful life devoid of anxiety, grief, or misery.

Backdrop of Book 1

BG has eighteen chapters called "Yoga" or paths dealing with various aspects of reality in the context of man's life and behavior. In this work each chapter is called a Book.

The first Book of BG is set in the context of a great civil war between two strands of the same royal family, the Kuru family. The two strands are headed by two sets of cousins: the "Pandavas" and the "Kau-

1

ravas". A devastating war is going to take place between these two clans. Book 1 describes the two armies assembled face to face. It describes the generals, the heroes, and the combatants. Arjuna is the supreme warrior on the Pandava side. And Holy Lord Krishna, who is Lord Vishnu Himself incarnated in human form, who is the source of all wisdom, is Arjuna's friend, counselor and also the charioteer of Arjuna's chariot in the battle.

Book 1 describes the gathering of the two armies before the battle actually starts. At this time, Arjuna inspects the heroes and armies on both sides. Then he becomes afflicted with great sadness, deep grief, and loses all enthusiasm for the battle. In Sanskrit this state of mind is called "Vishada". In his deep sadness, Arjuna realizes the horrific social effects the war will bring. He declares that he is not going to fight the battle. In BG, the battlefield and Arjuna's grief are described in superb poetry in Sanskrit.

Looking Ahead

Shlokas 3-6: Duryodhana (the evil son of Dhritarashtra) describes the commanders of the Pandava army.

Shloka 4: Vowel sound added to enhance rhythm.

Shlokas 7-11: Duryodhana's description of the Kaurava army.

Shlokas 12-20: The start of the battle is signaled.

Shlokas 20-24: The two armies are standing face to face. Arjuna wants to view them both.

Shlokas 21-23: Arjuna requests that his chariot may be held still in between two armies so that he can inspect the combatants on both sides.

Shlokas 29-30: Seeing his own relatives anxious to fight and kill each other the despondent warrior Arjuna laments. It is also a classic description of a panic attack descending on Arjuna.

Shlokas 31-29: Now the mighty hero Arjuna wails out his confusion, his grief overtakes him; he declares he will not fight.

Shlokas 40-44: The social consequences of civil war described in most beautiful verses.

Shlokas 45-47: Completely overtaken by grief, Arjuna the mighty hero declares he will surely not fight.

Reading Aid - Glossary:

In several places in this translation, the original Sanskrit words have been retained to improve rhythm and to provide a halo of the ancient scripture. In the text all these words have been underlined. They are translated and explained below. *All proper nouns and names of persons have been underlined but left as such without translating them inline.*

Adharma = Anti-dharma; lawlessness, unethical, broken structures etc.

dharma = ethics, laws, customs, duties, traditions.

Dhritarashtra = name of the blind king of the state and father of the Kaurav princes.

Sanjay = minister of Dhritarashtra, the blind king.

Duryodhana = The evil son of Dhritarashtra.

Achyut-a = immovable; it is one of many names of Lord Krishna.

Partha = Son of Pritha; it is one of Arjuna's many names.

Book 1

Arjuna-Vishada-Yoga

(Yoga of Arjuna's Grief)

<u>Dhritarashtra</u> said...

On <u>Kurukshetra</u>, the field of the <u>Kurus</u>;
    That field hallowed and holy too;
Gathered to battle are the armies;
    Of the <u>Pandavas</u> and of mine too. |

Oh <u>Sanjaya</u>, tell me what are they doing?
    Asked <u>Dhrutarashtra</u> the blind old king. || 1

<u>Sanjaya</u> said...

Sight of the <u>Pandava</u> forces ready for the fight,
Gave the <u>Kaurava</u> king not the slightest delight; |
Strolling slowly to the great Acharya "<u>Drona</u>",
Said the following the <u>Kaurav</u> King <u>Duryodhana</u>. || 2

Oh my Acharya please see the mighty army of the <u>Pandava</u>-ha; |
Arranged to battle by your disciple, the wise son of <u>Dhrupada</u>-ha. || 3

"<u>Bheema</u>" the Mighty hero and "<u>Arjuna</u>" the Archer Supreme-o |
  <u>Saatyaki</u> and the braves of the clans of "<u>Viraata</u>" and "<u>Dhrupad</u>-o";
All are standing, waiting to dive deep in the pool of the battle-o. || 4

Note <u>Dhristaketu</u>, <u>Chekitana</u>, and the King of <u>Kashi</u>;
    Each a glorious valorous Doyen; |
So are <u>Purujita</u>, <u>Kuntibhoja</u> and the mighty king <u>Sibi</u>,
    Each a strong bull amongst men. || 5

Striding forth is the bold <u>Yudhamanyu</u>,
    <u>Uttoamauja</u> both of supreme-a courage-a; |
Note <u>Subhadra</u>-son, <u>Draupadi</u>-sons too -
    All great warriors seething with rage-o. || 6

Oh Acharya note the valorous leaders of my army too; |
Please take note while I name these heroes for You. || 7
You, Your Lordship, <u>Bheeshma</u>, <u>Karna</u>, and Guru <u>Kripacharya</u>,
    All amassed many many glorious victories; |
<u>Ashwathama</u>, <u>Vikarna</u>, sons of <u>Somadatta</u>, and <u>Jayadratha</u>;
    All very brave who terrify their enemies. || 8

Also many heroes great in gallantry;
    Willing to die for me are in my infantry; |

All are skilled in battle they will never scuttle;
    Will use many different weaponry. || 9

Unlimited are our brave forces protected;
By the GrandSire the Great Bheeshma; |
Limited a lot, are Pandava heroes protected;
Though by the might of the great Bheema. || 10

Oh Our Lordships, Oh our commanders,
Please be ready for the battle will start; |
But never shall you hesitate to move,
To protect Grand-pa Bheeshma from any hurt. || 11

Then the Grandfather blew his war conch signaling to start the fight; |
It roared like a lion mighty and portent much to Duryodhana's delight. || 12

Sounded then the conches, kettle drums,
Cymbals and the hissing of the spears; |
Together at once they all blared, hearts got scared,
Deafening the heroes' ears. || 13

Standing on their fast and charming chariot-o;
Yoked by the very best galloping white horses; |
Holy Lord Maadhava and Arjun-o the archer suprem-o
Then each blew their own conches. || 14

Lord Krishn-a blew the Panchajany-a;
Arjun-a blew his conch Devadatt-a; |
Bheema Vrikodara sprayed-a terror-a;
Blowing Paundra his great conch-a. || 15

King-a Yudhisthir-a crisis-a cool-a,
Blew the concha-a "Ananta-Vijaya"-a |
Prince-a Nakula blows "Sughosh"-a,
Sahadev-a sounds "Moni-Pushpak"-a. || 16

Kashi-Raja-a supreme-a archer-a mighty brave-a Shiknadi too; |
DhristaDyumna and king-o Virata-ha mighty hero Satyaki too. || 17

Draupadi-sons Drupada-king Subhadra-son too;
All very brave, all are fierce!
Blew own conches loud blare and shrill-o,
Putting fear deep in enemy ears. || 18

That sound, that cacophony;
Tearing through Kaurava hearts made them edgy and flutter; |
That tumult that sound,
The ominous resound, that great roar the sky about to shatter. || 19

Seeing sons of Dhritarashtra ready for battle-a,
With weapons only braced to crush the foe-a; |
Raising his bow Arjuna, the archer supreme-o;
Said the following to the Holy Lord Krishn-o. || 20

Arjuna Vishada Yoga

Arjuna said to _Krishna_...

Standing apart are the two armies,
    Daring each other all are brave and tall; |
Oh _Achyut-a_ please hold the chariot-a;
    Still-a in the middle-a till I see them all. || 21

Please hold it still, till I feel, who these are hungry for war and fight; |
Hold it still till I feel who shall I fight with no fear and no delight. || 22

Let me see near and far who these braves are;
    Those craving to strife and to perish; |
Willing to perish in a pitch feverish as a favor;
    To _Duryodhana_ the evil and the devilish. || 23

Being so told by _Gudaakesh_-a, stopped the chariot-a Holy _Hrishikesh_-a; |
Armies on each side-a Oh king of _Bhaarata_, there is no place to hide-a. || 24

Said _Arjuna_ to Lord _Krishna_,
I See there the brave forces assembled by the family of _Kuru_; |
Grand-pa _Bheeshma_, other-a kings-a and my Guru _Drona_ too. || 25

Partha saw there standing:
    His paternal uncles, and grandfathers and his Teachers;
    So were his maternal uncles, and many cousin brothers; |
    As well as sons, nephews, grandsons all his very dear;
    And many many of his friends too, none having any fear. || 26

There in both armies did _Arjuna_ see with no glee;
    His Well-wishers, companions, friends and even in-laws; |
    All ready to strike, arrayed to battle forms with no flaws. || 27

Overcame with pity, _Arjuna_ the hero mighty,
    His voice sad and choking then told; |
Oh _Krishna_, anxious to battle, eager to die;
    Are my own relatives heroes and bold. || 28

My limbs are limp, limbs sinking; my mouth is drying; |
Trembling is my body, and my hairs are all bristling. || 29

"_Gandeeva_" the great bow of mine,
    Falling from my hands, my skin is burning; |
Am failing to hold myself to the present,
    Restless is my mind, it's wandering. || 30

Oh _Keshava_, if my own relations will be killed,
    If they are going to be dead; |
I see omens sinister-ous, none auspicious;
    Do not see anything good ahead. || 31

Oh _Krishna_, victory desire I not,
    Nor the kingdom nor the lust of royal hives; |
What would we do with the kingdom?
    Or the royal enjoyments in our own lives? || 32

Did we not desire the kingdom,
>   *Enjoyments and royal fun for the sake of those?* |
Those that are poised to fight,
>   *Riches and lives do they slight, posing as our foes.* || 33

Acharyas and fathers, uncles and brothers;
>   *Brother-in-laws all reveling willing to fight and die; |*
Grand-pas and sons, and in-laws not all are our fans,
>   *Maternal uncles not all unkind,*
>   *But many are raging blind, all vying to kill and die.* || 34

Oh Madhusudan-a, Oh Krishn-a,
I know the Kauravas will be killing, they will be vile and foul!
>   *Even then wish I not to slay them, I will not even howl. |*
Slay them shall I not even for Lordship of all the three worlds;
>   *Why then should we slay cousins only for this One world.* || 35

Oh Krishna,
Killing those evil witted Dhritarashtra-sons;
>   *Killing cousins who perpetrated vile aggressions;*
No joy shall ever come, nor can we be happy or sing;
>   *Sickened shall we be having committed a heinous sin.* || 36

Therefore, how would it be just if we ever kill;
>   *Sons of Dhritarashtra and our own friends and kinsmen; |*
How shall we enjoy peace and any joyous feel;
>   *How shall we ever be happy if we kill our own brethren?* || 37

Overpowered by greed,
Unholy desires unleashed,
>   *Cousins may not see such actions to be vile; |*
But destruction of family,
Treachery to the friendly ,
>   *Is wrong morally soaked in eternal evil.* || 38

With our visions clear,
With our judgment stern lacking any fear,
>   *How can we not know this to be a sin? |*
Forgiving their greed and wrath,
Can we not turn away from this path?
>   *Sure to destroy our whole kith and kin?* || 39

Destruction of the family, perishes the family "dharma" ; |
Dharma perishes, families get engulfed in "Adharama". || 40

Oh Krishna,
When adharma ascends, fine virtues of nations sure do get corrupted; |
With virtues debased chaos descends, so do vices and values wicked. || 41

Virtues fallen families sunken, ethics maligned dharma gets trodden; |
Respect for the past do wither fast, traditions too are soon forgotten. || 42

Thus, actions of sin of the destroyers of the leading family;
Do create dissonance of castes, values, and duties socially. |

Arjuna Vishada Yoga

Sinful actions blur the eternal duties;
   Of families causing great confusion;
Befuddling the duties of individuals;
   Of varying in status and occupation. || 43

Oh Krishna, Oh Janardana,
We have heard over and over and over again repeated,
When family laws, dharma get ignored and obliterated,
Men will live in hell till time itself comes to its very end. || 44

Alas, is the kingdom so alluring and pleasures royal are so encitin-g? |
That we are ready to kill our own kin and commit such heinous sin? || 45

If I do remain not resisting, unarmed and with not any weapon in my hand, |
(And then if) The sons of Dhritarashtra do kill me indeed on this very land, ||
Even then would I be happier;
   Then killing my own kinsmen to lord over this dear land. || 46

Heart heavy with pity, wailed Arjuna, Oh Maadhava, Oh Krishn-o;
   "Fight will I not, kill shall I not"; |
Dropping his bow and his arrow, Paartha the mighty great hero;
   Quietly sat down on his chariot-o. || 47

ﻌ   *End of Book 1, Arjuna Vishada Yoga*   ﻌ

Samkhya Yoga

Path to Bliss by Understanding Reality

Samkhya = Knowledge of reality gained through reason and rational processes, grounded in the material universe.

Yoga = A path of focused, disciplined effort to reach a goal.

BG = Srimad Bhagavad Gita.

What is in Book 2 - Samkhya Yoga:

The first ten sholkas in this book, is really a continuation of the description of Arjuna's grief and confusion from Book 1: Arjuna Vishada Yoga (Book of Arjuna's sadness and confusion).

Arjuna's grief, confusion and despondency are described in the very beautiful poem in the Book 1 of BG. First ten verses in Book 2, crystallize Arjuna's grief and confusion. How could Arujna fight in battle the very same people like his grandfather and his guru, whom he has loved and revered all his life? Should they be killed in the battle he would be enjoying pleasures soaked in the blood of people he loved. How could he do that? Should he do such a thing? This is a poetic description, though magnified, of confusion which many of us face in our lifetime. Whenever we face a situation when our righteous action will hurt someone we love, this very same issue comes up. Such situations span from apparently mundane to really serious ones. What we should do and how we should decide what to do when we face such a challenge which is likely to hurt some of our near and dear ones. Although there are variations, the problem itself is universal. This question is a segue to the philosophical deliberation in the rest of Bhagavad Gita (Books 2-18). In this piece Bhagavad Gita's advice is clear. When thus confused and you are at your wit's end, do not walk away from the crisis, surrender to the wisdom and expertise from someone who is a reservoir of wisdom and rational knowledge (Shloka 7). In sholka 7, the legendary hero, the exalted hero Arjuna now emotionally exhausted, surrenders to the Holy Lord seeking His advice.

BG's goal is to provide mankind a path to a happy, healthy, anxiety-free, successful life, free of miseries; that is, the goal is to help man attain a "divine" life. The axiom in ancient Indian philosophy is that only by understanding the true nature of reality can man achieve freedom from suffering, misery, and griefs. So, an understanding of the true nature of reality is essential to attain a divine life. Throughout the book, BG continues to provide insight into the true nature of reality.

In the rest of Book 2, BG deals with three topics directly relevant to this goal.

1. *Atman*, the life enabling entity in the living. Understanding the property of Atman helps man to understand the true nature of death. From this knowledge a man can overcome the grief and confusion associated with death which can bedevil even very successful men, for example Arjuna (Shlokas 11-32).
2. *Swa-dharma* and *Buddhi* Yoga: In this section BG encourages everyone to perform his duty and that man should adopt the path of rational intelligence abandoning the path of ritualistic practice. Performing his duty adopting Buddhi yoga, a man becomes successful and happy. (Shlokas 31-53).
3. *Sthita-Prajna* or Wisdom about the true nature of reality. It is Samkhya's axiom that man's failure and griefs are the result of ignorance of the nature of reality. So, by being wise about it, man will become successful and happy in life. He will enjoy a divine life. In Sholkas 54-72, BG describes what Sthita-Prajna or wisdom is; and how to acquire it.

Atman the Life Enabler and the Nature of Death

The crux of the issue is that a mighty hero, a great man of great knowledge and skill, has become despondent and basically dysfunctional, unable to function in his normal duties at the prospect of the death of his near and dear ones. How to get such a man back to his normal active and wise state of mind to perform his duties in the world? BG tackles the issue head on by analyzing the true nature of death. Following the postulates of the Samkhya Darshan (*Darshan* = view, philosophy), in Sholkas 11-32, BG describes very beautifully the properties of Atman, the life-enabling entity in every living being. According to BG, *Atman*, the life-enabling entity of living beings is actually immortal, immutable, unchangeable, inviolable. Though Atman resides in a mortal physical body and provides life-enabling properties, Atman itself never dies when the physical body, its container, falls apart and is not able to support the environment in which Atman can provide life-enabling functions. Thus, although the physical body dies, the "real" person, that is the "Atman" does not die, ever. So, there is no good reason to lament over the death of anyone. Neither a hero, nor anyone else should lament over the death of anyone. The "real" person in a living body is the Atman; the physical body is not the real living person. Without the Atman the body is nothing but a carcass. The Atman itself is immortal.

Residing in the physical container, that is the physical body, Atman enlivens the body. The Atman itself is immortal! So, BG's advice is why worry over the death of something which is actually immortal, unchangeable and everlasting! Worrying about the death of Atman is a delusion, a false view.

Postulates of Atman accurately map to the natural laws of the material world. Life thrives in a living being because the natural laws acting on the underlying organized material structure enables it to pulsate the characteristics which we call as living. Properties of every organized structure living or non-living is enabled by natural laws acting on the structure. This is the law of the material world. Structure begets function. It is also true that in the material world, every organized structure in the course of time will definitely get disorganized. Such is the law of thermodynamics! Once it is disorganized, the structure may/will lose its previous ability to support the functions of the organized living body. There is no exception. A structure previously supporting life when disorganized may not support the characteristics of life. Simply stated every structure enabling the characteristics of life will definitely come to a state when it will be regarded as dead. However, the principles, the laws that enabled the characteristics of living are themselves not mutated, nor changed, nor violated. The material structure is the one which gets changed or decays. The laws themselves remain immutable and permanent. _Atman_ is the spiritual name of these natural laws!

Forced by natural laws, material structures inevitably cycle through organization and disorganization. Whenever an organized structure is appropriate to support characteristics of life, by the power of natural laws properties of life will throb in it. Atman is then said to have permeated the structure making it living. When that organization is so disturbed that it cannot display the properties of life, it becomes a carcass. In Samkhya Darshan, this reality is described as the Atman impregnating a structure making it living; and eventually departing from it leaving a dead body behind. The Atman, that is the natural laws that enabled the properties of life themselves, is everlasting and immutable. A body may die; but its real resident the Atman never dies. Since this is an inevitable natural process, the advice is that *the death of any one is not worthy of a wise man to become so grieved that he becomes dysfunctional. No one should cease to perform his duty because of the death or of the possibility of death of someone he knows and loves. This is BG's advice.*

Swa-dharma and Buddhi Yoga

BG's advice is that man ought to perform his duty, no matter how hard it is. Man ought to perform his duty especially when facing a crisis. There is no permission to abscond from duty. Abstaining from duty is an appalling sin. These ideas are captured in verses 31-38.

Man ought to take shelter in *Buddhi Yoga; that is, use* rational intelligence to harness his actions in performing duty in every sphere of life. These ideas are beautifully depicted in a spiritual language in the verses 39-53.

BG's opinion is that a happy, divine life is built on performing your duty. Every one ought to perform his/her duty; or the person will live in ignominy, grief and shame!

"Sthita-Prajna" - Steady Intelligence - Wisdom

In the previous section, BG decrees that to attain a happy life free of grief and misery, man must perform his duty; man ought to perform "*nishkama karma*" (nishkama = lust free; karma = work, action); he ought not to evade his duties. In this section, BG advises that man must not only work, man must also develop wisdom. But what is wisdom? This block of eighteen Sholkas (54-72) describes BG's view of wisdom; and also, indirectly indicate how to develop that wisdom. Wisdom is to have an un-deluded view of the world; wisdom is knowing the true nature of reality. Freedom from delusion leads to happiness. A delusion free person is one whose intelligence is steady and unwavering. This quality is called "*Sthita-Prajna*" (*Sthita* = Established, unwavering; and *Prajna* = deep intelligence). This section describes the characteristics and behavior of a "*Sthita-Prajna*" person. This is a goal a man should pursue to attain a peaceful life free of misery and grief. This section also describes, in almost clinical detail, the root causes of delusion and how delusion gets established in the human mind and produces misery in a man's life. The description is both advisory and therapeutic. By following the advice, a man could recognize a "*sthita-prajna*" person and taking the behavior of a "*sthita-prajna*" person as a model, a man could with practice, become *sthita-prajna* himself. From this knowledge, a man could fashion appropriate exercises to eliminate delusion from his life; and consequently, attain a blissful life.

Looking Ahead:

Shlokas 1-10: Arjuna's grief and aversion to duty continues because of the fear of death of so many near and dear ones.

Shlokas 11-30 describe the properties of "ATMAN" - The life enabling entity in the living. The poetry is very beautiful and very enlightening. Hidden but based on material foundation, this deliberation of the nature of death is unique amongst all other philosophical thoughts on this subject.

Shlokas 22-30 describe the properties of Atman, the life enabling entity in the living beings. This enables one to understand the real nature of death, that death of a body does not signify the death or destruction of the real "person", the Atman in the body. So, one should not be overwhelmed by the prospect of death of the physical body.

Shlokas 22-25: These verses continue to describe the properties of Atman, the life-giving principle which makes a living being "living", without which any living body is but an inanimate carcass. The descriptions here are superbly beautiful. These verses are among the often-quoted verses of the *Bhagavad Gita*.

Shlokas 26-30: Together these verses describe fundamental properties of material nature.

Shlokas 31-36: These verses indicate why man should perform his duty. BG's advice is that everyone, including the highly accomplished leaders, ought to perform their duties, without exception. There is nothing to lose if one performs his duty honestly and earnestly. Shunning away from duty brings nothing but grief and dishonor. The activist philosophy of BG is in full display here.

Shlokas 39-53 describe Buddhi Yoga - the path of rational Intelligence and its virtues in life.

Shloka 47: This Sholka is especially noteworthy. It describes a truth of the world, often disregarded because of emotions and ego. It is one of the oft referred verses of Bhagavad Gita.

Shlokas 54-72 describe the virtues of "Sthita-Prajna", that is of steady intelligence and wisdom.

Shloka 62: Denial of fulfillment of lust is the root cause of anger ... so is being said. This is a deep insight into human psychology independent of any faith.

Shloka 63 describes how the anger arising from the denial of lust destroys a man's mind and intelligence.

Reading Aid - Glossary:

In several places in this translation, the original Sanskrit words have been retained to improve rhythm and to provide a halo of the ancient scripture. In the text all these words have been underlined. They are translated and explained below.

Acharya = Prominent teacher, spiritual guide

Achyut-a = Another name of Lord Krishna, Holy Lord Vishnu.

Bhaarata = Prince of the family of King Bharata; Often Arjuna is addressed by this name.

Bhaarata = King of "Bhaarat" the kingdom in reference to King Dhritarashtra.

Bheeshma and Dron-a = Name of Arjuna's grandfather and revered guru.

Brahma-nirvana = Supreme bliss; nirvana = extinction; Brahma = nature, reality. Together means one who has extinguished his ego and thus become one with reality; thus becomes free of delusion and attains supreme bliss.

Buddhi = Rational intelligence.

Dharma = Ethics, laws, properties; Also means righteous path; righteous path of behavior.

Dhritarashtra = Arjuna's uncle, the blind old king.

Govinda = Another name of Lord Krishna.

Guna = Mental propensity, mental tendency.

Hrishikesh-a = Another name of Holy Lord Krishna, who is Lord Vishnu in human form.

Karma = Work, actions.

Karma-Phala = Fruits, results, consequences of actions or karma.

Keshava = A name of Holy Lord Krishna.

Kshatriya = The caste, group of people entrusted to defending the state, laws, dharma.

Kunti = Name of the mother of Arjuna, the hero in this dialog.

MadhuSudana = Name of Lord Vishnu who destroyed the demon, Madhu.

Nishkama karma = Karma (work) done dutifully without lusting desire to cling to the fruit of the work.

Pandita = A wise person with deep knowledge of reality.

Paartha = Son of Pritha, a name of Arjuna.

Phala = Fruit, consequence.

Samkhya = Name of one school of ancient Indian philosophy based on reason and material foundation of the universe.

Sattva guna = Name of the guna that makes a man inclined to be curious, honest, logical; as opposed to being lusting, greedy, egotistic; or being lazy in body and mind.

Sthita-prajna = A wise man whose intelligence has become steady in reality, whose intelligence does not run around helter skelter.

Swa-dharma = Personal (or caste based) duty, obligation.

Vishaada = Sadness, confusion, dejection.

Book 2

Samkhya Yoga

(The yoga-path of Samkhya, rational knowledge)

Sanjay said...

Downcast eyes filled with tear,
Arjuna who never knew any fear,
> *Now is overcome with sorrow; |*

Seeing him so disturbed Lord Krishn-a;
Said following to the great Arjun-a;
> *His friend, the mighty hero. || 1*

The Holy Lord Krishna said...

Oh Arjuna
When serious danger is impending;
Wherefrom is your timidity coming;
> *To shun your duty seeing the enemy in the face? |*
Fits this not a brave warrior,
Fits this people far inferior,
> *This is no path to heaven nor to lofty fame;*
> *Sure is this a path to sink in lasting shame. || 2*

Abandon abandon thoughts decorating a coward-o;
Do these behoove you a legend and a great hero? |

Abandon abandon moanings of the faint heart-o;
Rise up, rise up Oh Partha, and scorch your foe. || 3

Arjuna said...

Oh Madhusudan-a;
How shall I fight against Bheeshma and Dron-a; |

How can I hurt them with my sharp deadly arrows;?
Worship them I do! They are my gurus, my heroes. || 4

In this world,
Far better is for us to beg, live on alms, and lazily tattle;
Than to slay our noble gurus even engaging in a battle; |

Desiring wealth and kingdom in the sway,
Destroying relations and gurus on the way;

Will bring fun and pleasures dripping only their blood;
Ne'er ever will bring peace or happiness in our world. || 5

Nor do I understand which is more noble more glorious;
Should we seek victory or should we not be victorious; |

Samkhya Yoga

Those, whom killing in battle, never ever do I wish to enjoy my life;
Those Dhritarashtra-sons are the ones facing me to fight and strife. || 6

Afflicted, damaged by the weakness of pity, my own spirit is poor;
Confused is my heart what "dharma" here is, my heart very unsure; |
I ask Thee, Thee I beg, Oh Krishna, always been I, a devotee of yours;
Tell me please Oh Achyut-a, the righteous path-a in the clearest prose-a.|| 7

Neither do I see what at the end shall dispel my deep drowning sorrow,
Sorrow that dries up my senses, wets my eyes said Arjun-a the hero; |
Even if we attain the empire unchallenged, how do we wipe off the sins;
How to dispel the grief of having to kill my Acharyas, Gurus and cousins. || 8

Sanjaya said...

Saying thus to Lord Krishn-a, the scorcher of enemies, the hero Arjun-a,
Crying "Oh Govinda", "Fight shall I not"; the mighty hero sat-a quiet-a. || 9

Oh Bharata, then with Arjuna sunk down with grief deep unending; |
In the center of the two armies, Hrishikesh-a spoketh the following. || 10

Part A: "ATMAN" - The life enabling entity in the living. (Shlokas 11-30)

The Holy Lord Krishna said...

(Oh Arjuna, thou)
Ought not lament things you are lamenting;
Words of wisdom thou seem to be speaking; |
Ought to know that Panditas not lamenting;
Nor weep either for the dead or for the living. || 11

Not indeed ever was a time when "I" didn't exist;
Nor was a time you or these rulers did not exist; |

Not ever in the fold of time will ever be a time;
When you, Me or they will truly cease to chime. || 12

"Atman" the Living in the body itself never changes;
The body itself do morph through the many stages;
  Childhood, to youth to infirmities of old ages; |

  At the end as the worn body falls apart,
  To a new body does the Atman depart;
Knowing this truth never grieve venerable wise sages || 13

Oh, Arjuna law of nature, contacts with matter in world;
Gives sensations of pain or pleasures; of hot or of cold; |

Impermanent are such sensations; they come and go;
So endure them Oh prince of the family of Bhaarata-o. || 14

A man unafflicted by these transient feelings is wise,
Man, unperturbed in pain and pleasures accrue no vice, |

Oh Arjuna this is my advice;
Attained is a life of unending peace and joy,
When Wisdom is taken as the surest ploy. || 15

That what is "untrue", "unreal" never ever does manifest;
That what is "true", and real never ever remains unmanifest; |
Both these are known to be truths of the world, of the reality;
To the wise sages, knowing nature of the world with certainty. || 16

Know **THAT** *which pervades the whole world is indestructible! |*
Not you nor anyone else can destroy which is never perishable || 17

Scriptures reveal only temporal, sure to perish is the body carnal;
But Atman, the life enabler residing in the body is forever, eternal;
Scriptures say, the Atman is too subtle to touch or be decimated;
Atman is subtle, immeasurable, nor can it ever be instrumented. |

Therefore knowing the truths of the life enabler Atman-a;
Oh Prince thou the best of the royal family of Bhaaratha;
Rise up, fight the battle, uphold dharma, Oh dear Arjun-a. || 18

Samkhya Yoga

Thoughts that Atman kills or can ever be killed is a delusion, is vain; |
Know the truth that the Atman never slays, nor can it ever be slain. || 19

Atman is never born, nor is it impermanent;
*   Having been there already, it will not un-become again; |*
Unborn, eternal, it is perpetual and ancient;
*   Body killed; Atman ne'er gets killed! Stop worrying in vain. || 20*

Know the Atman to be beyond destruction,
*   Eternal, unborn, beyond any change or mutation,*
*   Never in pain, forever beyond any consumption; |*

Oh Paartha, how could then any person,
*   Slay the Atman in another person,*
*   Or Cause the Atman to be slain? || 21*

As after throwing off worn out dresses;
Persons do dress in fresh new robes-es; |
So does the Atman throw away an old worn body;
Emerges into the fresh figure of a newborn baby. || 22

Weapons can never cut It; Fires cannot burn It; |
Water cannot wet It; air wilts It not even a bit; || 23

It can't be pierced, nor can It ever be burned;
Never It withers nor can It ever be moistened; |

Eternal, immovable every way, all pervading;
It is primeval, It is ancient, It is everlasting. || 24

Unmanifest, Incomprehensible, Unmodifiable It is; |
You ought never lament Its loss knowing all these. || 25

Even though eternally born or eternally dead you think It is |
Even then you, a mighty warrior ought not lament over this. || 26

Body born is sure to die, the dead is sure to be born; |
Lament not for them, nature's laws surely do move on. || 27

Unmanifest is the origin for every being;
Manifest is its middle, living and breathing; |
In death it is rendered unmanifest again;
So grieving over it would truly be in vain || 28

Some see It as wonderful, awesome fabulous;
Others speak of It being amazing, marvelous; |
Some others hear of It truly in great wonder;
Even after hearing only few become truly aware. || 29

The "dehee", the Atman in the living can never be killed or violated; |
Therefore Oh Bhaarata death ought not to be grieved nor lamented. || 30

Even if you look at your swa-dharma;
Ought there not be in you any dilemma;
Oh Kshatriya Prince! This is your duty, do thy karma,
Engage in action, banish hesitation, protect dharma. |

Nothing, nothing is nobler than fighting in an ethical war;
Don't waver, fighting a righteous battle is superior by far. || 31

Only by luck such opportunity for a brave comes to happen;
To fight a righteous battle that reveals the doors to heaven. |

Oh Paartha, lucky indeed is that brave warrior;
Who gets the opportunity to enter such a war. || 32

Now if you will abstain, not engaging,
    In this righteous battle to protect dharma; |
Sure then will you accrue sin unending,
    Tarnishing your glory, avoiding dutiful karma. || 33

Shunning a righteous war is sure to bring you loss of face;
Shame remaining forever, people will gossip your disgrace; |

You an accomplished warrior;
A mighty scorcher of enemies,
    Art thou not highly honored?
Living in disgrace, living a life with shame!
    Is that not worse than being dead! || 34

Walk away from this battle, other heroes are sure to say;
You were too afraid, of course Arjuna is a coward any way; |
The very same heroes who hold you in high esteem now,
Will think low of you, slight you, insult you every way how. || 35

They will speak words hostile, with much furor;
    They will speak many unspeakable words about you Oh! |
Will make mockery of your strength and valor;
    What can be more painful than that to a legendary hero? || 36

In the battle either you will attain the heaven if you die;
Or by winning you will enjoy the earth - that is not a lie! |
(Neither way do you lose!)
Therefore, rise up, Oh son of Kunti, Oh you the towering hero;
Firmly resolve to battle; protecting dharma; decimate the foe. || 37

Yoke yourself to the battle,
    Holding happiness and sadness alike,
    Holding profit and loss equal and alike,
    Holding victory or defeat not unlike but alike;
Yoke yourself to the struggle! |

Void thy emotions from the outcome ensuin-g;
Then you will not ever incur even an iota of sin. || 38

Part B: Buddhi Yoga - Path of rational Intelligence (Shlokas 39-53)

You have known that in the <u>Samkhya</u> <u>Yoga</u>,
*   The path, the truths are based on material reality;*
Hear now the wisdom of the <u>Buddhi Yoga</u>,
*   Where actions are powered by intelligence and rationality. |*

Oh <u>Partha</u>, when <u>Buddhi Yoga</u> harnesses <u>karma</u>;
Free will you be of euphoria and emotional trauma;
Results of actions will neither chain nor stain your mind;
Happily will you perform your duties protecting <u>dharma</u>. || 39

Working with <u>Buddhi Yoga</u> no effort is ever lost or wasted;
Exceptions, contradictions to this have never been beheld; |
If this discipline is practiced even with only a small little dose;
It rescues the mind from great fear, anxiety is not ever close. || 40

Oh <u>Arjuna</u> Oh the son of the royal Kuru clan;
*   The nature of resolute-purpose-bound-intelligence is just ONE;*
Countless are the branches of intelligence of a man;
*   Of an irresolute wavering mind, that count is anything but one. || 41*

Using many flowery languages,
*   Quoting delightfully from the scriptures and doctrines; |*
Naives do proclaim in all ages,
*   August Rituals are the only way, no other path wins. || 42*

Desiring to gratify own lusts, power, wealth and delights;
They offer rituals burdened with complicated knotty rites; |

They promise heaven and rebirths to be fruits of the ritual actions,
Though aiming covertly to gratify their own privileges and passions. || 43

Those whose thoughts and minds have been stolen away,
*   By attachment to pulls of pleasure, power and passion;*
Resolute-natured-<u>buddhi</u>, enlightenment is not in their way;
*   They are not granted resolute <u>Buddhi</u> even in meditation. || 44*

Scriptures discuss the three <u>gunas</u> Oh Mighty Heer-o;
Transcend the grips of the <u>gunas</u> on thyself Oh Arjun-o;

*   Seek shelter in Truth, shelter in the <u>Sattva guna</u>;*
*   That is the safe harbor for each and every one-a;*

*   Voids conflicts of opposites, confusions Oh Arjun-a;*
*   Anxieties will be gone forever leaving no agitation-a. |*

*   Worry thou not with thoughts nor of actions;*
*   Of adding to or protecting your possessions;*

Always do your duty, always be yourself Oh mighty <u>Arjuna</u>. || 45

When the country is flooded in every direction and everywhere;
Does a man have any use for a single well to get drinking water?

So much is the value of rituals and practices of a ritualistic yoga;
To a Brahman who is WISE and has understood the Buddhi Yoga. || 46

Your authority and power extend only to the "Karma",
Only to the actions you may choose for execution-a;
Never your authority, nor power extends to "Karma-Phala",
The results, the consequences created by thy action-a; |

Knowing this truth of nature as a law to reckon;
"karma-phala" should never be your inspiration;
Nor should you ever avoid duty and choose inaction. || 47

Renounce all attachments, do the best in your duty, be sure; |
Know that a yogi remains even to success and utter failure. || 48

Inferior is the ritual working,
Only fruits of karma coveting,
Is the path taken by the pitiable, really; |

Working in the Buddhi yog-a,
Sheltering in enlightenment-a,
Is the superior path of the wise, truly. || 49

If a man works in the Buddhi Yoga, in this world;
He is unburdened of any deed both good and bad; |
Yoked to Buddhi learning the skills of working,
Is the coveted art, is the Yoga of happy living. || 50

Remaining yoked to Buddhi, the wise sages,
Renounce fruits of actions, from their pages; |
They become free from rebirth, dodging bondages;
Go to happy abode freed from pains and anguishes. || 51

When your intellect will cross the thicket of deluded layers;
Interested will you be not in the ways of seeping rituals; |

You will have no desire for other ways you have yet to hear;
Nor will you be passionate about ways you have come to bear. || 52

When your intelligence remains unwavering,
Even if the scriptures need be disregarding,
If It remains steady without any vacillation;
Even in and even after the deep meditation, |
Then
You know thou have attained "Yoga" with surety;
You have achieved union with the truth of reality. || 53

Part C: "Sthita-Prajna" ... Steady intelligence - Wisdom (Shlokas 54-72)

Arjuna said...

Oh Keshava,
How to describe a "sthita-prajna", the wise man of deep meditation?
The wise man of steady intelligence, who also is deep in deliberation? |

How might a "sthita-prajna" sit, rest, or be moving?
What might be a "sthita-prajna's" style of speaking? || 54

The Holy Lord Krishna said...

When a person renounces by himself,
     All lusting desires arising in his mind; |
That person happy himself by himself,
     Is "Sthita-prajna"is wise and kind. || 55

A person Not hankering for happiness or pleasures dear;
Who is way past emotions of passion, anger, rage or fear;
Not succumbing to anxiety in misery, grief or at times agonizing;
Is said to be sthita-prajna, his intelligence is steady is unflapping; || 56

One who neither rejoices nor hates in any way,
     On obtaining a thing that is unpleasant or pleasant;
One who is unimpassioned, sober in every way,
     He is a sage whose wisdom is secure and radiant; || 57

Withdrawing its limbs on contact with unknown hindrances;
Is wisdom in the tortoises keeping it safe, looking very cool. |

Withdrawing his senses from objects fomenting the senses;
Sthita-prajna stands firm and tall in wisdom, he is not a fool. || 58

Wisdom turns alluring objects away from a wise man;
Though their "flavors" may linger in his mind's span; |

Realizing supreme Truth and wisdom never ever shun,
Fast does even the flavor fade in a Sthita-Prajna man. || 59

Even though a wise man may indeed be striving; |
His mind may still be stolen by senses harassing. || 60

With all senses restrained,
     Who sits yoked to Me unperturbed, |
Whose senses are controlled,
     His wisdom stands firm, never faltered. || 61

For a man,
Dwelling on an object, on any element;
Gives birth to desire for its attachment; |

Lust is the thirst for unrestrained desire;
Denial of lust breeds anger, rage and ire. || 62

Anger breeds delusion, corrodes reason;
Fleeting memory is the child of delusion;
Memory becomes shaky, as it goes wandering;
Destruction of intelligence will soon be coming; |
With his intelligence gone, and damaged,
That person is drifting and is all but dead. || 63

Self-restrained men even if engaged to objects through sensation; |
Attain peace and bliss if the mind is not soaked in hate or passion. || 64

In peace, is born cessation of sorrows and loss of craving; |
In mind at peace, intelligence soon is steady, unwavering. || 65

Any person not practicing own self-restraint,
Is not able to meditate, nor is he intelligent; |
Such a person finds no peace, nor even a bit of bliss;
Happiness comes only to those blessed with peace. || 66

Deep understanding is stolen away from the mind,
*   That moves around guided only by its sensors; |*
Such mind is like a boat pushed only by the wind,
*   Is drifting listlessly on waters without anchors. || 67*

Therefore, Oh mighty warrior, know this to be true:
*   One who willingly withdraws own senses*
*   From objects that do agitate his senses;*
*   Is wise with firm and steady intelligences. || 68*

Where it is night to most all beings,
*   There the wise man remains curious and awake; |*
What keeps awake most other beings,
*   Is where the "seeing" wise is asleep, unawake. || 69*

As when a river enters the ocean deep and wide,
*   But the ocean remains full, not overflowing;*
So do all desires enter a wise mind truly indeed,
*   Yet the wise mind remains calm not agitating,*
*   But not so for the desirer who is desiring. || 70*

The man who moves in the world and works in his life;
*   Abandoning all desires, free from lust;*
*   Freed from egotism, and pride's thirst;*
Unaddicted to wealth attains peace fast, with no strife. || 71

Who Stays in this divine state, on him delusion can never descend;
Thus he does reach Brahma-nirvana, the ultimate bliss at the end. || 72

∽   End of Book 2, Samkhya Yoga   ∽

23

Samkhya Yoga

Karma Yoga

Work – A Path to Liberation

Karma = Work or action.
Yoga = Focused effort to attain a specific goal.
BG = Shrimad Bhagavad Gita.

What is in Book 3 - Karma-Yoga

Bhagavad Gita is a very activist faith. It advises that man must work to attain a happy blissful life. One who avoids work has no happiness nor prosperity. This whole chapter is a treatise on the importance of work in man's life; also, it looks at work from different perspectives.

Although "freedom from work" is a goal of life, BG makes it clear that freedom from work is not abstaining from work; rather it is to work in a way that even after doing work, work does not feel like work. This is achieved by working sincerely but practicing to remain emotionally detached from the fruits of work. Work must be done knowing that the fruits of work are ordained by laws of nature and not by the desire of the person performing the work. Incorporating this truth in life, a man can get rid of misery, disappointment and euphoria brought by results of work. This is one of BG's core teachings; work hard without lusting for fruits of work.

Work, especially work of duty must be done to the best extent one can do. Taking a larger perspective, BG says that everyone must perform their duties in society. Only then can society and its people be happy and prosperous. People ought to engage in collaborative work for the common good of their society, their projects, their communities. This idea is illustrated through the deeply spiritual metaphor of "yagna" in Shlokas 10-19. Only if one never lives in society nor derives any of the benefits of social living can they be excused from their social duty of work. Those who live in the society but do not perform the yagna, do not perform their duties are nothing but thieves; they live in vain. That is BG's opinion (Shlokas 12-15). Working in the spirit of yagna brings freedom from grief; brings happiness and bliss.

Delving further (Shlokas 20 - 28), BG inspires man to never give up working, even if he has achieved enough for himself and even if he feels that there is nothing more he could or should attain. If not exactly for himself, the successful man ought to keep working his duties "to maintain the world". If leading people stop working, stop performing their duties then following them lesser more ordinary people would stop performing their duty. It would precipitate social chaos.

Following the guna theory of Samkhya yoga, BG asserts that the Gunas, that is the mental propensities of a man, propel him to act out physical actions. These actions in turn seal the fate of the man (Shlokas 27-29). The implied lesson is that man should strive to modify his guna if he wants to improve his life.

In the concluding verses (Shlokas 36-43), BG discusses the most important question which has eternally vexed people everywhere. The question is why do even very capable people commit evil, sinful deeds as if they are forced by some invisible entity (Shloka 36). In very simple words BG gives the answer: Lust (= uncontrolled desire to satisfy passion for sensory and / or egotistic pleasure) and anger, born out of failure of efforts to satisfy lust, are the causes propelling man to sinful actions. These two are the invisible and eternal enemies. In this context, BG provides the mental structure underlying the arousal of lusts. BG also assures that by practice a man can conquer lusting desire and root out lust. This is obtainable by focused persistent effort; that is Yoga, the Karma Yoga.

Reading Aid - Glossary:

In many places in this translation, the original Sanskrit words in "Karma Yoga", have been retained to improve the rhythm and to provide a halo of the ancient scripture. In the text all these words have been underlined. They are all translated and explained below.

Ahankara = Pride, vanity, ego.
Anna = Prepared food ready to eat, not raw grains etc.
Atman = The Life enabling entity in a living being. Without Atman a
    living being is nothing more than a carcass.
Bharata = Descendant of the clan of Bharata; often used to address
    Arjuna. Often it may also mean "Kingdom of Bharata", i.e., domin-
    ion of "Bharatbarsha" – the ancient name for the country India.
Bharatarshava = Prime bull of the clan of Bharata; really means the
    alpha male in the clan of Bharata; often Lord Krishna lovingly
    addresses Arjuna in this fashion; Arjuna is a prince of the Bharata
    dynasty.
Bramhan = Supreme Reality.
Buddhi = Rational intelligence.
Dharma = Ethics and practices which hold a man together (for happy
    living). In the realm of the physical world it means the properties
    of an object(s).
Guna = Mental tendency or attribute; see also Book 14 of BG.

Janardana = Mover, that is leader of men; often Lord Krisha is addressed in this fashion.

Janaka-ha = "Janaka" name of a very famous ancient king in the great epic "Mahabharata".

Keshava = One with fine hair; often an address for Lord Krishna.

Naishkarmanyam = State of "work-less-ness"; when you work hard to perform your task, but the work does not feel as if you worked, you are not tired in body or mind by doing the work.

Nishtha = Respectful practice with understanding of and attention to details.

Partha = Son of "Pritha"; name of Arjuna whose mother Kunti is also known as Prithaa

Prime-a = Prime; the vowel sound "-a" is added as rhythm enhancer.

Rajaha-guna = One of the three principal mental tendencies in human nature. Dominance of Rajaha tendency makes a man greedy, power hungry etc. make a man easily subjugated to passions. See also Book 14 of BG.

Samkhya = One of the six schools of Indian Philosophies deliberating the nature of reality. Samkhya is the path of understanding employing material observation and rational deliberation.

Shreya-ha = Supreme good for one's own self and for the community.

Work-aha = Work, actions. "-aha" is a vowel added as a rhythm enhancer (Shloka 20).

World-aha = World. "-aha" is a vowel added as a rhythm enhancer (Shloka 20).

Yagna = Willing Collaborative unselfish activity by a community to produce goods for the benefit of the community (team, project, society).

Yagna-karma = Actions performed in the performance of yagna.

Yagna-remainder = Whatever remains after distributing the results of the yagna activity to the participants of yagna.

Book 3

Karma Yoga

Work – A Path to Bliss and Liberation

<u>Arjuna</u> asked...

Oh <u>Janardana</u> if this is your conviction,
That <u>buddhi</u> is superior to actions by far; |
Then "<u>Keshava</u>" why is your suggestion
That I engage in the awful actions of war? || 1

Complex are your words, my friend, they are also not quite clear;
My intelligence is confused, my mind is puzzled oh my friend dear; |
Tell me only one thing that is very sure and also very clear;
Using which all may excel in life, be happy, leaving all fear. || 2

The Holy Lord <u>Krishna</u> said...

It was Proclaimed by Me in the beginning oh you innocent one,
That two paths to liberation do exist in the world for everyone; |

The Path of <u>samkhya</u>
the path of rational discourse and contemplating;
Also the path of <u>karma</u>,
The path of work for those who are seeking. || 3

"Freedom from work" is attained not by any one never;
Simply by him refraining from initiating any work ever; |
Joy and happiness are NOT in the path of any one either;
Nor ever comes bliss, to those renouncing work altogether. || 4

Never indeed can anyone ever;
Remain action-less totally even for a little bit; |
Forced by <u>Gunas</u> in his nature,
A man acts even if it goes against his own wit. || 5

One who keeps on thinking of sensual pleasures,
Who restrains work-organs, posing action-less in deed; |
Deep in mind pleasurable objects who measures;
Is really a deluded self; truly is he a hypocrite indeed. || 6

Who engages with no emotional aching;
His work-organs to the <u>yoga</u> of working; |
Who disciplines his sensual impulses with his own mind;
Is one who excels in his endeavors, is never left behind. || 7

Act you must always to uphold your duty, an obligation;
Know that an action is always superior by far to inaction! |
Even the journey of your own body do require your actions;
Journey of the body cannot be accomplished by inactions! || 8

Truth of the world Oh Mighty Arm,
    Yagna-karma yields freedom and happiness fast;
But bondage will surely do come;
    From selfish work done aspiring desire and lust; |

Therefore Oh Arjuna adopt the spirit of yagna to do your duty;
Always Do your duty unselfishly for the good of the community. || 9

In the beginning creating progenies and yagna-karma;
Said the Creator may practicing yagna be your dharma; |
May the practice of yagna-karma bring you prosperity;
May the yagna-karma be the wish-cow of your society. || 10

May your yagna cherish the gods; back will they you cherish; |
Thus cherishing each other may you all attain supreme bliss. || 11

Cherished by yagna, gods serve the enjoyments you desire ; |
Eating those gifts without offering them back to the grantor;
                    Makes one a thief truly indeed. || 12

Noble are the those eating yagna-remainder after serving others;
    Free and liberated are they, they not blemished ever; |
Wickeds cook only for the sake of themselves not regarding others;
    Suffering they endure, they are blemished forever. || 13

Creatures come into being from food, or anna,;
    Food is from rain showers, it is nature's dharma; |
Shower of prosperity is rooted in work of yagna;
    In yagna, the sacrifice begins in collective karma. || 14

Know that the yagna sacrifice is born from actions, from karma;
Bramhan, the imperishable supreme reality is source of all karma; |

Therefore yagna, the sacrifice is rooted in the all-pervading bramhan;
And the all permeating Bramhan is smoothly maintained by yagna-n! || 15

One who does not keep turning this wheel of welfare;
That has thus been set in motion, by the laws of nature; |
Rather delights only in his own sensual lusting sensation;
Is malicious indeed, Oh Partha, sure does he live in vain;. || 16

When completely contented in himself is a man;
    Who does not need any community around;
Yagna duties can such a man avoid and abandon;
    For such a man no social duty is to be found. || 17

Never does he have a purpose in any action ever;
Nor does in inactions he has a purpose whatever; |
Nor does he ever have any dependence on any single one;
Matters not if he has duties to be done or remain undone. || 18

Remaining detached from results, always doing the best in duty;
Is the hidden law that brings a man happiness, peace and clarity. || 19

Karma Yoga

Starting with "Janaka-ha" a many other great king;
Attained perfection with working but never quitting; |
Knowing this, you too ought to engage in work-aha,
Even if the only purpose is to maintain the world-aha. || 20

Whatever, whatever is the behavior;
Of men superior, those with divine savor; |
Whatever whatever they do manifest,
Others in the world often do them imitate. || 21

In the three worlds, Oh Partha, no duty do I have ever to be done;
 There is nothing that I have not attained;
 There is nothing that remains unattained;
 Nothing remains that ought to be attained;
Even then engage do "I" myself in karma no moments ever shun. || 22

If ever, indeed, "I" am not engaged in working,
 Tirelessly if Me not remain engaged in karma; |
Then everywhere men too will cease functioning,
 Following My way, they will ignore their dharma. || 23

If "I" do not perform any work,
 Worlds will sink, will perish; |
 (Confusion ushering, chaos springing, disorders will galore;)
Causing destruction of creatures and people;
 Disregarding duty is devilish. || 24

The way the un-wise people work hard, with vigor;
Remaining strongly attached to fruits of their labor; |

Same way, with same vigor must the wise work harder;
 To "hold the world together"
But detached should they remain from fruits of their labor. || 25

You ought not to create division;
 In the intellect of the work-addicted-ignorants; |
Wise should cause them, finding reason;
 To remain happily engaged in all their errands. || 26

Everywhere, all actions are caused,
 To be performed by Gunas of material nature; |
Only the ego (ahankara)-shrouded,
 Deluded fools do think that "I" am The real doer. || 27

The knowers of truth, Oh mighty hero,
 Know the distinct roles of gunas and material actions;
Thus they remain unattached Oh hero,
 To persons trapped in their very own specific conditions. || 28

Mesmerized by gunas of the material nature,
 The deluded ones remain stuck to guna-inspired actions;
Truth Knowers should not confuse this creature,
 The person of imperfect intellect happy in his delusions. || 29

Relinquish in Me all your deeds, Oh Arjuna my Hero the mighty!
  Meditating on the Supreme Being;
  Freeing self from all desires lusting, |
  Being totally dispassionate and sober;
  Being like one who overcame fever,
Engage, engage in the battle, Oh Hero, you must do your duty. || 30

Persons who do practice constantly this divine doctrine of Mine, |
Humbly un-sneeringly, are happy, free of the bondage of workin'! || 31

But those sneering-ones, not practicing this doctrine of true ways, |
Know them to be ignorants devoid of knowledge, suffering always. || 32

Even the wise, strives as gunas in his material nature allow him to; |
Creatures are forced by their guna-nature; what can punishments do? || 33

Senses are organized to evoke passions of desire or disgust,
Uncontrolled passion in a person gushes out as anger or lust; |

You should not come under the control of any raging passion;
Subjugation by passions hinders your growth and progression. || 34

Though may be viewed deficient, one's own dharma is superior;
Compared to higher regarded, better honed dharma of another; |

Far Better far superior is dying following one's own dharma;
Marching along different dharma invites dangerous drama. || 35

Arjuna asked:

Then, propelled by what does a man commit evil sinful deed;
Even unwillingly, seemingly enjoined as if by a force indeed? || 36

Holy Lord Krishna spoke...

Lust is this, anger is this,
  Springing from man's "rajaha-guna";
Mighty consuming, mighty harmful;
  Know these to be the enemy prime-a || 37

As fire gets enveloped by smoke,
  As mirrors get obscured by layers of dust; |
As membranes veil embryos,
  So does intellect too get blurred by lust! || 38

Dimmed is the intellect by the duo of lust and anger the vice,
These are the eternal enemies of men even those of the wise; |
Appearing in the form of lust it clouds; it blurs the intellect;
Like a difficult-to-extinguish fire, restive is the anger and lust. || 39

Senses, mind, and intelligence,
  Are said to be "its" places of restings; |
Obscuring knowledge and intellect,
  "it" deludes the embodied beings. || 40

Karma Yoga

Therefore, Oh you the mighty Hero of <u>Bharatha</u>,
Knowing true nature of lust, discipline your senses first,
    Destroy it totally, eliminate it completely,
    The knowledge-and-discrimination-destroying
    The harm-causing, evil-springing, sin-inspiring;
Vanquish the masquerading demon rooting out the lust. || 41

It is said that superior are the senses;
But the Mind is superior to the senses;
Superior to mind though is intelligence of a man;
Superior even to the mind is "this" - the "<u>Atman</u>". || 42

Therefore using intelligence, having learned even of the higher,
Upholding self by the self; defeat you can, conquer you must,
That hard to recognize enemy, the one masquerading as lust! || 43

⟄   *End of Book 3, Karma Yoga* ⟅

BOOK 4
Jnana Yoga
Path of Knowledge and Wisdom

Jnana = Knowledge and wisdom.
Yoga = Focused effort to attain a specific goal.
Jnana Yoga = Path of liberation focusing on knowledge and wisdom.
BG = Shrimad Bhagavad Gita.

What is in Book 4 - Jnana Yoga

In Book 4, Jnana Yoga, Lord Krishna engages in a discussion of wisdom and its purpose in the life of a man.

BG holds knowledge and wisdom in very high regard. To be liberated from miseries and the griefs of life every man ought to cultivate wisdom in his own life. In fact, BG says that wisdom is the holiest thing in the world; it is the most clarifying agent in reality (Shloka 38). The life of a person without knowledge and wisdom is an unending misery (Shlokas 29-40). What is the path forward for an average man? How does he proceed to gain relief from grief and misery? Shlokas 41-42 give a concise prescription. Any person can cultivate the prerequisites for gaining wisdom and gain happiness. This is a great message of hope.

BG states in detail those prerequisites in many of the Shlokas in Book 4. The reader may ask however, what is "knowledge" and "wisdom" in this context? It is clearly explained in Shlokas 35-39. Basically, knowledge is that thing which cures a man of self-deception and delusion, which allows a man to see that the same natural laws are operating in himself as well as in all other creatures. Wisdom is that thing that provides a true knowledge of reality without the distortions of emotional blurring and selfish emotional desire! Although one could split hairs on the difference between knowledge and wisdom in this narration we take them to be the same; and use them interchangeably.

Who can attain knowledge and wisdom? What is the process of attaining wisdom? BG's answers to these questions are in Shlokas 10-12 and also in Shloka 34. BG asserts that anyone who has practiced appropriate mental faculties (Shlokas 39-40) can attain wisdom. One mental habit, the ability to "sacrifice" is especially noted. In this context *sacrifice means to voluntarily give up something that one may like/enjoy in favor of activities and objects imbibing knowledge in the person*. BG describes many types of sacrifices in the Shlokas 25-32.

33

The beautiful Shloka 32 summarizes that there are many types of sacrifices. All sacrifices need work-effort and self-restraint. Simply speaking, these two practices along with respectful submission and freedom to satisfy curiosity by question and counter question and practice are necessary to gain knowledge and wisdom (Shloka 33-35). Without these qualities a man would not attain wisdom, which indirectly means that such a man will have an unsuccessful and miserable life. This is BG's assertion.

BG is composed in the foreshadow of a great war in the epic Mahabharata. So, it is not unusual for Arjuna, the hero of the war, to be curious as to why all through civilizations from time to time there are periodic social upheavals, war turmoil, etc. In Book 4, BG's answer to this question is expressed through spiritual Shlokas in 1-15. In the core, it is asserted that from time to time unvirtuous, greedy people gain control of the society and make life miserable for virtuous people. To remedy the situation there is divine intervention in the form of turmoil. In the process BG provides a deep insight into social organization (Shloka 13). This insight is valid in all societies through all ages.

Knowledge of reality and wisdom is adorable in every age and in every society. However, it so happens that from time to time this value gets tarnished, bringing misery to righteous people. At such times social upheaval does take place and must take place to restore righteous order. This idea is captured in the spiritual language in Shlokas 1-8.

BG's view of what is "Divine" is captured in the beautiful Shlokas 9-15. Note the absence of any reference to religion or race in this description. BG's description is truly universal, secular and time transcending.

What in short is BG's recipe in "_Jnana Yoga_" for a divine life? What should an individual do to enjoy a happy, prosperous, anxiety-free life? BG's advice/path/philosophy can be gleaned from the knowledge imparted in this chapter of "_Jnana Yoga_". In short a man ought to acquire wisdom, ought to sincerely engage in his duty sacrificing selfish desires (Shlokas 19-24) and free himself from the bondages of ignorance by severing ignorance with the knowledge-sword residing in his own heart (Shlokas 40-42). There is no implication of any god or any holy man in this process. A man has to do it himself; with proper practice a man can do it himself.

Reading Aid - Glossary:

In many places in this translation, the original Sanskrit words in "_Jnana Yoga_" have been retained to improve rhythm and to provide a halo of the ancient scripture. In the text all these words have been under-lined. They are translated and explained below.

A-karmana (a-kar-ma-na) = Inaction.

Arjuna = Name of the third Pandava prince who is a mighty hero, com-mander of the Pandava army; also, a great disciple devotee of Lord Krishna. In BG, Arjuna and Lord Krishna are having a dialog enumerating reality.

Atman (Aat-mon) = The Life enabling entity in a living being. Without Atman a living being is nothing more than a carcass.

Bharata (Bhaa-ra-ta) = Descendant of the clan of Bharata; often used to address Arjuna. Often it may also mean "Kingdom of Bharata", i.e., dominion of "Bharatbarsha" – the ancient name for the coun-try of India.

Brahman = Supreme Reality.

Dharma = Ethics and practices which hold a man together (for happy living). In the realm of the physical world, it means the properties of an object(s).

Guna = Mental tendency or attribute; see also Book 14 of BG.

Ikshvaku = Name of an ancient king in the epic Ramayana.

Jnana = Rational knowledge, wisdom.

Karma = Work, action, physical effort.

Karma-yogi = A Yogi or a practitioner who has adopted the path of karma (work) to understand the world, execute his project, etc.

Kuru = Name of the royal family; Arjuna is a prince of this family.

Manu = Name of an ancient King in the epic Ramayana.

Maayaa = Illusion (magic!)

Moksha = Ultimate liberation, liberation from ignorance and grief.

Parantapha (Pa-ran-ta-pa) = Scorcher of enemies; a mighty hero who is dreaded by his enemies.

Partha (Paar-tha) = Son of "Pritha"; name of Arjuna whose mother Kunti is also known as "Prith-aa".

Rajaha-guna = One of the three principal mental tendencies in human nature. Dominance of Rajaha tendency makes a man, greedy, power hungry, etc. Makes a man easily subjugated to passions. See also Book 14 of BG.

Samidha = Knowledge-fire, the fire that burns out ignorance and en-lightens the mind; also used in prayers of yagna.

Samkhya = One of the six schools of Indian Philosophies deliberating the nature of reality. Samkhya is the path of understanding em-ploying material observation and rational deliberation.

Shreya-ha = Supreme good for one's own self and for the community.

Veda = Book of knowledge, the Holy Book Of the Hindu Faith.

Yagna = Willing collaborative unselfish activity by a community to pro-duce goods for the benefit of the whole community (team, project, society). Collaborators sacrifice their effort for the good of the whole community.

Yagna-karma = Actions performed in the performance of Yagna.

Yagna-remainder = Whatever remains after distributing the results of the yagna activity to the participants of yagna.

Yoga = The knowledge or science of bringing body and mind in unison for the performance of meaningful effort; a path of focused sincere effort to reach a goal.

BOOK 4

Jnana Yoga

The Holy Lord Krishna said...

This immutable Yoga, the Jnana Yoga, is the Yoga of knowledge;
I told this Yoga to Sun the God; true it is, great it is at every age; |

Lord Sun gave this Yoga to his son Manu who thus became wise;
Manu gave it to his son king Ikshvaku unblemished by any vice. || 1

Thus receiving this yoga through generations,
    The king-sages became aware of it, were its host; |

Oh My mighty Brave, with the passage of eons;
    The great Yoga itself decayed slowly gaining rot; || 2

Now I narrate to you this ancient Yoga, the Yoga of Jnan-a;
    Know for sure this is truly the Supreme Knowledge-a; |
I reveal this secret Knowledge to you Oh my dear Arjun-a,
    You my dear friend, the greatest devotee in this age-a.|| 3

Arjuna Asked...

You, my Lord, have been born much later;
    The Lord Sun has been born much much earlier; |
How am I then to comprehend the nature,
    It was really You who did this knowledge declare! || 4

Holy Lord Krishna Said...

I have been born many, many a time in the past;
    And so did you too, Oh my hero Arjuna, my mighty Archer; |
I have knowledge of them all even that of the last;
    The dread of thy foes, Oh Parantapha, are not even aware. || 5

Even being birthless, I am the imperishable Atman;
    Of all that comes into being I am the Supreme Lord; |
Having established myself in the material domain;
    Only by My own "maayaa", am I manifest to the world. || 6

Oh Bharatha,
Whenever, whenever unvirtuous are in ascendance;
    Whenever righteous ethical living do get tormented; |
Whenever the unrighteous living grips dominance,
    Then, for sure indeed, I Myself do become manifest. || 7

To liberate, to protect the righteous from their misery and rages;
    To destroy the evil doers and the villains;
    To free the virtuous from their chains; |

    To establish dharma, to seed ethical vigor,
    To spring in their lives happy and virtuous tenor;
I come into existence Myself; manifest do I Myself in ages after ages. || 8

Jnana Yoga

Divine is My birth and divine are My actions ever;
    One who fathoms this truth becomes free of delusion; |
Having left his body, rebirth does haunt him never;
    Enlightened is he, divine, he comes to Me, Oh Arjun. || 9

Passions and fears forsaken; lust and anger quitting;
    Absorbed in Me, seeking shelter, refuge in Me; |
Many, purified by austerity, and knowledge attaining;
    Have reached My state entering into the Divine Me. || 10

Whoever, takes refuge in Me, in whatever way,
I love them, reward I them in that same way;
Oh Partha, men everywhere follow My path, that is the only way! || 11

Desiring success men worship their deities often indeed;
    Paying homage, performing sacrifices, doing work ritually; |
In this world, in the world of men, busily doing their deed,
    Success quickly emerges, born from work done faithfully. || 12

The Four "varnas", the four classes are My social creation;
Based are they on the gunas and the person's occupation; |
Even though "I" am the eternal Lord of this classic division,
Know Me to be the non-doer, eternal am I with no evolution. || 13

Actions do not tarnish Me;
    Nor do I covet fruits of any actions; |
One who thus fathoms Me,
    Is never fettered, by his own actions. || 14

From ancient times, those seeking "moksha", desiring liberation;
    Have done duties unattached to fruits of their action, |
Therefore, you too perform your duty, you too resort to actions;
    In the same way done by those throughout the eons. || 15

Actions and karma; inaction or non-action!
Even to the wise, these topics cause confusion. |
To you shall I explain karma simple, easy, and clean,
That insight will liberate you from all evils and sin. || 16

Karma, actions, obligatory duties each ought to be understood;
Malformed-actions, forbidden actions ought to be understood too;
"Inaction", a-karmana ought to be understood in thought and in deed;
Discourse on karma, on actions is truly deep, truly profound indeed. || 17

One, who sees inaction in action; also sees action in inaction,
    Who Is disciplined and steadfast in engagements;
Is the wise among men who is successful in his every action. || 18

Whose all enterprises have excluded intentions of lust;
    Whose karma has been made pure;
    Fire of knowledge who did endure;
Is the "one" the wise ones designated as "wise" and just. || 19

Forsaking attachment to fruits of actions,
    Always contented, ever independent he remains indeed;
Even though he does engage in actions,
    Not anything ever he really does, bind him to his deed. || 20

Desire-less is he, of restrained-mind-and-self engaged in actions
    Abandoning all desires to accumulate possessions;
    Thinking of the body only as a tool to perform actions,
Never does he gather mental dirt even by executing actions! || 21

Who is not elated by gain, neither in him loss cause dejections;
    Conflict of opposites who has transcended;
    Who Has become free from envy, greed or lure;
    Who Has become neutral to success and failure;
Never is he bound to karma even having performed actions. || 22

With attachments gone, when released from emotions agonizing;
    With knowledge firmly established in consciousness sway; |
With work performed in the spirit of yagna, sacrifice and giving,
    Bondage of Karma wholly dissolves; bondage does fade away! || 23

Dedicate I do all my work and all their fruits to the Brahman,
My work is my oblation, the Brahman is always my inspiration; |
The fire of yagna-sacrifice is indeed always from the Brahman,
Destiny of All my efforts is the Brahman their only destination. || 24

Some yogis
    Sacrifice the thrills of sensory pleasures with little fright;
    Sacrifice those Jnana yogis, those brave and the bright;

In the fire of the Brahman
    They give up gratification of own passions,
        Even the thrilling best; |
    Dedicate they do the fruits of their actions,
        For the good of the rest. || 25

Some do sacrifice pleasures of senses like hearing or touch;
    Sacrifice such pleasures in the fire of their self-restraint; |
Some give up the pleasures of an object they crave so much,
    Sacrifice they do in the fire of senses keeping no resentment. || 26

Some sacrifice actions aroused by sensory longing;
Some sacrifice by controlling rhythm of own breathing;
Inspired by thirst for knowledge and happy living;
In the fire of self-discipline the wise do the sacrificing! || 27

Some do sacrifice by practicing austerity;
    Some offer objects as sacrifice;
    Some pursue yoga as sacrifice;
    Wise ascetics perform sacrifice;
Through gaining the knowledge of reality. || 28

Some offer taking to giving; Others offer giving to taking; |
Yet others control both and make sacrifices for the living; || 29

39

Jnana Yoga

Others curb taking in food, ego, and powers;
      Making the act of taking as taking itself do they sacrifice; |
They are wise, _yagna_ and sacrifice knowers;
      Whose evils and sins get consumed through sacrifice. || 30

To the eternal _Brahman_ goes that sacrifice knower;
      One who enjoys remainders of _yagna_ as the divine nectar; |

Those not performing sacrifice nor _yagn-a_,
      Have neither peace nor bliss in this very world,
      What then to say of them for their after world,
Oh _Arjuna_, the best of the _Kuru_-clan-a. || 31

Know that many types of _yagna_ and sacrificin';
Are arranged in the mouth of _Brahman_; |
Sacrifices all are born of action of man;
Knowing this you will be free from grief and sin! || 32

Sacrificing knowledge is, Oh _Pa-ran-tap-a_,
Superior to sacrificing objects in possession-a;
Honest _karma_ always ends, Oh Paarth-a,
In birth of knowledge and wisdom, no exception-a! || 33

Know that knowledge is revealed to a seeker,
      Curious and of respectful submission,
      By question and by counter question,
      To one with deep penchant for learning,
      Service and self-effort in whom is not lacking,
In Knowledge and truth who does seek shelter. |

The perceivers of truth and surely some wise sage;
Will come to teach him wisdom and knowledge! || 34

Oh _Arjuna_, that is the knowledge which on knowing;
      You will not ever fall again into self deception; |
Through that, shall you see all creatures unending,
      In yourself and then in Me free from delusion. || 35

Even if you are the wicked most,
      Doing the worst sins among the sinners' deeds;
Taking refuge in the knowledge-boat,
      Shall you sail through the stream of sins indeed. || 36

Oh _Arjuna_ as a kindled-fire,
      Burns firewood emits light leaving only ashes,
So does _Samidha_ the knowledge-fire,
      Burns ignorance of life reducing them to ashes. || 37

Indeed in this world wisdom is the most holiest thing;
Nothing in the world exists that is any more cleansing; |

In time every _karma-yogi_ realizes this truth within himself!
Be you sure _Karma_ awakens wisdom in the yogi himself! || 38

Being respectful, with disciplined will,
*   A man does attain wisdom with ease; |*
Attaining knowledge-wisdom very soon will,
*   That man attain ultimate peace! || 39*

The ignorant, the irreverent,
*   The self-doubters do perish suffering only pain;*
They do not have this world;
*   Nor any later world, nor any happiness to gain! || 40*

One who has renounced his actions in yoga,
*   Who has severed his doubts through wisdom-a;*
One who has known "himself" through yoga,
*   Does not get bound by his actions, Oh Arjun-a! || 41*

Therefore with the knowledge-sword residing in your heart,
Sever this doubt-brewing ignorance leaving behind no part; |
Engage in the yoga of work, perform your duty;
Rise up, rise up, go forward Oh my Hero mighty. || 42

☙   *End of Book 4, Jnana Yoga*   ❧

Jnana Yoga

BOOK 5
Karma-Sannyasa Yoga

Path of work-renunciation

Karma	=	Work or action
Sannyasa	=	Renunciation
Yoga	=	Focused effort to attain a specific goal.
BG	=	Shrimad Bhagavad Gita

What is in Book 5 - Karma-Sannyasa Yoga

Karma is work. "*Sannyasa*" is a renunciation. Yoga is union, path, engagement, or tool. Together the title would mean the yoga or path of work-renunciation to achieve divine life. The concept of Karma-Sannyasa, that is of work renunciation, can stand a little explanation.

In an unsophisticated mind work leads to bondage, suffering. Man works to fulfill his desires, to obtain things he covets, to satisfy his greed and lust. As long as man is working, motivated by the prospect of material greed or lust or egotistic gratification, he is also inevitably dogged by the fear of failure and anxiety and agitation in mind. If his work does not yield desired results, he is frustrated, angry and miserable and may even act out in misdeeds inviting punishments. If the work yields a desired result, he is euphoric, agitated in a different way; may boost his own ego; may become arrogant, vain and may be deluded into performing misdeeds. And such is the nature of an unsophisticated mind, that he desires more and gets back to the cycle of working with the lust to obtain more material goods, to satisfy his reignited lusts or to boost his ego. Consequently, he inevitably enters into a new cycle of agitation, anxiety, and misery. Such a man works hard to fulfill his personal desires, but a peaceful, agitation-free happy prosperous life continues to elude him.

As long as a man lives in society, in the family, he is bound to work. There is no escape from it. So, what should the average man do? Should he live in a family, live in society, and keep on working in society resigning to a life without bliss? Or should he leave family and society, live like a hermit, renounce the path of work, and seek bliss following the path of contemplation and meditation? That path is chosen by the hermits, monks and others like them. For an average person this is a serious confusion. In order to attain a divine life should a person remain bound to the path of work by remaining in family and society; or should he abandon work and resort to the path of meditation perhaps through the path of monkhood or hermits?

Karma-Sannyasa Yoga

What is the right path? What is the right yoga for an average man?

Having gotten a taste of the activist philosophy espoused in the Bhagavad Geetha, we can guess what the answer is. In this book of "*Karma-Sannyasa Yoga*", Lord Krishna clearly states that the right approach for the average person is to follow the path of work. This is not a surprise to the reader – especially to those who have gone through Book 3, the "*Karma Yoga*" - the yoga of work. The interesting issue here is how can one be engaged in the path of work, live in the family and society and yet can be free from bondages caused by desire motivated work; that is, how can a man remain a working householder in the society and still attain liberation from anxieties and associated misery? What should the average man do; what should his motivation for work be, what should his view of the world be, so that he can work with maximal efficiency in life and also receive bliss, a life of health, wealth, and prosperity liberated from anxieties, sorrows, and miseries? The issue is phrased in spiritual language as: how can one attain "Moksha", that is attain liberation, while remaining deeply engaged in the world of work? This book, the yoga of "*Karma Sannyasa*", addresses this serious issue. Here Lord Krishna sketches out the path, the mindset, the worldview that a person should cultivate to work in society and also attain bliss at the same time. Without adopting this view, without this mindset, a man will work but will still remain in bondage to suffering.

In deliberating on this yoga Lord Krishna also teaches some truths about reality. We need to comprehend these truths to achieve a blissful working life. Firmly grounded on materialistic foundations, this chapter describes how persons following "Karma Sannyasa" should view the world. This serves as a model of behavior to emulate for those aspiring to follow the path of work renunciation. He describes the underlying (spiritual-neurobiological?) mechanism, which causes happiness or grief in the human mind. Based on such knowledge a man can choose a path, a yoga, where his work does not lead to bondage, to anxieties, and to suffering; rather this path leads to a life of bliss.

Based on natural laws Lord Krishna dispels some popular delusions that man often has about his deities. Man's delusions paint an unreal picture of the deities; delusion of reality causes a man to remain in the grip of suffering. If a man must believe in a deity, Lord Krishna shows how he should view his deity in a way that is consistent with laws of reality (nature). An un-deluded view of a deity leads to a happy, peaceful, harmonious, high-achieving life. Altogether the yoga of "*Karma Sannyasa*" provides a path for the average man who lives in a family and a community, to continue working in society and yet achieve happiness and bliss. All these are expressed in beautiful poetry which sometimes employ mystic spiritual symbolism. We shall explain them as we come to them in the text.

Looking Ahead

Shlokas 1-6: *The activist philosophy of BG always encourages the path of <u>karma</u>, engagement to work as a means of attaining a happy, successful life, over the path of <u>Samkhya</u> - the path of rational deliberation only (Shlokas 1- 6).* BG is not a prescription to become an ascetic. It is a prescription to train your mind and consciousness, to remain engaged in work, to enjoy a good life, and to understand the nature of happiness, contentment, and the properties of the real world (Shloka 2).

Shloka 3 provides a clear definition of a <u>Sannyasi</u>. "*One is always a "<u>Sannyasy</u>", who neither hates, nor covet anything eagerly;*" Thus a <u>karma-sannyasi</u> is one who works at his duties but is not strongly attached to the fruits of his work, <u>karma</u>. A <u>karma-sannyasi</u> works at his duty because duty ought to be performed in the best possible way; but he does not desire any selfish outcome from his work. This <u>yogi</u> performs his work but is not attached to the result of the work in any way. Such a person is a <u>karma-sannyasi</u>. A <u>karma-sannyasi</u> does not eschew his work or duty to the family or society. He simply does not remain strongly attached to the fruit of his work to satisfy his personal desires. According to BG, this person attains a successful life of happiness and peace.

Shlokas 7-11: BG first narrates the difference between the two philosophical schools of <u>Samkhya</u> and "<u>Yoga</u>" in Shlokas 1-6. Then BG quickly delves into the path of <u>Karma-Sannyasa yoga</u> defining it succinctly in Shloka 7. In this <u>yoga</u>, the "*<u>Yogi</u> acts with no greed, lust, or anger in his mind*"; That is, a <u>karma-sannyasi</u> should work without any attachment to the result of the work, <u>karma</u>. The question is if there is no lure of greed, lust, material pleasure, power, etc. motivating his work, then what is the real motivation behind the hard work of the <u>yogi</u>. BG is very clear, quite unambiguous, on this issue. *BG says* that the <u>yogis</u> work for "self-purification", that is to improve their knowledge of the true nature of reality, to clean themselves of the delusions and illusions about the nature of reality, the world, the <u>Brahman</u>. The <u>yogis</u> work hard but are not motivated by desires for selfish material gains (Shloka 11)[1].

---

1 This is not as unrealistic a proposition as it might first sound. Think of people like Isaac Newton, Bill Gates, Mahatma Gandhi, etc. Were they working hard spending their life for an increase in salary, earning a few more dollars or gaining a little more fame? Most likely they were not after any of this. They were busy solving a puzzle (gravity!) presented by nature; they are/were working hard to understand the paths needed to create a better life for a nation or for mankind. All these are

Attachment to the results of work for the purpose of personal selfish gain keeps a man in bondage to work. When a man overcomes those bonds by overcoming his attachment, a man, the karma-sannyasi, becomes free. In Shloka 10, BG uses a very beautiful simile to assert that working as karma-sannyasi, unfettered by the bondages of selfish desire, makes a man happy and highly productive. A man unfettered from such bondages can freely roam around different tasks without being stuck to any of them just as a drop of water moves freely on a lotus leaf, without wetting the lotus leaf though the lotus leaf is always in water.

In Shlokas 14-18, BG provides a refreshing view into the relationship between a doer, his action (work), results of his action and the nature of God (if any God really exists). The connection between an action/work and the result/consequence is embedded in the *material nature itself*; that is, in the laws of material nature. That is, the result/consequence of an action/work is determined by the physical laws prevailing in material nature and not by any hypothetical god or any other spirits.

Unlike the view of god in many other faiths where the god loves and bestows favor on those whom the god likes and punishes the folks who do not obey their god, BG's view is that a god neither takes any one's good deed nor his bad deeds ever. Essentially saying that no god is involved in the happiness or miseries one receives in life. Rather in straight language BG says the result of work/action is embedded in nature itself - no god has anything to do with the result of action; result of action/work is determined by the laws of nature. In other words, the natural law is the *Supreme Lord*! This is a stark contrast to the view of god in many other faiths. Since the results of one's work finally determines the quality of life of the person, BG is making it clear that quality of life is strictly dependent on a man's work and natural laws acting on the work. Understanding this truth enables a doer to focus on the work and remain detached from the result. Since the results of one's work finally determines the quality of his life, BG is making it clear that the quality of a man's life is strictly dependent on his work (and natural laws acting on that work) and nothing else.

The supreme Lord (the natural laws) is equally friendly to all. So is a karma-*sannyasi*! Relieved of emotional attachment to results of action,

---

puzzles in nature. They were all working hard to remove their own ignorance about the solutions to these problems, i.e., they were working for "self-purification", working to remove the blemishes of ignorance and delusions about some aspect, some slice of nature. We all do it in our modest lives whenever we are trying to solve a problem to make a successful project, designing better pathways for a happier life or family. When we view these as work to purify our minds of ignorance or delusion we are actually working as "karma-sannyasi". We all know this kind of attitude is the one which makes us all happy.

knowing that natural laws apply equally to everyone, a <u>karma-sannyasi</u> treats everyone equally, irrespective of his position or power (Shlokas 17-20). Recognizing this truth is wisdom.

Shlokas 20-26: A <u>karma-sannyasi</u> extinguishes his own sense of specialness; extinguishes his ego. He remains engaged in the welfare of the world. He lives in the middle path - no extremes. Control of lust and other sensory pleasures is a virtue. Controlling emotions is a virtue (verse 23). Like the <u>karma-sannyasi</u>, one should not be swayed by sensory pleasures. Such pleasure e.g., those induced by sensation of touch or taste, are transient. They are wombs of sorrow. (Shlokas 20-26).

Shlokas 27-28: BG is not only a set of abstract goals, it also shows some practices that when used can attain these goals. In Shlokas 27-28, BG describes one such <u>yogic</u> practice which enables a man to focus his mind better, which itself is key in solving his problems, recognizing delusions, and seeing truths of nature.

The last Shloka (Shloka 29) is a concise description of a path to bliss and lasting peace. In this Shloka "Me" is the deification of the supreme natural laws (Shlokas 14-15) is the opinion of this author.

Reading Aid - Glossary:

In several places in this translation, the original Sanskrit words in "*Karma-Sannyasa Yoga*" have been retained to improve rhythm and to provide a halo of the ancient scripture. In the text all these words have been underlined. They are translated and explained below.

<u>Arjuna</u> = Name of the third Pandava prince who is a mighty hero, commander of the Pandava army; also, a great disciple devotee of Lord Krishna. In BG, <u>Arjuna</u> and Lord Krishna are having a dialog enumerating reality.

<u>Brahman</u> = Supreme Reality, the material world.

<u>Brahmin</u> = A member of the priestly, scholarly class; widely respected by others.

<u>Chandal</u> = A person of the low class, with poor manners and meagre achievement.

<u>Karma</u> = Work, action, physical effort.

<u>Moksha</u> = Ultimate liberation, liberation from ignorance and grief.

<u>Nine-gated-city</u> = A reference to the human body; it has five doors (gates) through which the body exchanges material with the outside world. The nine gates are 2 nostrils, 2 eyes, 2 ears, 1 mouth, genital and anus.

Samkhya = One of the six schools of Indian philosophies deliberating the nature of reality. Samkhya is the path of understanding employing material observation and rational deliberation.

Sannyasa = Renunciation.

Sannyasi, Sannyasy, or Sannyasin = A person who has renounced something.

Yoga = The knowledge or science of bringing body and mind in unison for the performance of meaningful effort; a path of focused sincere effort to reach a goal.

Yogi or Yogin = Person who is a practitioner of Yoga.

BOOK 5

Karma-Sannyasa Yoga

Arjuna said...

Oh Krishna, You praise "Sannyasa" - renunciation;
And also you praised "yoga"- engagement in action; |
Tell me very clearly, without an iota of equivocation;
Which one of these two is truly the superior option? || 1

The Holy Lord spoke...

"Sannyasa" and Karma-yoga both bring peace and bliss too; |
Karma Yoga is viewed to be the more distinguished of the two. || 2

It is to be known that one is always a "Sannyasi",
        Who neither hates, nor covet anything eagerly;
Oh My Hero, a person free from conflicting tendency,
        Is liberated from bondages of misery quite easily. || 3

The path of "samkhya" is the path of rational deliberation;
And the path of Yoga is the path of engagement in action;
Only children and unwise say different are these two paths;
The wise never say or think these two to be distinct paths; |

Wise know that even when a seeker settles in one of the paths;
Finally, he harvests the knowledge attainable by the other path. || 4

That place that one attains by following "Samkhya",
Is also the same place one reaches practicing Yoga; |
One who sees this truth, truly gets, sees that really,
"Samkhya" and Yoga convey the same insight finally. || 5

But renunciation without resorting to yoga,
        Oh my Hero, is attainable only with great difficulty; |
However, a sage established in the "yoga",
        Quickly attains the Brahman, the truth about reality; || 6

Yogi acts with no greed, lust or anger in his mind;
This is the yogi, the one with an unblemished mind;
This yogi has shunted restlessness far from his mind; |

The Yogi who succumbs not to urges of the senses;
The Yogi who resists the temptations of the senses;
The Yogi who sees himself in all the other creatures;
When that yogi sees in himself those other creatures;
That yogi is never blemished by any of his duty-karma;
That yogi is free even after performing his duty in dharma.
That Yogi is a Karma-Sannyasi! || 7

49

Karma-Sannyasa Yoga

Those yogis are ones who are truth-knowing;
They know seeing, hearing, touching, smelling,
That eating, moving, and also dreaming;
That breathing, speaking, and defecting;
That grasping, and eyes opening, closing blinking;
Are all done by the senses for the sense-satisfying;
Sages realize that "I" do none of these acting;
The "Self" only enables the body to keep it living! || 8-9

One who does his work "offering" it to the Brahman, to the world;
Doing his duties renouncing attachments to fruits of his work; |
A sage thus working never gets stained by any sin whatsoever,
As water drop never wets a lotus leaf though it is always in water. || 10

The yogis use their body, mind, and their intelligence,
Their sensory organs, also organs of work;
They give up bonds to fruits of their work
To purify their own selves do they work;
Work they do to remove delusion and own ignorance. || 11

Engaged in work, renouncing the fruits of work,
The wise attains unending peace, success, and happiness; |
Unengaged to work, addicted to fruits of work,
Dimwits are stuck to anxiety, misery attain no happiness. || 12

Having controlled his senses and sensory appeals,
By his own wisdom the fruits of actions himself renouncing;
In the nine-gated-city does the happy self liveth,
Does nothing himself nor does make anyone do anything. || 13

The Lord, your god nor your deity creates neither your work;
Nor does He create for you the Lordship of your work;
Nor does He connect your work to the fruits of your work;
In material nature itself is embedded fruits of any work. || 14

The omnipresent does take no one's sin;
Nor does the Lord take any one's good deed;
With ignorance shrouding the knowledge within;
Living beings often are deluded of truth indeed. || 15

But, in whom that ignorance
Is destroyed by knowledge gained from self-effort, |
In them that highest knowledge
Do shine always like the bright sun unobscured. || 16

With intelligence who comprehend "That" (knowledge),
Whose "self" is firmly established on "That" (knowledge), |
With knowledge they do shake off the ignorance that blemish;
Unblemished pure they "go," the journey they not repeat afresh. || 17

Treats all equally both high and or low;
Be he a <u>brahmin</u> or may be a <u>chandal</u>-o; |
Same compassion attention to all big or tiny,
Be it an elephant, a cow or a dog quite puny;
That is the person who is "equal-seeing",
This is a mark of a pundit, a wise being. || 18

Those whose minds established in knowledge, in "equal-seeing",
In this very world do they transcend birth-death-birth cycling; |
The Supreme <u>Brahman</u>, the reality is flawless, is their conviction;
With knowledge wise becomes one with <u>Brahman</u> free of delusion. || 19

Euphoria is not what the wise ought to get getting the desired,
Anxiety is what the wise ought not get getting the undesired; |
With steady intellect <u>Brahman</u>-knowing wise is beyond delusion;
<u>Brahman</u> knowing wise remains established in reality not in illusion. || 20

Whose happiness not rests on sensory contact,
That wise finds happiness within self, it is a fact; |
That <u>yogi</u>, the one established in <u>Brahman</u>, in reality;
Finds happiness unending, enjoys calm and tranquility. || 21

(Oh <u>Arjuna</u>, the famed son of Kunti know you that ..)

Pleasures from touch are truly wombs of sorrow;
Such joys are transient the wise do well know; |
Joys born from touch do end with the touch receding;
The wise don't revel in pleasure that surely is fleeting. || 22

Able to endure physical agitation released from anger and lust; |
Is the <u>yogi</u> who on this earth itself enjoys happinesses to last. || 23

Who is happy with himself, one who is at peace with self;
Is a wise soul illuminated by the radiance of his inner self: |
Self-ego is his holy oblation, gets untethered from his ego lofty;
That <u>yogi</u> ascends to be One with <u>Brahman</u>, the supreme reality. || 24

From whom the confusion of duality has been cleaved away,
In that blemish-emaciated sage discipline and <u>yoga</u> holds sway; |
That sage engages in welfare of all beings with no selfish fire;
Is the One who easily extinguishes ego, sires no greedy desire. || 25

A mind that chips away lust, rage and vain;
A mind that reason curbs and keeps in rein; |
That wise thus knows his mind clear and well;
To him extinction of ego lies very close as well. || 26

Happily expelling all external agitations crowing;
Eye-gaze set in the middle of eyebrows fixing; |
Balancing inhalation-exhalation through the noses;
Without being restless One who does the practices; || 27

Karma-Sannyasa Yoga

Keeping intellect and senses in disciplined mind;
Abandoning lust, fear, and anger away far behind; |
Seeking <u>Moksha</u> that wise One who does the practice respectfully;
That sage that <u>yogi</u> is freed from anxiety, misery, and grief steadily. || 28

Know Me to be the enjoyer of all sacrifices;
Know Me to be the Supreme Lord free of vices;
Know Me to be the well-wishing-friend of every ones',
Knowing Me, engaging in work a <u>yogi</u> receives bliss,
The wise <u>yogi</u> ascends the dome of supreme peace! || 29

End of Book 5, Karma-Sannyasa Yoga

Abhyasa Yoga
Path of Practice

Abhyasa = Practice, repeated practice - NOT rote work.
Yoga = Focused effort to attain a specific goal.
BG = Shrimad Bhagavad Gita.

What is in Book 6 – Abhyasa Yoga

"Abhyasa'' means practice, repeated practice. "Abhyasa Yoga" refers to "union with the Divine" through practice. This chapter describes the "practices'', that is the "abhyasas", to liberate ourselves from the miseries and griefs of our lives and lead us to a life of excellence, life of joy, life of prosperity, to a life of union with the divine. The practices described here are doable by everyone, irrespective of faith, creed, and abilities. The practices or the "abhyasas" are of universal application.

In practical terms, union with the divine really means adopting divine behavior and cultivating divine spirit in ourselves, which in turn enables us to overcome the miseries of life and bestow on us a life of bliss. These "abhyasas" or practices lead the practitioner to a fuller understanding of reality, which in turn reduces/eliminates miseries from our lives. These are not practices to lead any one to an union with or to an audience with any mythical God. The practices prescribed here are collectively called "yoga" or union or path. The practitioner is a "yogi" or a "yogin". The practices do not require any difficult acrobatics of the body. It really is a technique to discipline your mind and develop a world view which conforms to the true nature of reality. When the mind is disciplined and a "correct" template is used to look at and understand the world, we do acquire divine habits and truly do achieve union with the divine. Again, the divine here does not imply the existence of any mythical God. It simply means integrating divine habits and outlook in one's life which leads to a life of bliss. This chapter describes the practices which will take the practitioner to the path of the divine.

The previous chapter ("Book 5"), the "*Karma-Sannyasa Yoga*" or "Union through Work-Renunciation", describes the virtues of work renunciation. Nowhere does it say that renunciation of work is equal to abandoning work; nowhere does it promote laziness. Work renunciation means refusing to identify one's own self with the result of his work. "Renouncing" here means renouncing the fruit of one's work to gratify his physical senses or his ego. Though this is one of the laudable goals, that chapter does not say how to achieve that state of mind. What to do, what practices to perform to elevate oneself to that state of mind and to incorporate the world view of a "yogi". This chapter concentrates on the methods which will enable one to achieve the state of mind of yogi. The path described here depends on practice alone; and is doable by everyone.

The path to the Supreme or the divine excellence in any discipline of human activity is through quieting of the mind. Mind is the vehicle riding on which a person can achieve excellence and can get in touch with the divine. There is no other vehicle.

An analogy may help here. One may wish to reach a distant destination riding on horse or driving an automobile. Whatever his chosen vehicle, there are two steps (stages) in the process. First, he must learn how to ride/control the vehicle; then he must be able to teach the vehicle the cues that the vehicle must obey to reach the desired destination. These two steps are true and required to successfully use a vehicle to reach the desired destination; it does not matter if the vehicle is a horse or automobile. Similar is the case when one's own mind is the vehicle. With his self effort, one must quieten his mind by specific practices (Shlokas 11-14); and also practice mental habits (the cues!) with which to direct the mind to look at and understand the reality. The practices are spread throughout this chapter - Book 6. Together these pieces of advice complete the practices which a seeker can practice to reach a highly productive life and attain bliss. BG also provides processes to follow in case the seeker has somehow veered away from the goal (Shlokas 37-47).

A quiet, controlled, unwavering mind is a prerequisite to achieving the divine, to achieving excellence. This is a central thesis here. This chapter provides an insight on how to quiet your mind through a specific set of practices. Then, it also describes the outlook which needs to be developed to achieve a blissful life.

Unlike some of the previous chapters, this chapter does not open with a question. It carries on the deliberation from the previous chapter and enters a new theme. The previous chapter (Book 5) was on the virtues of renunciation. A yogi is one who has renounced his attachment to the fruits of action. It is easy to declare renunciation of the fruits of one's actions to be a laudable goal, but how does one cultivate the mental habits and strengths to achieve such a state? How does one proceed on the path to be a yogin, to abandon the attachment for the fruits of action? This chapter describes the practices a person can undertake to develop such an outlook.

Looking Ahead

Shlokas 1-2 define who is a "Yogi" and its relationship with "sannyasa".

Shlokas 3-4 describe the two stages an aspirant must accomplish to be a "yogi".

Shlokas 5-6: Self-control is essential in the pursuit of becoming a yogi, as is harboring and nourishing a positive self-image. The importance of self-image, self-discipline, self-confidence, and lack of self-deprecation are described here. Make yourself your own friend and not an enemy – is the advice given to an aspiring yogi. Self-control is to be practiced relentlessly.

Shlokas 7-10 describe the attributes or qualities a yogi should cultivate!

Shlokas 11-14 describe a simple physical practice for the aspiring yogi to discipline his mind. It also sets the goal which a yogi ought to aspire to. The main idea is to minimize irrelevant movement and not attend to irrelevant visual stimuli to control the restlessness of the mind[1].

Shlokas 15-17: A yogi practices the "middle of road" lifestyle. Yogis avoid excesses of every kind.

Shlokas 18-19: A disciplined mind free from lusting desire, unwavering in its pursuit of the true knowledge of reality is the hallmark of a yogi. A very beautiful simile is in Shloka 19.

Shlokas 20-23: A mind made free of agitation by the practice of yoga is the gateway to ultimate happiness. That is, Yoga helps one conquer agitations in his mind; and this leads to ultimate happiness. Yoga is the mechanism which causes "dissolution of union-with-pain". A yogi does not need external stuff to be happy (Shloka 20). Neither does a yogi depend on pleasure of the senses for bliss (Shloka 21), since the Yogi knows that pleasures from senses are temporary and are actually the "womb of sorrow" (see *Book5 - Karma Sannyasa Yoga*). Sloka 23 provides a succinct spiritual definition of yoga.

Shlokas 24-25 indicate the importance of abandoning lust as the driver of life, a path which a yogi should practice.

Shloka 26 recognizes the ever-wandering nature of the untrained mind; but BG assures us that through practice (Shloka 11-14), such

---

1   The theory is that by controlling voluntary activation of the muscular system, one slowly quiets a restless mind; a quiet body quietens the mind (brain) which is the original source of controllable muscular functions. Physiologists will be better able to say if the theory is correct or not.

wanderings can be disciplined and a path to unblemished happiness does open up.

Shlokas 27-28 describe the beautiful concepts of "Union with <u>Brahman</u>" and "contact with <u>Brahman</u>". These are two expressions of the same concept. Implementing them in life leads to bliss and life of uninterrupted joy. Here <u>Brahman</u> means reality.

Shlokas 29-32: The <u>yogi</u> understands the principle of "one-ness" – which reduces confusion. "One-ness" is the understanding that every being is controlled by the same natural laws, which is not partial to anyone over another. The Divine Lord ("Me") is the spiritual deification of the natural laws in the opinion of this author. Understanding the true nature of <u>Brahman</u>, i.e., the true nature of reality, a <u>yogi</u> acquires imperviousness to the turbulent conditions (sadness or feisty-ness) of life.

Shlokas 33-34: <u>Arjuna</u> remains skeptical of the notion that mind can really be controlled!

Shlokas 35-36: First Krishna agrees that <u>yoga</u> is difficult to be mastered by an undisciplined mind, however He assures that with sustained practice mind can be brought under control; and can be slowly, incrementally detached from the lust and passion driven way of acting and living.

Shlokas 37-39: <u>Arjuna</u> seeks clarification, especially about the fate of those who sincerely aspired to become a <u>yogi</u> but failed because of a lack of self-discipline though they were well intentioned! It is the story of most of us; it is a very valid inquiry. Krishna's answer is in the rest of the Shlokas of this chapter.

Shlokas 40- 45: Krishna assures us that well intentioned effort is never totally in vain. Though not reached to perfection such efforts lead to continued improvement in vision and life. With continued striving the <u>yoga</u>-aspirants seek out the company of people of similar or higher ability and continue to ascend in the path. Well intentioned effort leads to improvements in knowledge and life. It is never a waste!

Shlokas 46-47: <u>Yoga</u> and <u>yogi</u> (as described above) are asserted to be better than ascetics and ritual workers! Also, <u>yoga</u> performed with love is higher than <u>yoga</u> performed with rational understanding alone; so it is said.

Reading Aid - Glossary:

In several places in this translation, the original Sanskrit words in "<u>Abhyasa Yoga</u>" have been retained to improve rhythm and to provide a halo of the ancient scripture. In the text all these words have been underlined. They are translated and explained below.

Arjuna = Name of the third Pandava prince who is a mighty hero, commander of the Pandava army; also, a great disciple devotee of Lord Krishna. In BG, Arjuna and Lord Krishna are having a dialog enumerating reality.

Brahman = Supreme Reality, the material world.

Brahmin = A member of the priestly, scholarly class; widely respected by others.

Karma = Work, action, physical effort.

Karma-phala = Karma is work, effort, action; "phala" is fruit. Together it means the fruit of work or effort.

Kusha grass = A type of tall grass normally growing on riverbanks.

Moksha = Ultimate liberation, liberation from ignorance and grief.

"Raja-ha" guna = Second of the three principal mental propensities defined in Indian philosophy. "Rajaha guna" is the propensity underlying unusual attachment, lust, and greed for objects and ego. A much more complete deliberation is in "Book 14 - *GunaTraya Vibhaga Yoga*".

Samkhya = One of the six schools of Indian philosophies deliberating the nature of reality. Samkhya is the path of understanding employing material observation and rational deliberation.

Sannyasa = Renunciation.

Sannyasi, Sannyasy or Sannyasin = A person who has renounced something.

Shabda-Brahman = "Shabda" is sound; "Brahman" is reality. Together it may mean that something which transcends Brahman riding on sound. Since in older days, in the days of Vedic civilization, knowledge could only be transmitted orally. This expression could mean spreading knowledge in all corners of reality. It is a Vedic recitation; this author knows little about.

Tapasvi = An ascetic.

Yoga = The knowledge or science of bringing body and mind into unison for the performance of meaningful effort; a path of focused sincere effort to reach a goal.

Yogi or Yogin = A person who is a practitioner of Yoga.

Yoga-stha = Established in yoga, deeply engaged in yoga.

BOOK 6

Abhyasa Yoga

The Holy Lord Krishna said...

Forsaking pleasures of home and hearth does not make one a "tyagi";
One who forsakes attachment to the results of karma is the true "tyagi". || 1

Listen Oh Pandava, renunciation and yoga are basically not different;
But none is a yogi who has not renounced karma-phala attachment. || 2

Karma effort is the tool feeding a man's yoga inspiration;
Core of a yogi's victory is a calm mind free of agitation. || 3

When indeed one stops clinging to work to gratify his own senses;
He is a savvy yogi who renounceth them beyond his mind's fences. || 4

One should set the self free by efforts of the self;
Not discourage nor deprecate the self by the self; |
The self indeed is the noble friend of the self, helps you grow;
And self alone can be a vile enemy of the self, you should know. || 5

In whom, the self has been conquered by the self,
Self remains in that self as a great friendly help; |

In a self in whom the self remains uncontrolled;
In that self the self is an enemy hostile and bold. || 6

The disciplined mind succumbs not to anxiety ever;
Always serves the Supreme Lord with great fervor; |
In hot or in cold, in anguish or in joy, honored or insulted;
Yogi, that noble soul, is always calm never is he agitated. || 7

Whose self is satiated with rational discriminative knowledge;
       Conquered are whose senses, whose passions not bold;
Established is who, immovable-standing-at-the-top not at an edge;
       Equivalent to whom are clay, stones or a bar of gold;
Is the one who is called a great Yogi! || 8

Who remains un-emotional to all be they allies, enemies or friend;
Standing in the middle of friend and foe to neither does he bend; |
Impartial is who to both a virtuous and a heinous;
Is the hallmark of a yogi distinguished and famous. || 9

Remaining in solitude, thoughts free of desire and bondages of possessions;
Yogi should constantly yoke himself to self, not thinking of lust nor passions. || 10

On a firm ground not too high, nor too low but is neat,
       Yogi should spread his kusha grass seat;
Keeping his mind calm fixed and restrained would he sit;
       The Yogi would remain still not moving a bit. || 11

A single thought focused in mind, senses all ruled by the self;
Fixed on yoga sits the yogin seeking purification of his inner self; || 12

His body, neck and head straight and erect, steady with no motion;
Eyes gazing at the tip of his own nose looking not in any other direction. || 13

With mind calm, apprehensions all banished,
In the practices of a "brahmachari" established; |
Disciplining mind, thoughts riveted to Me,
Concentrated he should sit, devoted to Me. || 14

The yogi's mind and his own self always thus yoked to Me;
Goes to peace, to that nirvana supreme, in union with Me. || 15

Overeating is not a Yogi habit, nor too indulgence in starvation;
Nor oversleeping nor keeping over awake is in a Yogis bastion. || 16

Moderated in food and play; efforts and actions balancing;
Disciplined in sleep and awake, the yogi destroys suffering. || 17

Mind completely controlled, established in the self fast;
When free from longing, free from desire of last bit of lust;
Then is the Yogi said to be the "disciplined" saint at last. || 18

As the flame of a lamp in a windless place is motionless without flicker;
Thoughts in a mind engaged in yoga of the self also does not quiver. || 19

When yoga practice restrains the self, when the mind stands stilled;
When Yogi sees self by the self, with happiness his mind gets filled. || 20

Ultimate happiness is grasped by intellect alone by the senses never;
Knowing this truth, the yogi remains satiated with happiness forever. || 21

Attaining which, Yogin regards nothing else to be a superior gain;
And staying at which not shaken is a yogi even in profound pain[2]. || 22

Know you all that dissolution of union-with-pain is yoga's definition;
Practice it with a mind un-dismayed and unwavering determination. || 23

Lust driven intentions all completely renouncing;
Mind and senses controlled and fully disciplining; || 24

Intelligence firmly grasped, little by little actions ceasing;
Mind fixed in the self; the Yogi should worry about nothing. || 25

Whenever, wherever, wanders the restless mind hither or thither;
Yogi himself restrains his mind controlling it right then and there. || 26

The passion-calmed serene mind,
The yogi unblemished and kind,
    Remains always at peace; |

Freed from gnawings of "raja-ha" gun-a;
Yogi becoming one with Brahman-a;
    Yogi enjoys ultimate bliss. || 27

---

2 Which equals the ultimate happiness in Shloka 21.

Abhyasa Yoga

Engaging himself always in yoga,
Yogi is liberated from evil and ego; |
Then with ease no doubt does the Yogi attain;
Supreme happiness of contact with Brahman. || 28

Himself established in all beings,
And All beings established in himself;
Thus sees the yoga-disciplined self,
Everywhere he is equal-seeing. || 29

Who sees Me everywhere; sees every existence in Me;
Never am I lost for him, nor ever is he lost to Me. || 30

Who sees Me, honors My presence in every being in existence,
Whose faith is established in one-ness,
In Me does that yogi dwell in every state of his own existence. || 31

Oh Arjuna, In happiness or in sorrow, in every situation,
One who sees everyone the same as the self,
No doubt is he the supreme yogin, that is my opinion. || 32

Arjuna said...

Oh Krishna, the yoga that you spoke of now;
To be practiced through the even-ness of a calm mind;
I do not perceive this would be possible how;
Relentless restless mind is the nature of the human kind. || 33

Oh Krishna, truly restless, indeed, is a man's mind,
Harassing, strong and obstinate is nature of mind; |
I think restraint on the human mind;
Is as difficult as restraining the wind. || 34

Lord Krishna said...

No doubt, not easily quiet nor is at peace,
Naturally restive is a man's mind, not easily restrained;
But my Hero know this sure-o that with practice,
And detachment, mind too can be subdued and be trained. || 35

My opinion, oh hero, yoga truly remains very far from an uncontrolled self;
But with practice and discipline, yoga do indeed become a part of Yogi's self. || 36

Arjuna asked...

Those, who came with faith but in discipline if they are low;
Those, whose minds have veered away from yoga;
Those, who have failed to attain perfection in yoga;
Oh Krishna, please tell me which way, where do they go? || 37

Having been cut-off from both worlds, these failed men;
Cut-off from world of yogis and from the more mundane;

Do they get lost forever, rudderless do they just wander;
Disconnected do they just float like clouds of little thunder;

Having failed to establish himself in yoga, what paths do remain for this man;
Is he deluded forever from path of truth, reality; away from path to brahman? || 38

Oh Krishna, only You can burn away my deep confusion;
Leaving no residue please do cut away all my delusion;
Other than you, none else can be the splitter of this doubt.
None else do I see who can steer me to the shore of truth. || 39

Lord Krishna said...

Indeed, not "here" nor "there³" is a yoga desirer destroyed ever;
Oh my hero you should know, misfortune grabs the virtuous never ever. || 40

Attaining the world of the virtuous folks, dwelling there for many years;
The one fallen-from-yoga reappears in a house that is pure and illustrious. || 41

Or else he comes to be born in a wise yogi family by his virtuous deed;
In this world, gaining such birth is more rare and quite difficult indeed. || 42

There he (re)gains the state of his former self⁴ Oh great hero Partha;
Then joined by intelligence, striving toward perfection he remains yoga-stha; || 43

Indeed by it, by habit of prior practice continuing;
Inquisitive of yoga gradually this wise soul striving;

Slowly gets moved forward to perfection;
May be not always with conscious action;

But practice of yoga-habits does purify the seeking man;
Do know that in time this yogi surpasses Shabda-Brahman. || 44

From sincere striving aided with the mind disciplined;
Yogi attains supreme goal becoming pure, unblemished;
Attaining perfection that yogi over many births of practice;
Yoga-siddha becomes the wise Yogi freed from every vice. || 45

Superior to an ascetic tapasvi, is the yogi;
Greater than a learned man is said to be a yogi;
A ritual worker remains far behind him, the yogi;
Therefore, oh Arjuna, strive, strive to become a yogi! || 46

Even, among all the yogis that honor Me;
One who has merged his inner self in Me;
With love and respect who adores Me;
That yogi is viewed as the one most attached to Me. || 47

ॐ *End of Book 6, Abhyasa Yoga* ॐ

---

3 heaven
4 spiritual

BOOK 7
Jnana-Vijnana Yoga
Path of Knowledge and Rational Discrimination

<u>**Jnana**</u> = Knowledge
<u>**Vijnana**</u> = Knowledge obtained through experience/experiments and rational discrimination.
<u>**Yoga**</u> = Focused effort to attain a specific goal.
BG = Shrimad Bhagavad Gita

What is in Book 7 - Jnana-Vijnana Yoga

"<u>Jnana</u>" means knowledge and wisdom. "<u>Vijnana</u>" means knowledge obtained through experience/experiments and rational discrimination. The words "science" and scientific method normally translate to "<u>Vijnana</u>". <u>Vijnana</u> means that kind of knowledge, which is obtained through experience, which stands experimentation, is reachable and confirmed by rational discourse. "<u>Jnana-Vijnana Yoga</u>" would mean Union with the Divine through the *path of knowledge and rational discrimination*. Union with the Divine means attaining a divine life; a life of happiness, free of stress and anxieties.

This path described in this seventh book of BG is based on material experience, discriminative knowledge, and rational analysis. It is not a path of blind belief or hear-say. The road to success and happiness, the path to resolve your crisis and confusion is through "<u>jnana-vijnana</u>", i.e., through the application of knowledge and rational discrimination and by believing that everything in the world is governed by natural laws. Through rational discrimination one would avoid blind faith and irrational ways. This is the underlying philosophy expounded in this chapter, in beautiful spiritual language.

Looking Ahead

Book 7 concisely describes BG's concept of the structure of reality. It is an axiom in the Upanishad school of philosophy and in BG, that man's unhappiness and miseries stem from his lack of true knowledge of reality. So, it is very rational that BG opens this chapter straight away by defining the structure of reality. It illuminates what is divine by simple examples. It deliberates on why most people fail to see the truth about the nature of reality and suffer in their lives. It describes the categories of people who spend effort to understand the true nature of reality and with effort ultimately reach divine life.

Shlokas 1-7 describe BG's view of the structure of reality. It divides material nature in two layers or two planks: the inferior plank or the lower layer contains objects and forms which are sensed innately by everyone. This includes the five main components which are manifest. It is worth noting that BG includes the mind, intelligence, and egotism also as components of the lower layer. This is quite reasonable because ultimately these components are based in material structures as well. The upper layer or the superior plank of reality contains the Supreme power which sustains the world of objects and forms.

Many do not recognize or believe in the Supreme Component; and hence they fail to discover or understand it. The Supreme Component is unseen by our sense organs, but it controls all changes in the universe. It is visible only through intellect and realization. This component is deified in the form of Lord Krishna. Throughout this book, Lord Krishna says "I" or "Me" as a proxy for this superior component of nature. We will see in the narration that this superior component of material nature has properties attributed to God in popular faith. So, if Lord Krishna is deified as the Supreme Lord, the deification is not unjustified! The Supreme Lord of the universe is/are the natural laws which govern all facets of reality. So, a proper interpretation of the Supreme Component is that the Supreme Component contains or is the natural laws (physics, mathematics) which determine the state of every object in the world. In the demystified interpretation of BG, we equate the Supreme Component with natural laws. Once we accept this equivalence all the mystical expressions in this Book and elsewhere in BG become simple, easily understood by everyone. It ought to be noted that though the supreme element and the natural laws are unmanifest, their effects in controlling the events of the world are very manifest. For example, gravity is unmanifest, but the falling bodies to the ground are very manifest. So, equating the unmanifest Supreme Being to the natural laws is very appropriate.

Shlokas 8-11 give examples of divinity or divine qualities from among objects we experience in our everyday life. This part is beautiful.

Shlokas 12 and 13 introduce us to the concept of three "gunas" and "guna-states" which are present in all material forms. The gunas determine the behavior of human beings. This is a fundamental concept and is useful in understanding the behavior of entities of the world. Guna means attitude and mental propensity. BG and Samkhya Yoga deal with Guna pretty extensively[1]. Readers should look at Book 14 - "Gunatraya Vibhaga Yoga" of BG for a more complete deliberation on the Gunas.

---

1 This is one of the more fundamental contributions of BG in the author's opinion.

Shlokas 14 and 15 introduce the concept of "Maayaa". It is another fundamental concept in understanding the true nature of reality, and our own behavior. A close English translation of Maayaa is a delusion (error in judgement). In these verses lie an answer to a common question as to why some people discover or "see" underlying principles of the world and others cannot / do not see it. To be deluded by Maayaa, is to remain stuck in the lower strata of material nature and falsely imagine that the view of the lower layer is the complete view of the universe. The veil/grip of Maayaa can be eliminated only by vijnana - rational discrimination (Shloka 14).

Shlokas 16-19 describe four categories of people who are able to loosen the grip of 'Maayaa' on them, partially or completely; and are able to perceive the true nature of reality to the corresponding extent. It also states categorically that it takes a long cycle of efforts (the spiritual expression is the cycle of death and rebirth) to understand the truth about reality. It takes a long and often varied series of experiments before the law/principle controlling a system becomes clear to the investigator!

Shlokas 20-23 describe the nature of faith in the human mind. It implies that gods in different faiths are actually different facets of the Superior plank of material nature - deified as the one Supreme God. It shows how different faiths are subsumed within the universal view of a Supreme God as the deification of the Superior plank of reality. In turn it indicates how different faiths, poly-atheism, etc. are actually localized views of the Superior plank of reality. It also indicates how people charmed by their own desires follow specific gods or faiths, rather than following to understand the Superior plank of material nature. Essentially their limited desire encourages them to follow gods or paths who they think are capable of only bestowing limited or restricted gifts. Wise people / yogis however are driven to *understand* the true nature of reality; that is, they are driven by the desire to understand what laws/processes govern the system; they strive to understand the nature of the upper layer of a system. Such people are not distracted by limited gains from worshiping gods promising specific power or gifts. For example, the driving forces in these successful people are not money, raises at work, stock bonuses, etc; their driving force is to understand the laws governing the behavior of the system.

Shlokas 24-25 emphasize the un-manifest, imperishable, eternal nature of the Supreme Lord; that is the eternal, unchanging nature of the natural laws - the upper layer of reality. For example, the gravitational principles never change; they are eternal and active throughout the material universe.

Shloka 27: Here creation = birth, initiation of a project, or similar activities; All projects in life start with ignorance, desire, delusion, etc. But slowly through worship, work, and rational thinking these are cleared up; that is the idea. Through work and rational thinking everyone can get rid of their delusion.

Shlokas 26-30 provide a great message of hope. Although everyone at birth is gripped by the duality-delusion propped by emotions, with faith in rational discrimination as a tool, everyone can explore and understand the true nature of reality and thus be liberated from the grips of confusion, ignorance, grief and misery.

Reading Aid - Glossary:

In several places in this translation, the original Sanskrit words in "_Jnana-Vijnana Yoga_" have been retained to improve the rhythm and to provide a halo of the ancient scripture. In the text all these words have been underlined. They are translated and explained below.

Amruta = The magical potion conferring immortality.

Arjuna = Name of the hero, a principal character in BG and the epic Mahaabharata.

Brahman = The universe, the reality.

Buddhi = Intelligence, specifically rational intelligence.

Dhananjaya = A nick name of the hero Arjuna.

Jnana and Vijnana = Jnana means knowledge; Vijnana means knowledge obtained through experience, experimentation and rational deliberation based on material reality.

Prakriti = Material nature.

Kunti = Name of Arjuna's mother.

"sattva", "Rajaha", "Tamaha" = Names of the three principal mental propensities or attitudes.

Guna = Mental propensity.

Maayaa/Maya = Delusion; some time may mean illusion too.

Vasudeva = A name of Lord Krishna; here indicates the Superior layer of reality.

BOOK 7

Jnana - Vijnana Yoga

The Holy Lord Krishna said...

Arjuna, please heed this message from Me;
When your mind is always attached to Me;
When your mind always takes refuge in Me; |

When mind engages in Yoga relentlessly;
When mind becomes free of doubts fully;
Then you surely will know Me completely! || 1

Hear now about jnana and vijnana;
About knowledge and rational discrimination-a;
Knowing these nothing else on earth;
Remains for further deliberation-a. |

I will tell you completely the truths of jnana and vijnana;
Knowing these, nothing else to you will remain unknown-a. || 2

Of thousands of men, scarcely a few strive to be perfect;
Even amongst the striving only a few do become perfect;
Even among only a few who do understand Me perfect;
Few are those who realize My nature that is unmanifest. || 3

Eight components build up "prakriti", the material nature;
Earth, water, fire, wind, space, its five manifest features;
Mind, "buddhi" and egotism complete the architecture; || 4

These eight items in Prakriti form its lower layer;
Now then do hear the mystery of its upper layer; |
Power of the upper layer, the world I keep on holding;
With which I sustain everything living and not living. || 5

Know you sure that this upper layer of Mine;
It is the womb of all things living or nonlivin-; |
I am the root; I am the origin of whole world;
In Me also lies the dissolution of the entire world. || 6

Oh "Dhananjaya", nothing else does exist in the world;
Which is higher or superior to Me;
Like flowers strung on a garland are the entities of the world;
The thread holding them is none but Me. || 7

Oh, son of Kunti, in water I am the life giving Amruta, know it for sure;
I am the radiance in the sun and the moon, don't you doubt anymore; |

In all the Vedas the holy sound "Aum" is My expression;
In the space I am sound, I am the manhood in the man. || 8

I am the holy fragrance of earth, its aroma, its holy scent;
I am the life in all the living who will come, who came and went; |

Jnana-Vijnana Yoga

I am the energy of the sun beaming out its vigor;
In the ascetic I am the austerity, rigidity, and rigor. || 9

In all creations both in the past and future;
I am the eternal seed of all the creatures; |

I am the intelligence in the intelligent;
I am the radiance in the radiant! || 10

In the strong, I am the strength, free of lust and attachment;
In all creatures, obeying Dharma, I am the desire, love fervent. || 11

The three attitudes "sattva", "Rajaha", "Tamah-o"
All do indeed come from Me; |
I am in none of them though, is what you ought to know;
But know that they are all in Me. || 12

The three gunas are seated in every being, and creature in nature;
Charmed by the gunas, the deluded ones know not my true feature;
They fail to discern, they fail to perceive;
That supreme, imperishable, perpetual is my true nature. || 13

Unearthly supernal, heavenly indeed is the guna-induced Maayaa;
Very difficult is it to pierce through that cloud, that veil of Maayaa;
Only those who take refuge in Me, transcend the illusion of Maayaa. || 14

The evildoing, the deluded ones, the lowest among men,
They do not seek resort in Me, nor bring Me in their life;
Knowledge stolen by Maayaa the wretched amongst men
Trapped in demonic attitudes, they get life with a miserable vibe. || 15

Oh Arjuna,
Four types of good-doing people honor me and rise;
Those in pain, those who are curious,
Those who desire prosperity, and those who are wise. || 16

Amongst them, the wise, the eternally steadfast one;
The one with undivided devotion, is indeed the special one;
I am very dear to the wise, to me the wise is the dearest one. || 17

Indeed, all these people are noble and kind;
But the wise with his unwavering mind; |
But the wise is My very own self, that is my opinion;
Remains fixed in Me, as supreme goal, no hesitation. || 18

Piercing the veil of Maayaa, tossing out doubts from mind;
*   After many births do the wise finally seek refuge in Me;*
*   "Vasudeva is the ultimate of everything", he does see;*
Know that such a great wise soul is really difficult to find. || 19

Their intelligence stolen by lust,
Many resort to other deities wishing objects they lust;
Fixated only on trite rituals fast,
They remain limited, gaining only the object of lust. || 20

Whoever worships whatever form or deity,
    Willingly with devotion and faith;
    On him do I indeed bequeath;
Resolute enduring faith in that form or deity. || 21

He who respectfully performs for pleasures of his god;
And from that effort he receives some fruits,
Know from Me alone have those fruits been ordained. || 22

Short lived are the fruits of effort and action;
To gods go the god-worshippers with devotion;
Small things folks of small-intelligence do obtain;
My devotees proceed to Me, never in vain. || 23

Not knowing My higher state
The unintelligent thinks
My lower form is "Me" that is manifest;
Even though in My higher state;
I am eternal, I am un-manifest,
Supreme am I in my higher state || 24

In this world confused by the Maayaa cover;
Not everyone can see My invisible feature;
Nor can everyone realize My true nature;

Few know that imperishable I am, eternal I am; || 25
They know not birth-less and ever present I am. || 25

I know all beings all the creatures of the past,
I know the living ones too, forever none will last; |

I know all the beings that will come in the future;
But only a wise few will ever know My true nature. || 26

Swayed by the swelling up of desire-hatred-duality and delusion,
All beings come to be deluded at the beginning of each creation. || 27

Those whose sinful actions have ended;
In virtuous actions who have fully blended; |

Liberated from the duality-delusion,
They Worship Me with firm resolution. || 28

Those taking refuge in Me, who seek shelter in Me;
Strive for liberation from frailty and death,
Brahman the Supreme Self they knoweth;
Completely they know all the actions as well as Me. || 29

Those who know Me to be the Supreme Being;
Supreme God is none but Me, thus knowing;
I am the Lord of all sacrifice, so believing;
They Know Me thus with faith unwavering;
Are at peace even at the time of their departing. || 30

ॐ End of Book 7, Jnana-Vijnana Yoga ॐ

Akshara-Brahma Yoga

Path of Imperishable Brahman

Akshara	=	Permanent, unchangeable, imperishable.
Brahma	=	Reality
Yoga	=	Focused effort to attain a specific goal.
BG	=	Shrimad Bhagavad Gita.

What is in Book 8 - Akshara-Brahma Yoga

"Akshara" means something which does not change, mutate, or disappear. Akshara is something which is permanent, unchanging and is imperishable. In contrast, "kshara" is something which is impermanent, which is transient, mutable and which shall arise and disappear in time. Brahman is a central concept in philosophy. Its simplistic meaning is "reality". Everything that exists, whether one sees it or not, whether one knows about it or not, whether one can think about it or not, is in Brahman. Whatever you see, do, know, or are ignorant about, but if it exists, it is in Brahman. There is nothing beyond Brahman; there is nothing beyond reality.

The previous chapter (Book 7: *Jnana-Vijnana Yoga*) described a model of reality in two layers. The tangible portion of reality is composed of objects with forms. The tangible portion of reality is "*kshara*", meaning which is transient, which does change with time. The "*kshara*" layer of objects and forms can be felt by our senses. Behind the "*kshara*" view of reality, is the core from which all objects and kshara forms arise, change and dissolve into. This core is the "*Akshara*" or permanent or immutable component of Brahman. *Purusha* is the more common name for the Akshara component of reality used in Bhagavad Gita. The "*akshara*" form that is the *Purusha* is not tangible through our senses; it has to be realized through intellect, rationality, and consciousness.

This chapter is a conversation to understand this imperishable immutable component of the Brahman, which is the "*Akshara-Brahman*". *Akshara-Brahma Yoga* is thus the Union with Divine through the path of understanding the *Akshara* nature of the Brahman, the reality.

In the Shlokas to come a reader will see that the postulated properties of Purusha are exactly the same as those of natural laws that we know today. That is why in our demystified narration Purusha is equated to be the same thing as natural law. Purusha is postulated to be the creator of the world. According to BG, all manifest objects emerge from the unmanifest by the power of Purusha; are transformed to other objects and forms and finally dissolve into unmanifest; all by the power of <u>Purusha</u>. This is exactly the view held by modern theories of Physics. When the great physicist Stephen Hawking says that the universe has been created and is continually changing by the "creative" forces of physics, Hawking is actually restating the model of reality proposed in the Bhagavad Gita in 20th century language. The creative forces of Physics are being ascribed the same properties ascribed to <u>Purusha</u> in BG. It would be interesting to see how this very modern thought is foreseen, introduced, and developed in this ancient text.

A reader will see in the narrations below, that the attributes, properties, and characteristics of the <u>Akshara Brahman</u> or the <u>Purusha</u> as described in this chapter of the ancient book and those of the universal laws as we understand today are virtually identical. In fact, they are so similar that our narration will assume that *Purusha* and universal laws are different names of the same thing, the imperishable component of reality, the <u>Brahman</u>.

Though this chapter opens with the definition of the philosophical terms "<u>Adhi-bhuta</u>", "<u>Adhi-daiva</u>" and "<u>Adhi-yajna</u>", its main thrust is on <u>yoga</u> or union with the imperishable <u>Brahman</u>. Union with imperishable <u>Brahman</u> means understanding the nature of the imperishable component of reality, that is understanding the nature of *Purusha*, (in other words understanding the nature of natural law) and integrating these teachings in our outlook and behavior. This is all done in beautiful poetry veiled in spiritual language.

What the "imperishable <u>Brahman</u>" is has been described in the previous chapter. This chapter is a deliberation of: How does one realize this imperishable <u>Brahman</u>? What happens when one realizes the imperishable nature of the <u>Brahman</u>? How does such understanding change a man's life? In short, what is the impact of understanding or not understanding the nature of the imperishable <u>Brahman</u> in one's own life on the understanding of his own universe? A simple answer is that understanding the imperishable <u>Brahman</u> will liberate the seeker from his sufferings in this world. The answer is not mysterious at all. We know that knowing the components of a system and the laws which regulate the system, we can interact with the system more effectively and make fewer mistakes. A man's life interacting with the world constitutes a system. The more a man knows about the laws governing the behavior of a system, including the one comprising the man and his world, the more a man can work effectively in the system. Being more effective and being more efficient with the system means a man is more successful with the system and reap the rewards of success more often; it means that such a man suffers from failures and their consequent miseries a lot less often. This is the same as saying that by realizing the nature of the *Akshara Brahman* one will attain a happier, more productive, and prosperous life. Knowing the akshara part of nature prepares a mind to see and appreciate unseen but real truths (laws) about nature and keeps such a knower free from delusions and sorrows.

Looking Ahead

Shlokas 1-2 present Arjuna's questions about the concepts of "*Adhibhuta*", "*Adhi-daiva*", "*karma*", and "*Adhi-yajna*".

Lord Krishna's answers start at Shloka 3.

Shlokas 3-4 provide concise definitions of these technical concepts. They are important to understand since this is the opening to the broader discourse on this subject.

Shlokas 5-8: In essence these verses declare the universal truth that through intentions and effort, a man will finally become what he wills to be; there is no doubt in it. They provide a path to be in union with the divine; the path is to remember the divine at all times in all your efforts, integrate the divine ways in all phases of your life.

Shlokas 9-14: These verses give a concise beautiful description of the Purusha, the imperishable component of Brahman (the reality). Purusha is the one which enlivens every being in the universe, and which permeates every object space in the universe. These verses also lay out a path toward understanding the nature of the Purusha. Purusha is the law(s) controlling the transformations in the universe and is imperishable though the forms created by the power (action) of the purusha are temporary and perishable. This is the central thesis. This fundamental theory of the universe or the Brahman is depicted in five short verses. Imagine! From our knowledge of modern physics, we arrive at precisely the same understanding of the nature of the universe.

Shlokas 15-19: These verses describe a central concept of the *Indian/Hindu* view of the universe as a dynamic system, which is in eternal flux from creation through sustenance to dissolution and back to creation again under the control of the Purusha. These verses use the metaphor of day and night of Brahma as the birth and dissolution cycle of the universe. Readers may note that this view is true for the personal universe of every person as well.

Shlokas 20-26: These verses talk of the un-manifest nature of imperishable Brahman; they use the metaphor of re-birth to indicate that man undergoes the cycle of birth and death till he has shed his ignorance of the true nature of reality; till he has realized the nature of the un-manifest yet all-pervading laws of akshara Brahman.

Shlokas 27-28: These verses emphasize there are only two paths in the world: the path of light (enlightenment) and the path of darkness (ignorance)! They talk about the characteristics of each path. Finally, it declares that the path of light leads to understanding the nature of the imperishable Brahman, which is the ultimate destination of every wise person. Understanding the nature of the imperishable Brahman is to attain the union with the divine.

Reading Aid - Glossary:

In several places in this translation, the original Sanskrit words in "*Akshara-Brahma Yoga*" have been retained to improve rhythm and to provide a halo of the ancient scripture. In the text all these words have been underlined. They are translated and explained below.

Akshara = Imperishable, immutable state of reality.

Arjuna = Name of the hero, a principal character in BG and the epic Mahaabharata.

Adhi-bhuta = Impermanent mutable destructible state of reality

Adhi-daivata = The supreme divine agent in reality; also called Purusha.

Adhi-yajna = Lord of sacrifice; final goal of sacrifice.

Adhyatma = The inherent nature of person(s).

Brahma = Creator of the universe according to Indian mythology.

Brahman = The universe, the reality.

Kalevara = Body; poetically also used to mean the environment a person lives in.

Karma = Action; creative power that causes origin and changes in beings.

Paartha = Another name of Arjuna, the hero in the epic.

Purusha = The supreme divine agent in reality; natural laws in this narration.

Uttarayan = Season of the year when the Sun is in its northern passage. In this season the days become brighter and longer in the northern hemisphere. Equating light to enlightenment, in the poem the Suns passage in "Uttarayan" symbolizes a higher and higher level of enlightenment in the seeker.

Veda = The Holy scripture, book of knowledge.

Yajna = Collaborative work, project where participants congregate work, according to their skill for the welfare of the community.

Yuga = Technically it means twelve years. However, in mythological or astronomical literature it is much more than that. I do not know the exact number.

BOOK 8

Akshara-Brahma Yoga

<u>Arjuna</u> spoke...

<u>Brahman</u>, Supreme self, <u>Karma</u> what are their meaning;
Please teach me all these Oh my Lord;
What in the world is declared to be the Supreme Being;
What is said to be the Supreme God? || 1

Oh Lord, in this body what is "Supreme Sacrifice"?
What is its shape or form? What does it look like?
How will a devotee, a disciplined yogi also wise,
Will know "You" when it is time for his final hike? || 2

The Holy Lord Krishna said ...

"<u>Akshara</u>" <u>Brahma</u>n is the imperishable, is the supreme of all beings;
The creative power that causes origin and changes in all the beings;
Is the definition of "<u>Karma</u>", known as action;
"<u>Adhyatma</u>" is the inherent nature of a person. || 3

The impermanent mutable destructible state of reality is "<u>Aadhi-Bhuta</u>";
Known as <u>Purusha</u> the supreme divine agent in reality is <u>Aadhi-Daivata</u>; |

In this world "I" am the "<u>Aadhi-Yajna</u>"-a,
"I" am the Lord of all Sacrifice-a;
You should know you great hero <u>Arjuna</u>
"I" am the final goal in all sacrifice-a. || 4

At the end-time while he is Me remembering;
When from his own <u>kalevara</u> he is departing; |
My states and attributes he will be attaining;
Know this is true there should be no misgiving. || 5

At the time of departing from his <u>kalevara</u>
The attributes a man remains engrossed consuming; |
Know that on his return to a new <u>kalevara</u>
Similar are the attributes with him he will be bringing. || 6

So remember Me always dedicate your genius to Me;
Commit your intellect, your ability always only to Me; |

Engage in the struggle, in the challenge tho bitter;
You will surely come to Me, doubt you not it ever. || 7

With disciplined practice of <u>yoga</u> he abandons anxiety and jitter;
Directs all thoughts to the <u>Purusha</u> not rambling hither nor thither;

The yogi who remains absorbed in meditating on the <u>Purusha</u>;
Is astute, is the wise who surely attains the Supreme <u>Purusha</u>. || 8

Akshara-Brahma Yoga

That birthless the eternal, that _Purusha_ governor all beings, is the ultimate;
    Who is subtler than the subtlest;
    Even subtler than atom lightest;

    That _Purusha_ is the holder of every single thing;
    His form is beyond imagination beyond all seeing;

    Darkness runs far far away from His brush-a;
    Bright (Radiant) as Sun is He; all obey Him the _Purusha_;

On Him, on that Supreme _Purusha_, the wise, the seers do happily meditate. || 9

At departure, practicing _yoga_, his steady mind unwavering;
With respect, faith and devotion to Him the Yogi firmly latching; |

Focused on the middle of the eyebrows, yogi's vital breath steadily holding;
When merged deeply in _Yoga_, Yogi attains the _Purusha_, that Supreme being. || 10

Veda wise folks assert imperishable immutable is "That";
Losing all emotional bias, the seekers do enter in "That"; |
Shunning excesses who lead life in the holy path;
In brief I describe to you now that virtuous path. || 11

All gates of the body disciplining;
The mind to the heart restricting;
Vital breath in the head holding;
Establishing self in _yoga_ concentrating; || 12

One syllable HOLY sound "OM" uttering;
Faithfully humbly on Me meditating;
Who goes forth his body abandoning;
That wise sage is the one Supreme goal attaining. || 13

Yogi whose mind cease wandering;
Who is ever busy of Me thinking; |
In Me who is always happy staying;
That great soul finds Me easy attaining. || 14

Those great wise souls, to Me they do cometh;
Transcend they do the cycle of life and death; |

In the home of sorrow and frailty, their presence does come to end;
Reaching the highest perfection, in MY abode they reside to no end. || 15

All beings in all worlds of _Brahman_;
Are made to return again and again;
Cycle of death and birth is all in nature's rhyme;
Breaks only by attaining Me the Supreme divine. || 16

Knowers of truths (time) of day and night the wise do say;
That man's thousand _yuga_ spans _Brahma's_ only one day;
And after a thousand man-_yuga_;
    One _Brahma_-night comes to end, so they say; || 17

When a Brahmaa-day is breaking;
    From the unmanifest appear all forms manifest;
At the arrival of a Brahmaa-evening
    All manifest forms dissolve into the unmanifest. || 18

In the world of living and of the nonliving too, all that are manifest;
All those existent, time and time again all with forms come to exist; |

But they remain unable, remaining powerless they;
They do fade away at the dusk of the Brahma's day;
Even then again become manifest they;
At the dawn of Brahma's very next day. || 19

But there is even a higher entity that has no form, that is always notable;
That entity is the Supreme, invisible, is eternal, and never is that mutable; |

That Supreme Being never is it damaged, never is it impaired;
Even after the living, or non-livings do perish, or get impaired;
That Supreme One remains eternal, remains fresh, remains ever unimpaired. || 20

It is said "That" is indestructible, unchangeable "That" is unmanifest;
Wise souls contend that That Supreme is man's destination ultimate; |

Achieving that goal, the wise never return from that holy estate;
That exalted place, that divine abode is where I am the resident. || 21

Listen Paartha, that Supreme, the Purusha, is heavenly, divine nevertheless;
Only by unwavering effort is He to be attained not findable by any path else;

In Him resides all beings living or not, animate and inanimate;
He extends over the whole universe, every being He does permeate; || 22

The "time" a yogi goes, departs from the world;
Conditions if he returns or not back to the world;

Now then hear oh My great Hero you are my dear friend,
I will tell you all about times when Yogi may choose his end. || 23

In bright day, in bright lunar fortnight, in fire bright, and in Uttarayan;
Departing in these conditions, Brahma-knowing folks go to Brahman. || 24

In smoky air, in dark lunar fortnights, in nights when light is dim;
In Sun's southern passage of shortening days daylight getting dim;
Then departing, a yogi goes to the lunar-heaven making there his own way,
Enjoying pleasures there for a while, yogi returns to earth for another day. || 25

Truly, eternally in the universe there are only two paths for a seeker;
Path of light is of knowledge, darkness of ignorance shroud the other; |

Walking the path of light, the yogi gets liberated from bondage of rebirth;
Striding on the other man remains tied to the cycle of death and rebirth. || 26

Knowing these two path-a,
    A wise yogi is never in delusion, never does get deluded;
Therefore at all times Oh Paartha,
    Remain steady in yoga, not ever should you get annoyed. || 27

Akshara-Brahma Yoga

Studying <u>Vedas</u>, charitable giving, performing <u>yajna</u> deeds;
Disciplined non-pompous living in life are all virtuous deeds;
Scriptures have ordained fruits for doing all such holy deeds. |

But fruits do not charm the yogi's wise mind blind;
Continuing practice of <u>yoga</u> with unwavering mind;
Knowing truth of <u>Brahman</u>, of immortal <u>Purusha</u> Supreme-a;
Beating such fruits, the yogi attains the pristine abode Supreme-a. || 28

‽   *End of Book 8, Akshara-Brahma Yoga* ‽

BOOK 9

Raja Yoga / (Raja-Guhya Yoga)

Yoga / Path of Royal Importance

Raja = King or Royal.
Guhya = Concealed, secret.
Yoga = Path, Focused effort to attain a specific goal.
BG = Shrimad Bhagavad Gita.

What is in Book 9 - Raja Yoga

Raja means King or Royal. Why is the chapter named *Raja Yoga*? Just as the King is the first among the people of the kingdom, so is the "*Raja Yoga*" thought to be the prime amongst the set of yogas described in this Holy book. Just as the King epitomizes the kingdom, as the king is the symbol of the kingdom, so is this Book 9 on *Raja Yoga*. *Raja Yoga* epitomizes the beauty of the other paths. This chapter is a subtle summary of the lessons of the other yogas in this book. "Raja Guhya" means the concealed secrets worthy of the royalty, known to the royalty. This chapter discloses truths which normal people do not know or may not care about. These are known, believed, and acted on by the wise (the Rajas) in the society. Both of these terms actually mean the same thing; a set of truths which are of great importance among the other paths which lead man to a happy, anxiety free, successful life.

In this Book 9, the fundamental nature of reality is going to be described; it will also connect to our spiritual thinking; it will demystify our view of the world in which we live in, and our own relationship to the world.

Having a good understanding of the true nature of reality liberates a man from miseries in life! This is the underlying thesis of the *Upanishads* as well. This idea is the core behind the deliberations in this book.

This "yoga" is *Raja Yoga* or the Royal Path. It means that amongst other paths this path is of royal importance. It is not a path prescribed or restricted only for the kings. This path is of royal importance since it deals with the description of that part of reality which is not immediately tangible to physical senses but the part which controls the manifest nature of reality. One could think of it this way: although the king himself is rarely seen by the subjects; the king's laws control all aspects of the kingdom. The part of reality, the natural laws, are themselves concealed to the senses; but their effects are visible and manifest in the life of every person. The laws are the kings; they are of royal importance.

As in other places in BG, in the Book 9 also, the Divine or the divine lord Krishna is actually the deification of the natural (physical and spiritual) laws of the world. Once we view the mystical reference to the Divine as the hidden reference to the natural laws, the mysticism in this chapter completely disappears. We will see whatever attribute of the Divine is being narrated here, are actually the properties of the natural laws narrated in a spiritual language. The underlying teaching is that the universe is law bound, law driven; that all transformation in the universe and in life are controlled by laws (and thus in spiritual language, controlled by God or the Divine); that the laws (that is, the Divine) is impartial, they apply equally to everyone. It is futile to attempt to influence the laws to act in your favor or work against your enemies. The Divine cannot be persuaded by pomps or exuberance in your actions or worship. The only way to please the Divine is to strive sincerely with undistracted devotion to the Lord. The underlying truth is that a life of egoless service to others (family, organization, society, flag, nation etc.) brings unending happiness and success. Life devoted to gratification of ego, selfish lust produces a mixed bag of euphoria, misery, and grief. This knowledge is a royal secret, royal knowledge, available to everybody but only the wise adopt it as a way of life. This is the path following which the wise may attain unending peace, happiness, and prosperity.

Therefore, the advice is that wise men should ceaselessly attempt to understand these laws and comply with these laws in their life and activities. That is, stated in spiritual language, they should always worship the Divine sincerely all the time without entertaining distractions. Worshiping the Divine will end the seeker's delusion about reality. And reduction of delusion will usher in happiness, prosperity, and peace. This is the summary of _Upanishadic_ thinking abstracted in this chapter of _Raja Yoga_ – the yoga of royal importance.

Reader, whenever in this chapter you encounter "I", "Me" or "My", replace those references in your mind with the concept of "natural universal laws", and find for yourself if the meaning of the Shloka is based on physical reality or not. With such replacement the entire Shloka will appear de-mystified and will appear to be a true description of reality, and an effective path for a happy successful life.

Looking Ahead

Shlokas 1-2 introduce this royal yoga, the royal path. The path, the deliberations here are based on rational discrimination, not on blind faith. The path is available to everyone, not restricted to royalty of any kind.

Shlokas 4-7 describe the attributes of the Divine Lord, a spiritual proxy for the natural laws. The Divine permeates the entire universe, so do the natural laws. Divine and the laws are concealed from the physical senses, they are not seen; they are not manifest. But they are known by their effects on the manifest world. The laws cannot be seen but their effects are seen all over the universe all the time.

Shloka 9 also Shloka 29: The Divine Lord, the natural laws, is not partial to anyone or anything. In stark contrast to the God(s) in many other faiths, BG's Divine Lord is not partial to His followers nor is he vengeful to those who are not. It is easily and perfectly understandable when you equate the Divine to the natural laws of the world. (Example: laws of gravity do not favor or hate anyone.)

Shlokas 11-12 lucidly describe the attributes of ignorant deluded people.

Shlokas 13-15 describe the attributes of wise people.

Shlokas 16-19: All activities, individual or collaborative, are under the control of the Divine. Belief in this idea will reduce the ego of the individual and inspire the believers to do their best in their effort. Actually, nothing anyone can ever do which is not permitted by the natural laws. This is a physical reality. In beautiful spiritual language these Shlokas are defining the properties of the natural laws which are the sole controller of the world.

Shlokas 20-22 are a poetic description of how man's life cyclically passes through phases of pleasures and lack of it, till they find the path and adopt the path to undistracted peace and happiness (Shloka 22), by having full faith in the Divine, the natural laws. Then they attain unending peace and happiness.

Shlokas 23-24 are a beautiful description of how Bhagavad Gita subsumes all other faiths (Shloka 23), though the idea may not be charming to some of the other faiths. It is possible because Bhagavad Gita resorts to the true reality of the world; that the world is governed by natural laws. BG does not depend on any mythical or imagined entity as the controller or creator of the world. Nothing can persist unless it is based on natural laws (Shloka 24).

Shlokas 26-27: In worshiping the Divine Lord in BG, love and sincerity is the key; no need for pomp. Actually, pomp or theater does not do any good, since the Lord is strictly impartial to everything and everybody (Shloka 29). All that is needed is sincere and respectful effort. To succeed in any endeavor is obeying the Lord, that is, complying with the natural laws with rational discrimination.

Shlokas 27-29: A recipe for a happy prosperous life is being indicated here. A life dedicated to egoless service to others is a happy, agitation free life. This idea is described in many other places in BG as well. Readers may note the special applicability of this advice to the mighty hero Arjuna, who is to engage in a very serious and may be a calamitous battle. Only when Arjuna is acting without ego and doing his best as a service to others (the society, the nation, etc.), is he going to be happy and live peacefully forward no matter what the result of the battle is. The advice is true for everyone from a commoner to the king in all ages in all places.

Shlokas 30-34: These Shlokas are actually messages of hope and a path to redemption for everyone. Anyone, even those raised in a defective environment and following wicked paths, can redeem themselves to happy peaceful life if they surrender to the Divine Lord honestly and pursue life according to the teachings described here. This is concisely spelt out in Shloka 34.

Reading Aid - Glossary:

In several places in this translation, the original Sanskrit words in "*Raja Yoga*" have been retained to improve rhythm and to provide a halo of the ancient scripture. In the text all these words have been underlined. They are translated and explained below.

Arjuna = Name of the third Pandav prince in the Epic Mahabharata. He is the principal disciple of Krishna.

Dharma = Ethics, ethical behavior; loosely it means religion.

Kalpa = In Hindu cosmological thought a Kalpa is one thousand Maha Yuga. Essentially it is a very very very long period of time. A Kalpa is marked by the beginning of creation of the manifest world. At the end of a Kalpa all manifest things dissolve into unmanifest, nothingness. This is the concept of Kalpa. Inherent in the idea is the concept that the world and universe comes to be created and dissolved many many times.

Partha = another name for the hero Arjuna.

Vedas Rig, Sama and Yajur = Vedas is the principal Holy Book of the Hindus. Veda actually means knowledge, the book of knowledge. Rig, Sama and Yaju-r are three main sub books in the Vedas. These are really large books written in the ancient form of Sanskrit. Mythologically speaking Vedas (that is knowledge) are the creator's gift to mankind.

Yajna or Yagna = Collaborative effort of a group of people for the common good of the group, society etc.

Yoga = Focused practice to achieve a goal.

BOOK 9

Raj Yoga / Raja Guhya Yoga

Holy Lord Krishna spoke...

Now I reveal to you that knowledge;
Which is the most secret of all;
Don't you sneer at it, nor do ignore it,
it is the greatest knowledge of all; |

I shall tell you this supreme knowledge;
Combining with rational discrimination;
You will be cleansed by this knowledge;
Of dirt and defects of ignorant persuasion. || 1

This royal knowledge, this royal secret;
Know it to be supreme; Know it to be pure,
It is visible, is understandable be you sure;

Righteous it is; happy, pleasant to practice it is;
Indestructible, imperishable, and also eternal it is. || 2

In this dharma, in these truths those ignorant ones those devoid of faith;
Not attaining Me, remain stuck into the unending cycle of life-and-death. || 3

The whole universe do I pervade it is living or inanimate;
Concealed to all senses am I to none am I ever manifest; |

All beings reside in me always, whether living or not;
They all live in me, but in any one of them I live not. || 4

Divine is My yoga power, listen to its essence;
Moving or not, I bring all beings into existence; |
Animate or inanimate, every being is sustained by Me;
None do abide in Me, nor ever does anyone capture Me. || 5

Just as even by staying in the sky, great wind soaks everything;
So too all beings are immersed in Me, I do drench every being. || 6

At the erosion of a Kalpa,
Material beings come back to Me at the end;
At the advent of new Kalpa;
Recreating new beings back them do I send. || 7

Propped up by My own material nature,
I create, I send them forth time and time again;
Entire multitudes do I send, resistance is in vain;
From My control of material nature. || 8

Oh Arjuna,
No karma ties me down, nor am I addicted to any karma;
Indifferent do I sit, unattached unclinging; that is My dharma. || 9

Oh son of _Kunti_,
Forced by Me as the Principal Sublime and Supervising;
Material nature creates animate and inanimate being(s);
Because of this reason, the world keeps on changing. || 10

The deluded ones do hate, do despise Me;
    When human form is My impression; |
They know not that the higher form of Me;
    Is the Mighty Lord of all Creation. || 11

Indulging in vain hopes, satiate they do in vain actions;
They take resort to vain knowledge and poor cognitions; |

Wicked in nature they are, their nature likens more to a demon;
And they do seek shelter, not in enlightenment but in delusion. || 12

Oh _Partha_, the wise souls do take shelter in My divine sanction;
Worshiping Me with steady mind indulging in not any distraction;
They know Me to be the origin of beings immune to destruction. || 13

Singing My glory and striving with firm determination;
Eternally they worship Me, honor with deep devotion. || 14

People worship Me in many many ways:
Making sacrifices in many umpteen ways; |

Some do knowledge sacrifice, others sacrificing objects they do adore;
Some keep faith in monism, others worship gods many many more;
Only the wise knows My presence in all directions is truly galore. || 15

In all sacrifices, in all _yajnas_, I am at the beginning I am also the end;
I am the plan, the ritual, I am the sacrifice without vice;
I am the offering; I am the cure in the medicinal plant;
I am the fuel, I am the holy text, I am the sacred chant;
In all efforts I am at the beginning through the middle to the very end. || 16

Of this universe, I am the creator, I am the father;
I am the mother, the grandfather also the arranger;
I am the object of all knowledge;
    I Am the final goal of every seeker; |

The soul cleansing holy sound "Om" in the core really is about Me;
I am in the Holy _Vedas Rig, Sama and Yajur_, they are all about Me. || 17

I am the summum bonum of each and every seeker;
Of the whole wide world, I am the supreme sustainer;
I am the observer; I am also the examiner;
I am the great Lord of all, none is greater. |

I am the final abode; in Me all have a divine shelter;
I am the greatest friend of all, none else is greater;

I am the origin, also the world do dissolve in Me;
Lord of maintenance of the world is none but Me;
I am the treasure,
    The imperishable seed of the world is also Me. || 18

Raja Yoga / (Raja-Guhya Yoga)

"I" warm up (the world); I send the rain; I am the warmth-a;
I am <u>Amruta</u>, the nectar of immortality; also, I am the death-a;
I withhold, I let go!
I am holy, also I am unholy that is dreadful yet is the truth-a. || 19

Knowers of the three Vedas, the divine drink Soma drinking;
Cleansed of evils, through sacrifices, <u>yagna</u> and worshiping;
These men do pray for their goal, that of heaven attaining; |
Earning merit, they go towards heaven to the world of gods;
Enjoy they do their divine pleasures in the company of lords. || 20

Having enjoyed the wide heavens, their merit exhausting;
They enter and re-enter in the world of the mortal being;
Thus par three laws of the Vedas they do keep conforming; |

They do cycle through going and coming;
And objects of desire they keep on having. || 21

Those who ignore distractions, on Me meditating;
Those who are worshiping Me with hearts loving;
Eternally steadfast who are happily Me-honoring; |
From Me they receive whatever they are needing;
Whatever they have I am the one who is protecting. || 22

Even those who are devoted to other gods wilfully;
While they do worshiping the other Gods faithfully; |

Even they, Oh Paartha are worshiping Me and Me only;
Though, not according to rule, not knowing the truth fully. || 23

"I" am The Supreme; the final Enjoyer is Me ;
Lord of all sacrifices, all sacrifices come to Me; |

But those who do not understand me to be as such;
They sure will fall, will vanish from their perch. || 24

Those devoted to Gods, to the Gods those devotees go;
Those devoted to ancestors, to the ancestors they do go; |

Those devoted to the spirits, in spirits they find their home;
But those sacrificing for Me, surely come to My shining dome. || 25

A leaf, a flower, a fruit, even only simply a little water;
Offering With love and devotion for Me without a flutter; |

Given with love and devotion, I take all their offerings for sure;
When gifted by those whose Self is dedicated and hearts are pure. || 26

Whatever you do, whatever you eat, whatever way you do live;
Whatever you sacrifice, whatever you cede, whatever you give; |

Whatever austerity you practice, whatever it may return;
Do all that as a sacrifice unto Me asking nothing in return. || 27

Surely shall you be released from all elation and agony;
From bondages of all your actions, good, bad and any; |

Disciplined through the "yoga" of renunciation;
You shall attain Me; you shall achieve liberation. || 28

Impartial am I to all beings; all are equal to Me;
None do I hate, nor is any one a darling to Me; |
All those with devotion who do worship Me;
I am in all of them, they also are all in Me. || 29

Even if the worst evil doer do take refuge in Me,
Undistracted if he firmly takes to worshiping Me; |

Having ditched the evil path, that soul ought to be considered virtuous;
Since he firmly resolved on My path, the path right for the righteous. || 30

Quickly that man becomes virtuous; he does attain peace unending;
Oh Arjuna be you sure that My disciples are impervious to destroying. || 31

Even when raised in evil womb if one takes Me as his final outlet;
Be he a Vaishya or a Shudra or even a feeble hearted effeminate;
Receiving My grace all of them will surely attain the peace ultimate. || 32

Then what about the Brahmanas,
*   The holy, and the royal sages who too are devoted?*
Having received the impermanent unhappy world,
*   Devoting themselves to Me, they will also be liberated. || 33*

Be you Me-minded, be you devoted to Me,
*   Bow you down to Me; Be Me-sacrificing,*
*   Be Yourself steadfast in yoga Me-remaining;*
*   I am the supreme goal thus always holding;*
No doubt soon shall you be coming unto Me; || 34

ॐ *End of Book 9, Raja Yoga* ॐ

BOOK 10
Bivuti Yoga

Path of Realizing Splendor of the Divine

Bivuti = Splendor, grandeur, brilliance.
Yoga = Focused effort to attain a specific goal.
BG = Shrimad Bhagavad Gita.

What is in Book 10 - Bivuti Yoga

"Bivuti" means glory, magnificence, opulence etc. Here Bivuti means the glory, magnificence of the Divine. "Yoga" is union, the path, the process, the practice(s) which takes a person from one state to another. In this case yoga is the path which can take a person from the life of wants and grief to a life in union with the Divine, that is, to a divine life free of anxieties and miseries. "*Bivuti Yoga*" is the path of union with the Divine through the understanding of the glories and magnificence of the Divine. Recognizing the glories of the Divine helps a person to understand what divine or divinity is; and incorporating the divine virtues in one's own life the person can transcend the sufferings and confusions of his own life. Just as recognizing the effects of electricity lets us understand what the nature of electricity is, similarly, recognizing and appreciating divinity makes us aware of the nature of the Divine. However, an untrained mind cannot "see" electricity and the mechanical laws working behind a functioning electrical motor. A teacher has to point it out and explain the role of the invisible power moving the manifest objects. Similarly, an untrained mind does not see the glory of the Divine which is powering and sustaining the ever-changing visible world. That the ever-changing world is being maintained and sustained by the invisible, yet the real glory of the Divine is to be pointed out by a teacher to his enquiring student. This is the context of the tenth chapter of this Holy Book. Here Lord Krishna, the teacher, is pointing out to Arjuna, the disciple, many entities from reality as manifestations or glories of the Divine. The entities are all around us. Unless pointed out by a teacher an untrained mind does not see them as expressions of Divine glory. When the student sees many such examples, he gets an idea of what the Divine is; and this understanding leads him to a life of bliss!

Previous chapters had described the yogas, that is the path to the Divine, through the path of work and understanding of the nature of reality. The previous two Books (Book 8 and Book 9) described the nature of reality in both practical and abstract conversations.

Bivuti Yoga

Abstract conversations are always difficult for the untrained mind to comprehend fully. Compared to abstract conversation, an average mind understands much better when the abstractions are connected to something tangible. With something manifest, something tangible and visible to his senses, a person can "see" the ideas much more easily. This is the technique employed in this chapter and the two ensuing chapters.

The question that may be hovering in the mind of the student, is what is the Supreme Lord, the Divine; how can one feel or see the Divine; how can one be one with the Divine; that is, how can a person develop the divinity within himself? These questions are answered in this chapter by describing the "<u>Bivuti</u>" of the Divine or the Supreme Lord. "*Bibhuti*" means splendor or magnificence or grandeur, in this case the splendor of the Supreme Lord. Even if one is unable to follow the abstract nature of the narration of the Divine it is hoped that when the splendor of the Divine is pointed out to the student, she/he will get it! The student will get an understanding of what the Divine is and what Divine attributes are since the splendor, or the magnificence, are manifest and are visible to his senses. Once the seeker realizes the splendor, the attribute of the divine, he may practice and adopt the splendors in his own life. And that is the way, he will slowly acquire divine characteristics; that is how the seeker will merge into the Divine and be liberated from the miseries and griefs of his life. This path of understanding the "<u>Bivuti</u>" of the Divine and practicing the divinity in one's own life is a "<u>yoga</u>". Since this <u>yoga</u> is built on understanding the <u>Bivuti</u> or splendor of the Lord, the <u>yoga</u> is called "<u>Bivuti Yoga</u>" – the path through realizing the splendor of the Supreme Lord.

Most of the examples of the splendor or <u>Bivuti</u> cited in this chapter, are characters or objects in the rich mythological stories of India. In this space, it will be impossible to fully narrate the splendors of these mythological beings without telling the mythological stories themselves. That will be really beyond the scope of this conversation here. Instead, this narration shall provide short descriptions of these exemplars and leave the reader to read up on the stories himself. These mythological stories are gorgeous, lucid, engaging and filled with lessons for leading happy, prosperous lives. An inquiring mind will not be disappointed reading these stories.

As a reader proceeds through this chapter, it will be obvious that each exemplar indeed is the Supreme and excellent instance of the class to which it belongs. The underlying idea is that excellence in any field of endeavor is Divine; and that if one wants to achieve divinity, one should pursue excellence in all spheres, in all walks of his/her life, in all efforts of his/her life. The mantra or the path implied in *Bivuti Yoga* is that "Excellence is Divine!" Incorporating the habit of pursuing excellence in a person's life will liberate a person from the miseries and griefs of life. This is the path of "*Bivuti Yoga*".

Most of the Shlokas in this book are actually examples of some aspect of the Divine splendor. The examples are often people or some objects that we know of. In each instance, an attempt will be made to indicate what specific property or attribute is so magnificent that it is cited as an example of Divine Bivuti (splendor). It should be noted that although specific personalities or objects are chosen as exemplars, it should never be assumed that other objects or persons do not harbor divinity. That would be a misunderstanding, a misinterpretation; since in many places it is made abundantly clear that the Divine pervades everything, absolutely everything; Shloka 20 provides an example of this idea. The grandest of each class (man or objects) are cited as examples of Divine splendor because every seeker can easily see and appreciate the gorgeousness and magnificence (both physical, cerebral or spiritual) of the chosen instances.

In many Shlokas it is mentioned that some special virtues, etc. described in that Shloka are from "Me", that is, from the Divine. We interpret it to mean that these virtues, habits, and mental abilities are noble in quality; such virtues are to be strived for – because such virtues and abilities are divine indeed. These are goals that an individual should strive to attain – whether a distinct God or the Divine actually exists or not. Describing the Bivuti of the Divine is a way of making it clear to the rest of us what virtues are noble and desirable. In every Shloka, we shall examine each example of splendor narrated in the Shloka trying to figure out what essential attribute of the item (man or object) is being advocated as the divine virtue. The aim of understanding these virtues lies in the hope that one can cultivate such virtues in his own life.

One might argue that virtues espoused in some of the Shlokas in this chapter may not actually be noble nor might they represent divine nature. Some may argue that the qualities indicated in some exemplars are not divine at all; or that they are not practical at all. Such arguments may be raised for almost anything. This chapter and the two succeeding chapters are collectively called "*Bhakti Marga*" or the path of devotion. (*Bhakti* = devotion; *Marga* = Path). What we need to remember here is that in the "*Bhakti Marga*" or the "Devotional Path", the devotee does not argue with Divine; nor does he get into a heated debate with the Divine whether a certain statement is true or acceptable. In the devotional path, the devotee believes the Lord wholeheartedly and attempts to follow the path shown by the Lord in his/her own life. And that is how the reader could try to understand this chapter and the two subsequent chapters. Attempts will be made to understand the meaning of the Shlokas in terms of our modern world and then assume that these Shlokas are actually describing the nature of the Divine, that is, these Shlokas are defining the divine qualities practicing which one can get closer to the Divine.

This chapter starts with Lord Krishna describing the Divine through rather abstract concepts. Then Arjuna the disciple makes a direct request to the Lord: "Oh Lord tell me more, point out to me the things which are expressions of your glory; tell me how I should think of you". (Shlokas 12-18). The Lord never disappoints the sincere devotee. So, Lord Krishna goes on pointing to objects, people, animals, and many (cerebral, spiritual) qualities, which are examples of Divine opulence. Through this He also claims that reality itself is the expression of the Divine splendor. (Shlokas 19-42).

There is a practical challenge in reading through this chapter. The exemplars often are names of people or objects from Indian Mythology. Indian Mythology is rich, gorgeous, and engaging. The names are actually representations of spiritual qualities, both good and some may not so good, depending on the reader's point of view. People not familiar with the mythological stories may find it difficult to understand the significance of the qualities. In most cases an attempt has been made to accommodate the meaning of such names, inline in the translation. Where it is difficult, they are included as notes in the glossary section. Hopefully, it will help the reader appreciate the inner meaning of many of the Shlokas.

Looking Ahead:

Shlokas 4-7: A description of people who devote to yoga with unwavering devotion.

Shloka 41: This Shloka is a concise summary of what comprises the splendor of the Lord.

> *"Everything that is true, that is noble, that which is marvelous;*
> *All that is vigorous, all that is glorious all that which is gorgeous;*
> *They are just a small part of My infinite splendor;*
> *Know that they are all only a fraction of My power;*
> *In this do not ever doubt Oh My great hero. || 41 "*

Reading Aid - Glossary:

In several places in this translation, the original Sanskrit words in "*Bivuti Yoga*" have been retained to improve rhythm and to provide a halo of the ancient scripture. In the text all these words have been underlined. They are translated and explained below.

"A" = First letter in Sanskrit alphabet and in most other Indian languages; pronounced as "ah".

Adityas = Sons of "Aditi", the mother of the gods. Collectively the gods are referred to as Adityas.

Airavat = Name of the most powerful divine elephant, born from the ocean while the ocean was being churned for Amruta, the nectar of immortality. Also see Ucchaisrava.

Ananta = Name of the greatest constrictor. Ananta means endless. In mythology, Ananta the constrictor forms a coil on the ocean and forms a resting place for Lord Vishnu.

Arjuna = Name of the third Pandav prince in the Epic Mahabharata. He is the principal disciple of Krishna.

Aryama = Chief of the dead ancestors in the world of the ancestors.

Asit, Debal, Vyasa = These are names of three great sages of the ancient. Amongst these the most famous is Vyasa, who is believed to have written the "MahaBharata", the greatest epic created by mankind ever.

Asvattha = Name of a type of large tree very common in India and other tropical places. Botanically, this tree is possibly in the family of fig trees. This large tree can be home to many birds at a time. There are not many trees in India which grow as large as an Asvattha tree.

Atman = Self; the life enabling element in all living beings, big or small, stationary, or moving. Also called "aatma".

Brahman = supreme reality.

Brihati-Saama = The Holy text "Saama Veda", the second of the three Vedas (see below), is sung in musical tunes. Amongst these, the most complex and difficult to master tune/meter, is called "*Brihati-saama*". "Brihati" literally means big. Krishna denotes that among the musical tunes in which this Holy text is sung, the "Brihati" melody is an example of Divine opulence. Perhaps it means that those objects and capabilities, which are difficult and subtle to understand and acquire in your faculties, are indeed examples of Divine luster. The musical meter "*Brihati-Saama*" is sweet and pleasing to our senses and the mind. At the same time this meter is complex, subtle, and difficult to be proficient in. Such objects are examples of Divine splendor. They, like the "Brihati-Saama" are subtle and complex to understand, difficult to be proficient in, yet at the same time they are pleasing to the senses and enriching and nutritious to the mind and soul. These are some of the attributes of an object displaying Divine splendor. The "Brihati-Saama" is cited as an example in keeping with the age when the Holy book was composed. But we can find such examples in our lives in every age. In these objects divinity comes from the fact that they are subtle, that is why they are difficult to comprehend; from the fact that it takes hard work to gain mastery in these activities; yet they bring joy and happy melody in life and mind.

Brihaspati = Name of the Guru of the gods.

Bhrigu = Name of a very great wise sage who was also very competent in military arts.

Daitya = Demon.

Dwanda samaas = "Samaas" is a grammatical device to compound two or more different words into creating one new word. In the "dwanda" type of samaas, the component words retain their own meaning and importance in the compounded word. It is like adding two words through the conjunction "and" to create a new word.

Dharma = Ethics, ethical behavior, properties; loosely it means religion.

Dhananjaya = Conqueror of wealth; it is another name of Arjuna.

Gandharva and Chitraratha = Gandharvas are entertainers of heaven; they are experts in music, dance and all other forms of fine arts. Chitraratha is the name of the king of Gandharvas.

Gayatri and "chhanda" = "Chhanda" means a rhythmic poem, a chant, a mantra. Of all the "chhandas" or mantras, the "Gayatri" mantra is being declared as the holiest. Why? One can go on a long discourse on this, but we will make a very short argument. The Gayatri mantra is a prayer which admires the Lord Sun who is the giver and sustainer of all living forms as we know. Lord Sun is the only god who is visible to everyone, who touches every life. The prayer requests the Lord Sun that the darkness of ignorance in our mind be removed; that the mind of the one who is praying be enlightened. This is the ultimate one could desire from a living God whose existence is never questionable. This is a good reason to think why the Gayatri mantra is the holiest mantra. Lord Krishna declares that amongst the chants, the "Gayatri" chant is the one in which the Divine resides. It is an indirect way of saying that to enlighten your mind through appropriate practice is a divine activity.

Himalaya = Name of the long and lofty mountain range in northern parts of India.

Janardhana = A name of Lord Krishna. It means mover or leader of men.

Janhavi = Name of the river Ganga (also called Ganges in the west), regarded as the holiest river by Hindus. It is the river which keeps north India fertile and prosperous.

Japa = Chanting some holy prayer or mantra repeatedly putting your mind and body in the act of chanting.

Kandarpa = Name of the lover god who grants the blessing of procreation.

Kamdhenu = Wish-cow owned by the sage Vashishta. Mythology has it that when sincerely prayed, the Kamdhenu grants the wish of the person.

Kaplia = name of a very wise sage. Kapila is credited to have authored (compiled?) the Samkhya Yoga, one of the six schools of classical Indian philosophy. Samkhya is completely based on rational deliberation, not mysticism. Even in modern times, Samkhya is regarded as the pinnacle of the rational philosophical treatise.

Keshava = A name for Lord Krishna.

Krishna = Name of Arjuna's counsel and teacher, a great friend of the Pandavas. Krishna is also the king of the clan of Yadus. Krishna is the one who is explaining the philosophy of life, death, karma, and nature of reality to his friend and disciple. His words are the words of Bhagavad Gita through which He is showing how people should live a life of success and bliss.

Kuru = Name of the royal house which ruled the city of Hastinapur and much of north India at the time of creation of "MahaBharat". Arjuna is a prince of the house of Kuru.

Manu = Name of the first man on the earth. Mythology says Manu was born from thoughts of Lord Brahma, the creator of the universe, not by biological reproduction.

Marichi = Name of the god which controls the violent storms.

"Marga-sheersha" = Name the first month in winter. The month of "marga-sirsha" in the (ancient) Indian calendar is the month between mid-November to mid-December in the modern calendar. This month is being cited as an example of Divine splendor. I believe the reason is like this: In the Indian subcontinent, this is the time when oppressive summer recedes, the monsoon rains fade; the cool month brings relief from the hot and humid days; agricultural produce is in abundance and the granaries are full. Altogether, the month of "marga-sirsha" is a prosperous and relaxing time of the year. Prosperity and peace are divine attributes. If one wishes to aspire to divinity, then one should make peace and prosperity the cornerstone of life, is the message it seems.

Meru = Name of the lofty mythical mountain where the gods reside.

Naarada = Name of the wise sage of heaven. In the mythology, Naarada often acts as Vishnu's ambassador to the world of men.

"OM" or "AUM" = The one syllable holy sound, often chanted in prayers. It means the Lord is everywhere from the beginning to the end.

Pandavas = Sons of the King Pandu; Arjuna was the third of the five Pandava brothers.

Partha = Son of Pritha; it is also a name for the hero Arjuna.

Pralhaad = The most noble and virtuous king amongst demons. Although born in the demon royal family and raised amongst them, Prolhaad got very enlightened and became a great devotee of Lord Vishnu. He is best among demons. (See also Daitya).

Purusha = Spirit; laws which control changes in the material world.

Rama = Name of the virtuous legendary warrior; the king of Ayoddhya who destroyed the demon King Ravana of Lanka. Rama is the hero and principal character in the Indian Epic Ramayana. Rama is the epitome of dutifulness, truth, and justice.

Rudras = "Rudras" are gods engaged in destruction and renewal. They perform an essential function in the world. In the mythology there are twelve "Rudras". But amongst them the "Shankara" form of Rudra, also known as Lord Siva, is the best.

Shankara = Name of the most popular Rudra (above); also called Lord Shiva. Among the Rudras Lord Shiva is the best. Lord Shiva is the Supreme lover, the Lord of fertility and also the Lord of dissolution of existing forms. Shankar is that form of "Rudra", which exemplifies love, fertility, as well as the force which dissolves current forms and regenerates the world. This majestic quality of simultaneous love and regeneration is a magnificent display of the Divine. (In the eyes of those who are willing to cling on to a static, unchanging view of the world, regeneration is death and destruction of the current form of the world and therefore abhorring. We should note that such a view of a static unchanging world is unreal and ridiculous!)

Skanda = Name of the commander of the armed forces of the gods.

Ucchaisrava = Name of the divine horse born during the churning of the ocean for Amruta, the nectar of immortality.

Usana = Name of a poet of great fame.

Vasu = Name of a group of eight (?) demigods in the mythology.

Vainateya = Name of the biggest bird. Mythology has it that this big bird also serves as the flying chariot for Lord Vishnu, who uses it to travel around the world. Think of it as the Air Force One for Lord Vishnu.

Vedas Rig, Sama and Yajur = Vedas is the principal Holy Book of the Hindus. Veda actually means knowledge, the book of knowledge. *Rig*, *Sama* and *Yajur* are three main sub-books in the Vedas. These are really large books written in the ancient form of Sanskrit. Mythologically speaking, Vedas (that is knowledge) are the creator's gift to mankind.

Vaasava = Name of the king of gods.

Varuna = Name of the Lord of the creatures in water.

Vaasudeva = Another name of Lord Krishna.

Vasuki = Name of the king of serpents.

Vishnu = One of the three gods in Hindu Trinity. Vishnu maintains the world. Think of Him as the chief maintenance engineer who keeps the world functioning.

Vrishni = Name of the clan whose king was Lord Krishna.

Yama = Lord of death the ultimate disciplinarian; after death all people are brought to Lord Yama to face justice for their actions (karma) when alive. Yama's judgment is final.

Yajna or Yagna = Collaborative effort of a group of people for common good of the group, society etc.

Yakshas, Kubera, Vittesha = Yaksha (and raakshas) are mythical characters who are hoarders of wealth rather than creators of prosperity (value!). (More like bankers in the contemporary world). These characters are sometimes hostile, sometimes neutral to virtuous people. Divine magnificence is found amongst the Yakshas and rakshasas as well. Vittesha, means the lord of wealth. His popular name in mythology is "Kuber". The richest "Yaksha", that is, Kuber, is an example of divine magnificence. In the mythology, hoarding is normally frowned upon and is not encouraged. Perhaps, that is why there is no worship prescribed for Kuber, even though he excels in the art of hoarding and is very wealthy. In the Indian tradition, wealth alone does not make you worthy of worshiping. But even then, why is Kuber being cited as displaying divine magnificence? Perhaps because Kuber is displaying a high level of skill and competence in his trade. And the underlying meaning is that excellence in your skill and trade is a splendor of the Divine.

Yoga = Focused practice to achieve a goal.

BOOK 10

Bivuti Yoga

The Holy Lord <u>Krishna</u> spoke...

Oh great hero, hear again, though you are very wise;
Even then I will still give to you this supreme advice; |

Oh my dear friend I shall tell you all this;
Wishing you success and desiring you bliss. || 1

Neither the gods nor even the wise venerable sages;
Nor do they know that I am the source of the ages, |
None does know My true form nor of My beginning;
Nor that I am the source of gods and of everything. || 2

Who knows Me as birth-less, who knows me to be eternal;
Whose faith in me as the Supreme Lord is never on trial; |
Amongst the mortals he is the one without delusion;
He is the one liberated from all sins, free of confusion. || 3

Whose intelligence and knowledge is clear and steady;
Honesty and forgiveness are his companions and ready; |

Free of delusion, disciplined are his own body and mind;
Happiness and pain are not far from each other in his mind. || 4

Non-violence, impartiality, fulfillment and austerity;
Reputation and notoriety, cruelty as also generosity;
From Me alone come these tendencies to humanity. || 5

Four <u>Manus</u> and the great seven seers in the sky starring;
Know they all came, were created from thoughts of Mine;
From them in the world came streams of all living being; || 6

These truths of My splendor who are truly adoring;
Are united with Me remaining in <u>yoga</u> unwavering;
Oh hero in these truths you should never be doubting; || 7

I Am the origin of all,
    From Me do roll everything living and nonliving;|
Thinking thus worship Me,
    The intelligent and those capable of meditating. || 8

Thinking all the time about Me;
Dedicating all their efforts to Me;
    Always do they enlighten each other; |

They talk about Me all the time;
Their mind is happy and sublime;
    Happiness, bliss fill their life together. || 9

Who remain engaged to Me ardently;
With affection who worship Me lovingly; |

They receive intelligence-yoga as gift from Me;
Using that yoga unwaveringly they come to Me. || 10

Out of mercy for their haplessness;
*   Dwelling within their own being;*
I destroy their ignorance-darkness;
*   With the lamp of knowledge shining; || 11*

Arjuna *said...*

Oh Lord the Supreme Brahman is none but YOU;
The supreme abode, the supreme purifier is only YOU; |
The Divine the eternal Purusha is also only YOU;
The pristine, the birth-less the all-pervading is none but YOU; || 12

All wise sages through the ages bring us this same message;
Even Naarada of heaven says so, and he is the holy wise sage; |

Asit, Debal, Vyasa all sages of great fame do speak so;
And even You, You my Lord, yourself have told me so. || 13

Hey Keshava, all these what you are telling me;
*   Believe them I do to be true in the core of my heart;*
Oh Blessed one, hey Krishna you are friend of me;
*   But to know your manifestation none knows where to start; |*

May they be gods, or they may be demons none have any spark;
About glimpses of Your material expressions, they all are in dark. || 14

Only You alone know Yourself by Yourself, Oh The Supreme Being;
Oh Lord of universe, oh god of gods, You bring welfare to all beings. || 15

You are the Lord of world;
Please describe to me, please, please do not leave anything out;
Tell me your self manifestations which are all divine in and out;
By which manifestations you permeate the worlds inside and out. || 16

Oh Yogi, how may I know you;
By always meditating on you;
In which which aspects Oh my Blessed Lord;
Should I be thinking of You? || 17

Oh Janardhana again and again in detail and in the essence;
Please tell me Your Yoga, Your splendor, Your magnificence;
Hearing the nectar of your words never ends my exuberance. || 18

The **Holy Lord** *said...*

Oh the best of the Kurus,
Oh mighty hero, divine indeed are My splendor;
Endless indeed are My glories and grandeur;

So I shall narrate only the ones those most notable;
End of MY glories, end of My bibhuti is not reachable. || 19

Bivuti Yoga

I am the Atman the eternal and imperishable;
*   I Am the self in every being;*
I am the beginning, I span through the middle,
*   Also I am the end of all being. || 20*

Among the Adityas, the gods, I am Vishnu the supreme;
Among the storm gods I am Marichi, the storm extreme;
Among the givers of light, I am the brightest, I am Sun;
In the star studded sky at night, I am the lover's Moon; || 21

Amongst the "Vedas", "Saama-Veda" is what I am;
Amongst the gods, king of gods "Vaasava" is who I am; |

Amongst the sense organs, the mind is Me;
In all creatures the consciousness also is Me! || 22

Amongst the "Rudras",
*   The supreme lover "Shankara" is Me;*
Amongst the Yakshas,
*   Most competent Kubera Vittesha is Me; |*

Among the Vasu demigods the all purifying Fire god is Me;
Amongst all the mountains, Meru the home of gods is Me; ||23

Among the chief priests know that Brihaspati is who I am;
Among commanders of forces Skanda is who I am;
And among bodies of water know that Ocean is where I am. || 24

Among the greatest of seers Bhrigu is who I am;
Among utterances, the single syllable "OM" is I am;
Among all yagnas, the holiest Japa yagna is I am;
Among the immovables the Himalaya is what I am. || 25

Among all the trees, hugest the Asvattha is what I am;
Of divine seers, Narada, the sage of heavens is who I am; |

Among Gandharvas the king Chitraratha is who is Me;
Among the perfected ones the sage Kaplia is none but Me. || 26

Among horses Ucchaisrava the one born of nectar is My name;
Among the great elephants the mightiest "Airavat" is My name;
Among people, Lord of the people adoring the crown is My name; || 27

Among all weapons thunder is what I am;
Among all cows Kamdhenu is what I am;
I am Kandarpa, the power to procreate is Me;
Among serpents, Vasuki the king is none but Me. || 28

Among constrictors, Ananata the greatest is Me;
Of the creatures in water, lord Varuna is Me;

Among the ancestors, the chief Aryama is my name;
Amongst disciplinarians the final one Yama is my fame. || 29

In the clan of Daityas, the great Pralhaad-a is Me;
The goal of time-calculators, Time is none but Me; |

Of all the beasts, the king of the beasts always is Me;
Of birds Vainateya, the bird-chariot of Vishnu is Me. || 30

Of the purifiers, "Pavana" the sweet breeze is Me;
Of the legendary warriors, Rama the virtuous is none but Me;
Of all alarming creatures in water, the ravenous shark is Me;
And of all rivers, the holiest of holy, the river "Janhavi" is Me. || 31

In every chapter, in its beginning, and at the end is Me;
Also in the middle that what resides is none but Me; |
Of all knowledge the knowledge of Self is I none but Me;
Among the debating styles the logic-centric style is only Me. || 32

Of the letters in alphabet, the first vowel "A" is Me;
Of compounded words the type "dwanda" is Me; |
The infinite imperishable Time is also none but Me;
The only arranger facing in all directions is also Me. || 33

The all destroying death is none but Me;
The Future germinates from none but Me;

Among the adorable feminine virtues,
Fame, prosperity, speech, memory, are truly Me;
Wisdom, endurance and Forgiveness are also Me. || 34

Of the Vedic musical meters, Brihati-Saama is Me;
Of the poetic "chandas", "Gayatri" is none but Me;
Of the months in a year "Marga-sheersha" is what I am;
Of the seasons, the one the mine of flowers is where I am. || 35

In the cheats, dishonesty is what I am;
In the gambler, gambling tendency is Me;
In the victorious the victory is what I am;
In the diligent, the honest effort is only Me;
In all who are virtuous, the virtue is what I am. || 36

In the Vrishni clan, Vaasudeva the divine is I am;
"Dhananjaya" the best of the Pandavas, is who I am; |

Among the greatest sages, Vyasa is my name;
Among poets I am "Usana" of greatest fame. || 37

In the authorities, the power to punish is what I am;
In those desiring victory, the just principles is where I am; |

In all secrets, silence is nothing but Me;
In the knower, the knowledge is only Me. || 38

And that which is the seed of all being;
That seed is only Me;
Nothing whether stationary or moving,
Could ever exist without Me. || 39

Divine are my splendors, divine is this knowledge;
They have no limit, nor do they have any edge; |

Bivuti Yoga

You heard these with many examples from Me;
All these are true, all that are told to you by Me. || 40

Everything that is true, that is noble, that which is marvelous;
All that is vigorous, all that is glorious all that which is gorgeous;

They are just a small part of my infinite splendor;
Know that they are all only a fraction of my power;
In this do not ever doubt Oh my hero the great archer. || 41

But Arjuna there is no need for such detailed description;
Know that just by using My powers only a tiny fraction;
I maintain the whole universe without any interruption. || 42

❧   *End of Book 10, Bivuti Yoga*   ❧

Vishwa-Roopa-Darshana Yoga

Path To the Divine Realizing the Big Picture View Of The World

Vishwa = World, Universe.
Roopa = Form, figure, look, structure.
Darshana = See, view, realize, understand.
Yoga = Focused effort to attain a specific goal.
BG = Shrimad Bhagavad Gita.

What is in Book 11 - Viswa-Roopa-Darshana Yoga

"Viswa" means the universe. "Roopa" is a form or figure. "Darshana" is a view or vision. Yoga is a focused effort to attain a specific goal. In BG it means a path or process of union with the divine. Together this would mean the path of union with the Divine by realizing the big picture of the universe. The cosmic view would perhaps be a better translation of the word "Viswa-Roop-Darshan" but the translation "seeing the big picture" is retained here since it seems that average readers seem to connect to this expression much easier. This expression will be used throughout Book 11 to convey the sense of "Viswa-Roopa-Darshana". In essence both expressions convey the same sense. If one understands the nature of the universe, if one understands the true nature of reality, then the individual is absolved of ignorance. That is enlightenment. Enlightenment is the path to the Divine. Enlightenment is the root cause of man's happiness, health, peace, and prosperity. Ignorance is the cause of the same things missing from a man's life.

Gaining an insight into the big picture means gaining awareness of what other objects, entities, and forces are shaping an individual's material and emotional life; and in turn what other objects, entities, etc. are influencing the primary effectors in his life; and so on; and so on. Continued understanding of these big and bigger pictures makes a person more and more aware of the fundamental truths about reality; that is, brings the individual closer and closer to the Divine, who is the Truth in reality.

The Big picture is the big picture both in space and time. The big picture in space is understanding the other objects and entities in the universe which are influencing the nature of your universe at any time. The big picture in time means a realization of what the universe was in previous times and how it will be in the future and what is causing the changes, which may or may not be directly perceptible to you. Efforts to understand the big and bigger picture enlighten your mind about the truths of reality and take you closer to the Divine. That is the idea – I think.

The underlying idea is that man should try to discover and appreciate the "big picture" in his life, in his world. Searching for and understanding the big picture is actually searching for and understanding the Divine. It is the search for the big picture that leads us from the limitations of our local observations, which are often colored by prejudices, to more universal principles. It is the search for the big picture that leads us from individual events to natural laws. That search expands our mind and provides a deeper clearer understanding of reality. As a result, it leads us to a happier, more productive life; that is to a life of bliss.

For example, the falling of an apple is a local event. The search for the big picture of the relationship between the apple, the fall, the ground, leads us to the concept of gravity. Gravity is the big picture whereas the fall of the apple is a local picture. A search for and understanding the big picture leads us to discover and appreciate the laws of the universe, which in turn leads us to a happier, less confused, and more blissful life. It is really remarkable that *BG* recognizes the truth that searching for the big picture is a "<u>yoga</u>", is a path to take us closer to the Divine. The idea is so rational, so scientific, and so unique! There is hardly anything mysterious in its narration. The implied advice is that we should adopt the habit of searching for the big picture in our daily life. Examples like these are everywhere. Through adoption of advice like these, which are strewn throughout the Gita, the BG becomes a practical tool to improve our own lives!

The big picture or "**<u>Viswa Roop</u>**" is narrated as a didactic between the disciple <u>Arjuna</u> and the teacher Lord Krishna. In the previous book (Book 10), Lord Krishna described the glories or magnificence of the Divine. Hearing that, the disciple (<u>Arjuna</u>) gets a pretty good idea of what Divine is and how to incorporate divinity in his own life. The disciple has listened faithfully. This has only intensified his hunger for more! Now he wants to "see" the Divine. He requests the Lord, that, if possible, could he see the Divine – see Him in all His multitudes of forms and expressions. The Divine Lord Krishna in his kindness for his friend and disciple empowers him to see the Divine. What the devotee sees, how he gets overwhelmed by the sight, and how he praises the Divine is the theme of Book 11.

We can pause here for a moment and wonder about the impossibility of the situation! Here, a simple straightforward request has been made. Can one see the Divine? In other words, can one see God? How does God look? How does one see the Divine? In some faiths even the question of how God looks is generally avoided; and in some faiths even the question could be blasphemous! So how does *Gita* answer this question truthfully and in a way that stands up to rational analysis? Through charming poetry in this Book 11, Gita's answer is that understanding the true nature of reality is seeing the Divine! To see the Divine, you need to awaken the eye of your intellect; in the poetry here the eye of intellect is called the "divine eyes". In a real masterpiece of poetry, *Vyasa* the author, presents this message through a didactic between Lord Krishna and his disciple Arjuna. How the disciple sees the big picture of reality and what he sees is the subject of this chapter.

The student wants to see the Divine; he wants to see the big picture of the reality. This is really a very difficult desire to fulfill. It is impossible to see the big picture through his human eyes because of their limited range and depth. But Lord Krishna fulfills the desire of the disciple by granting him "divine" eyes, divine vision (Shloka 8). With this extraordinary vision, Arjuna sees the "Viswa-Roop" or the "big picture" of reality as we call it here. Arjuna transcends the limitation of his own sensory vision and "sees" the manifestation of the Divine – the reality. That extraordinary ability is the enlightenment of the mind, which enables man to overcome the limitation of his biological sensory apparatus. With this eye of the intellect, man sees the unseen; overcomes the limited views of his surroundings, gets to "see" global laws and processes. This big picture clarifies his mind and encourages him to act dispassionately. This is not mystical at all! We know from our own experiences of learnings in life that most of the reasoning, understanding of mechanisms, appreciation of laws, are accomplished by the eye of our intellect. Our physical eyes are capable of seeing only superficially; it is only with our intellect we are awakened to a deeper understanding of the nature of things.

When a man is able to see the big picture, the man will understand the mechanisms and laws behind the manifest reality. That understanding itself is beautiful; that understanding is divine! That is to say, as you wake up to mysteries of the big picture, you find that the reality is not random; you find that it is law driven; that it is simultaneously creating new forms (birth of new life) and removing old forms (death); that each form is proceeding towards its own dissolution, governed by laws in reality; that reality is simultaneously graceful, nurturing life; and also cruel and destroying life. This realization of the nature of reality, is very beautifully narrated in this chapter in deeply devotional language with deep symbolic imagery.

When the divine eyes are developed in you, you realize the nature of reality hitherto unknown to you, hitherto unseen by you. Recognizing the nature of reality, your mind becomes unconfused; recognizing the law driven nature of the world, you see your path in life more clearly, more unambiguously, and devoid of anxiety. This is a definition of attaining divinity or receiving Divine Grace. When you strive to see the big picture, you recognize many possibilities; you will find many divine things present around you, which makes your life happier and more meaningful; ignorance about the world and about your life will dissolve.

As long as you remain clammed up in your shell and do not strive to see the big picture (spiritually speaking as long as you do not strive for the grace of the Divine), you do not see much other than your own limitations. A very common way to remain clammed up is to be self-absorbed, to be arrogant, is to live in a "me-me" and "me-centric" mode of existence. In such a mental condition, the big picture of reality, that is the nature of the Divine, remains out of your view; since your view remains local; restricted to your own shell. But to be able to see the big picture, you need to work for the Divine, you need to depend on the Divine. In practical terms it means you need to break out of your selfish mold; you need to overcome your ego and prejudices; you need to develop your intellect; you need to approach the world in a rational, objective, unbiased manner; you need to have faith that there is more to the world than what is in range of your physical vision, that there is a bigger picture beyond your immediate vision; that the universe is not random, that there is order and laws which drive the reality. This is how one receives the "divine eyes"; this is the path to attain divinity. These ideas are very succinctly described in the last few verses of this book.

The literary style of this book in the original text is unsurpassed. Perhaps no translation can bring out that beauty. The narration is very much about the search for a meaning based on our experiences in material life. That effort inevitably causes loss of beauty and charm as well. The author sincerely hopes that every reader will make an effort to read the poetry in the original text.

Looking Ahead:

Expressions like "*the universe lives in You*", "*You are the home of the world*" are repeated in many places in Book 11 and many other places in BG. Though the expressions appear mystical, really they are not mystical. It is consistent with BG's view that the universe is law bound, everything in the universe is always under the control of natural laws.

When we assume that "Lord" is a poetic symbolism, a deification of the natural laws, the poetry in BG becomes clear and non-mystical. Since the universe is controlled by natural laws end to end, it is easy to understand the meaning of the expressions that the world lives in the laws, that is, the universe lives in the Lord; that the Lord is the home of the universe, etc. In poetic symbolism BG assumes the Lord to be the natural laws governing the world.

Shlokas 1-4: Arjuna requests that he be able to see God, the Lord.

Shlokas 5-8: Krishna grants the wish but only after gifting him the divine eye, the eye of intellect. Without the intellect being awakened, no one can see the Vishwa-Roop, the big picture of the world or the big picture of one's own life.

Shlokas 9-14 describe the Viswa-Roop as Arjuna was seeing. *Sanjaya*, the minister to the King *DhritaRashtra*, rather than Arjuna, is speaking these few verses. But why is Sanjaya speaking rather than Arjuna? The reason is that by "seeing" the Viswa-Roopa, Arjuna was wonderstruck. Arjuna was overawed and unable to talk or express himself.

The wise Sage Vyasa (author of Mahabharata) had given Sanjay the special power, that during the period of the war, Sanjay would see, hear, and relay to the blind king whatever Arjuna was seeing, thinking, hearing, and saying in the battlefield. Assume that Sanjay was gifted with some kind of remote vision with which he could see the happenings in the battlefield and narrate them to the blind king DhritaRashtra. This is why Sanjay is able to "see" Arjuna's thoughts and express it in words, even though Arjuna himself was too overwhelmed to speak. Arjuna was seeing the "Viswa-Roopa" and being wonderstruck, became speechless; Sanjay was seeing whatever Arjuna was seeing and was narrating the same to the blind King DhritaRashtra. (In the story, this extraordinary power was to last for the duration of the battle only).

Shlokas 23-31: The stern unkind destructive face of the Divine, the reality is described here. Previous verses have described the kind, gentle, life giving, nourishing face of the Divine, the reality. However, the big picture is that the Divine, the reality, is both kind and stern, life-giving and life-destroying, all at the same time. Continually it creates new forms, and also changes and removes existing forms. Now Arjuna starts to realize this stern, the unkind face of the Lord; he starts seeing unforgiving aspects of reality!

Shlokas 28-30: This is a part of the bigger picture. Death and destruction of the living (or any organized form) is inevitable. So, to be dysfunctional at the thought of someone dying, even if they are your near and dear ones, is not a wise thing.

Shlokas 32-34: In these three verses (32-34), the Holy Lord not only tells the devotee why He is assuming such terrifying form, but also seems to be stating some other facts (truths?) about the world. First, He says that the battle or conflict is a divine mechanism to cause attrition in the existing world (verse 32). We can and some of us will always argue if the attrition of the old structures of the world is a good thing or if it is a divine mechanism or not. In spite of all arguments, the fact remains that in time, old orders and old structures are inevitably removed and replaced by other new orders. The attrition of the old order must take place, be it personal, societal, or civilizational. This is an inevitable fact – a natural law. The process of change or attrition of the existing are driven by natural laws, that is, by the hand of the Divine.

It is pointless, to remain depressed or resort to inaction when duty calls. Rather BG's clarion call is that one must engage in his duty and perform the best one can. Looking dispassionately, non-egotistically, everyone in an organized activity, be it a battle or a profit-making project is merely a cog in the big wheel of actions. This is BG's advice on this issue (Shlokas 33-34)

Shlokas 36-40, 43-50: On realizing the big picture of the Lord (nature and its laws) admiration for the Lord gushes out from the devotee. Knowledge of the big picture of reality scares away the demons of ignorance and let us see the truths.

Shlokas 41-42: BG's unique vision of the relationship between the devotee and his God (Lord) is portrayed in these two beautiful verses. The fact that the God and his devotee can be portrayed in a deep sincere loving friendship is a unique contribution of BG. The relationship is not of fear, punishment, and obedience, but of deep love and sincere affection between friends and lovers.

Shlokas 52-55: A question that invariably goes through a reader's mind is this: If realizing the Viswa Roop or the big picture of his life is so important for a man to attain a divine life, how can an average man realize the Viswa Roop. Like an expert clinician, BG lays out the path in simple terms. Shloka 53 says just by following prescribed rituals one cannot be awakened to the big picture. What to do is in Shlokas 54-55, the summary of which is that man should conquer his ego, should free himself from the dungeon of his ego and serve others. Ego or egotistic outlook keeps man tied to himself, to the restricted view of the world. Only by serving others without ego can a man get a glimpse of the big picture. By providing such prescriptions in practical terms, BG transcends from a scripture to a practical guide for happy and successful living.

Reading Aid - Glossary:

In several places in this translation, the original Sanskrit words in "_Vishwa-Roopa-Darshana Yoga_" have been retained to improve rhythm and to provide a halo of the ancient scripture. In the text all these words have been underlined. They are translated and explained below.

Adharma = Anti dharma; dharma = ethics, laws,

Adityas = Sons of Aditi, generic name for gods.

Agni = Name of fire god; Fire burns away impurities.

Asvins = Name of the twin brothers who are physicians of gods.

Arjuna = Name of the mighty warrior, disciple of Krishna; the conversation between Krishna and Arjuna is the content of Bhagavad Gita.

Basus = A group of eight demigods.

Bhakti = Devotion.

Bharatha = Prince of the kingdom of Bharat (India); nick name of Arjuna the hero.

Bhishma, Drona, Karna, Jayadratha= Names of famous heroes.

Brahma = One of three principals in Hindu Trinity. Brahma is the one who created the world and gave knowledge to the world.

Dhritarashtra = Name of the blind King, Regent of the kingdom.

Gandharvas = Entertainers of heaven.

Gudakesha = A man ready for action. Often Arjuna the warrior is addressed by this name.

Janaardana = Leader of men. Often Krishna is addressed by this name.

Keshava = Another name of Lord Krishna.

Kiritee = Name of the exceptional jewel adorning the crown of Krishna.

Maha-bahoh = Mighty Armed.

Maruta = Gods of storms.

Pandava = Sons of king Pandu; here it refers to Arjuna who is the third son of Pandu.

Partha = Son of Pritha, a nickname for Arjuna.

Prajapati = Lord of people.

Purusha = Supreme Being who/what controls the universe.

Purushottama = The best among men; here refers to Lord Krishna.

Rudras = Gods in charge of destruction and regeneration.

Sadhus = Wise sages.

Shashaanka = Name of Moon as a god.

Sri Hari = Name of Lord Vishnu, the principal god of Hindu trinity.

Ushmapa = Steam drinker.

Varuna = God of all aquatic creatures.

Vasus = A group of eight demigods.

Vaasudeva = Another name of Lord Krishna

Vayu = Wind or wind god.

Vishnu = Name of the principal god in Hindu Trinity.

Viswa = the universe.

Vishwa-Roop = Vishwa means the world, the universe. Roop means form, figure, and beauty. Together it means a view of the entire world/universe.

Yadava = Chief of the Yadu clan. In the story Krishna was the chief of this clan.

Yakshas = Wealth hoarders of heaven.

Yama = *Lord of death*; after death every person is brought to Lord Yama for judgment of their actions in their life in the world. Yama's judgment is final.

BOOK 11

Vishwa-Roopa-Darshana Yoga

Arjuna Said...

Favoring me in your grace you yourself Oh my Lord,
Spoke to me the highest secret in your own word; |

That secret that knowledge of the Supreme Self;
My delusions have now receded far from myself. || 1

Heard from You in detail nothing remaining;
Secret of creation and dissolution of all being; |

Oh my Lotus-Eyed Lord I did hear in entirety;
About Your immutable eternal Divine Majesty. || 2

That is how Oh You my Supreme Lord;
You yourself did say so in your own word. |

Now Oh Purushottama, You the greatest of all Beings;
I Love to see your divine form Oh the Supreme Being. || 3

If you, my Lord, think by the power of yoga;
*   If it is possible for You to be seen by me;*
Then oh You the Supreme Lord of Yoga,
*   Please show Your imperishable Self to me. || 4*

Holy Lord spoke...

Oh Partha, behold Me, in my splendor;
In shapes and forms and divine color;
In hundreds rather thousands of figures raving ;
Many many shapes and forms far beyond counting. || 5

See the Adityas, the Basus, the Rudras;
See the Asvins as well as all the Marutas; |

Many wonders not seen by any one in past-a;
Behold them too, Oh the prince of Bharatha. || 6

Oh Gudakesha, see now at one place in My body in My being;
Exists the whole universe of objects stationary and moving;
See in my body whatever else you wish you could be seeing. || 7

All these with your own eyes;
*   You will not be able to see; |*
I shall give you Divine eyes;
Then only My Divine majesty can you see. || 8

Sanjaya said...

Thus saying Sri Hari, the supreme Lord of Yoga, Oh King;
To Partha did He unveil His ultimate Supreme form Divine. || 9

111

Many faces, many eyes, all very very amazing;
Many wondrous many looking most fascinating; |
Many Divine decorations, many divine ornament;
Many many divine tools all ready for engagement; || 10

Many with divine garlands, with garments divine;
Many with divine perfumes, with cosmetics divine; |
Infinite, facing in all directions;
Is the all-wonder-containing-Lord the Divine. || 11

If in the same sky a thousand suns should arise all at once;
If brightness such as that would exist ever, then that radiance;
That would be the brightness of the Great Self, His brilliance. || 12

There as within one place was the entire amazing world;
Divided and subdivided in many ways neat and grand; |

Thus, did see the Pandava the great hero amongst the great;
In the body of the Lord of Lords many many forms elegant. || 13

Then stunned in utter astonishment;
With all his hair standing on their end; |
Bowing head to the Lord in amazement;
Palms folded in reverence Arjuna said at the end. || 14

Arjuna said...

In the Divine body of yours I see all the many gods;
Crowded together are many creatures in their pods; |
I see there Lord Brahma seated on the Lotus,
See all sages, also many divine serpents perilous. || 15

Many arms, bellies, eyes, and faces,
See Your endless forms and senses;
Everywhere on all sides I see only You,
Oh My Lord it is a magnificent view. |

Oh Lord I do not see where is Your beginning,
I do not see Your middle nor see Your ending;

None of these do I see Oh the Lord of the Universe;
You pervade everything You are the whole Universe! || 16

With Crown, Club and your divine Disc shining,
I see You who is difficult to completely beholding, |

Your Massive splendor, Your shine floods in every direction;
You are immeasurable, You have radiance of the fiery sun. || 17

You are the supreme, everlasting, you never change;
You are the ultimate to be known in any knowledge;
You are eternal, You are forever fresh, You never age. |

Final home of the universe, the immutable is You;
The eternal defender of "dharma" is always You;
The ever-existing ancient Purusha I think, is none but You. || 18

You have no beginning, no middle, you are endless;
I see your radiant oblation-eating strange fiery face; |

Infinitely vigorous strong are You;
Infinite number of arms have You;

Oh Lord, Sun-and-moon eyed are You;
With His own energy, who warms the universe;
My Lord is that not YOU! || 19

The heaven and the earth and indeed the space connecting,
Is penetrated in all directions by You alone Oh The Greatest Being; |

Seeing this form of yours wondrous and stern;
The three worlds do shake in fear and churn; || 20

Here indeed,
  entering Thee;
Are crowds of gods and goddesses;
Some afraid, offering reverential praises; |

Entering Thee;
Are throngs of perfected sages;
Greeting You profusely with their praises; || 21

Rudras, Aadityas, Vasus, and the Sadhus;
Viswa gods, two Ashvins, and the Marutas;
Gandharvas, Yakshas, demons also Ushmapas; |
And all those the perfected accomplished ones,
All gazing at You with utmost wonder in their eyes! || 22

The great form of yours with many mouths and eyes,
Oh Maha-bahoh, with so many arms, feet and loins; |

Many bellies, many many tusks that do inspire fear;
Having seen these the whole world shiver and quiver;
And so do I! || 23

Lofty sky touching, huge mouth gaping;
Many colors that from You are radiating;
Huge are Your eyes bright and dazzling; |
Seeing you my heart continue pounding;
Courage, peace of mine are both deserting;
Oh Vishnu You are the Greatest Being. || 24

And the many terrible tusks of your mouths glowing;
Looking indeed as if "time" itself on the fire burning;
I do not know the direction to which I should be running;
Nor do I find any refuge, any shelter I should be entering;|

Oh the Dwelling of the universe, You are the final sanctuary;
Oh Lord of Lords please shelter me in Your immense mercy. || 25

Here in mad race to enter in You, DhritaRashtra sons are rushing;
To enter in You droves of rulers of earth too are busy hastening; |

Vishwa-Roopa-Darshana Yoga

Bhishma, Drona, Karna "son of the charioteer" and others;
And also, with them are entering ours' own chief warriors! || 26

Hastily, do they enter Your open mouth;
With those terrible gaping large tooth; |

In the spaces between these bites some are clinging;
Some are seen with their heads crushed and hanging. || 27

As rivers with mighty torrents rush to the ocean as if in loving; |
So even heroes fearlessly rushing in Your gaping mouth blazing. || 28

As in the glowing flames enter insects and moth;
With great speed for their own destruction; |
So are the people entering Your fiery mouth;
With a very great hurry for their own dissolution. || 29

You lick and swallow the world from every turn;
With your mouth gaping and blazing; |
Oh Vishnu, Your intense rays do the universe burn,
With Your radiance the whole universe filling. || 30

Who are You in this mighty yet terrible form, may I know;
Please spell it out for me Your deeds, please help me know; |

I wish to know You, the origin of every being is You,
Am unable to fathom You, the inner nature of You;

I bow to Thee, beg Your mercy, God of gods is You! || 31

The Holy Lord Spoke...

I am "Time"; the mighty One That makes the world meet its attrition.
Engaged now I am in bringing the current order to its own erosion; |

Even without you, none of the warriors will exist in near future;
All Those who now are settled in the opposing ranks waging war. || 32

Therefore, get up you great hero, attain glory fighting;
Conquering the enemy, enjoy the kingdom flourishing; |

I have already destroyed all these warriors, indeed;
Arjuna, you are only a device in this momentous deed. || 33

Drona, Bhishma and Jayadratha all of lofty fame;
Even Karna the Great and heroes of famous name; |

By Me, they have all already been packed to their destruction;
Oh Arjuna, kill them in the battle, keep not slightest hesitation; ||

Fight! You shall be victorious in this holy strife;
None of the adharma-clinging enemies will survive. || 34

Sanjay said...

Having heard all the words <u>Keshava</u> said,
Trembling and with both palms folded, |
Bowing head in deep reverence, frightened,
Falteringly did <u>Arjuna</u> to Krishna said; || 35

<u>*Arjuna*</u> *said...*

Rightly, Oh <u>Hrushikesha</u>, the whole world rejoice,
Delighted, gratified by Your essence and grace; |

Scared, the demons dissolve away in all directions,
To You, accomplished ones bow heads in reverence. || 36

Oh, Great Soul, and why would they all not bow to You,
Greater even than <u>Brahma</u>, the original creator, is You;
You are the Lord of gods, the infinite the endless is You;
The eternal home of the universe is nowhere but in You
The existent, nonexistent, and everything beyond that is You || 37

The root of all gods is no one else but You,
The spirit most ancient yet ever fresh is You;
Home of the entire universe is truly only You. |

Thou art the supreme knower,
Thou art the supreme state the wise wish known;
Thou pervade entire nature known and unknown,
Thou art of infinite forms and power! || 38

You are the ancient, the great grandfather of all deity;
<u>Vayu</u>, <u>Yama</u>, <u>Agni</u>, <u>Varuna</u>, <u>Shashaanka</u> also <u>Prajapati</u>; |

I bow to Thee, a thousand times I do bow to Thee;
And again and again, I bow to Thee, I bow to Thee! || 39

Bow to Thee from front, from behind too I do bow to You;
Reverence to You always and from every side, every view |

Thou art of infinite valor; boundless might is Thine;
You penetrate everything large, and small, coarse or fine;
Therefore, You are ALL! outside of You there is nothin-g. || 40

Oh Krishna, Oh <u>Yadava</u>, You the Supreme, Oh my Friend;
Of Your this greatness, I was so ignorant my dear friend;

You are a dear friend always I was thinking;
While playing, relaxing or also during dining;
Whatever I uttered without my own realizing;

In my delusion, and even in my love for you;
Even in jest, at times I behaved rudely with You,

Alone or in front of others, Oh dear Krishn-a;
Please forgive me, Oh the Boundless One-a. ||41-42

Father of all the three worlds is You, none but You;
Father of all that is moving and non-moving is You;
The one to be worshiped most in all worlds is You;
More esteemed than even an honorable Guru is You;
No one else exists who is even comparable to You,
The one of matchless grandeur in the worlds is You only You; || 43

In front of You, Oh the most honorable Supreme Lord;
My whole body lies low, bows to you in reverence;
As does a son to father, I do beg your forgiveness;

As a lover asks the dear beloved,
As a friend seeks from a friend;
I beg your mercy; I beg your grace;
Oh Lord please, tolerate me please,
Shower me please with your kindness. || 44

Seeing this form of Yours seen before ne'er;
Delighted I am, but my mind shakes in fear; |

Please show me (again) You're that Divine loving figure;
Please be merciful, Oh my Lord, my heart pounds in fear;
Oh, the God of gods, the universe dwells in You forever. || 45

I pray to see You as before with kiritee, club and disc shining;
Oh, the thousand armed one, in You is the whole universe living;

Console me again with your loving four-armed figure assuming; || 46

The Holy Lord spoke...

In My compassion to you, Oh Arjuna, you a hero like no other;
Were you shown this supreme form by My own yoga power; |

This infinite fundamental splendorous view of nature;
That which has not been seen before by none other. || 47

By reading Vedas, yajna performing, or by gift giving;
Or by performing austerity, or by harsh ritual practicing; |

In the world of men, I can't be seen in My this cosmic view;
Oh the great amongst the Kurus by any one other than you. || 48

Oh Arjuna,
Seeing My complex-terrifying vishwa-roop in your fore;
Shudder not in fear anymore, nor be confused no more; |

Let go of your fears, with your heart filled in joy,
Behold My familiar form again, don't you be afraid or shy. || 49

Sanjay said...

Vaasudeva having said this to Arjuna, looking very pale;
Again, showed him His own previous form as in human tale; |

Reassuring the frightened hero, looking fearful and forlorn;
The Great Soul re-assumed His wonderful loving form || 50

Arjuna Said...

Seeing the human form of Yours, Janaardana oh my loving buddy;
Now I am calm, peace now reigns in my mind that was unsteady. || 51

The Holy Lord Krishna said...

Very remote is my Vishwa-Roop for most to be able seeing;
To most My Vishwa-Roop doesn't even shine;
Even though the divine the wise persons are always longing;
Many still fail to see the Vishwa-Roop of Mine; || 52

Not by reading the Vedas only, nor alone by austerity,
Not also by gifts, nor too by doing rituals with sincerity, |
Not can anyone see this Vishwa-Roop-a form of Mine;
The way you saw the grand beauty, the immensity of Mine. || 53

Oh, the scorcher of the enemy,
Indeed, with unwavering "bhakti" unflinching devotion;
It is possible that I be known in devotees' realization; |

And only through the truth alone can Me be entered,
Seeing This form can the limitations be conquered. || 54

One who
Does all his work for Me;
    To whom the supreme is Me;
    Is Devoted entirely to Me;
One who
    Is All Attachments-abandoning;
    Does his work ego-conquering;
    Does not feel animosity to any being;
Is the one who comes to Me, Oh Pandava! || 55

∾   *End of Book 11, Vishwa-Roopa-Darshana Yoga*   ∽

Bhakti Yoga

Attaining The Divine Following the Path of Devotion

Bhakti = Devotion

Yoga = Focused effort to attain a specific goal.

BG = Shrimad Bhagavad Gita.

What is in Book 12 - Bhakti Yoga?

"*Bhakti*" means devotion; and Yoga is a path, tool, or process to reach a goal. In this book the goal is to be one with the Divine by following the path of devotion to the Supreme Divine. Simply speaking the goal is to attain a divine life. A divine life is a happy, healthy, prosperous, blissful, fulfilled life; it is free of fear, anxiety, confusion, worries, mental tension, anguish, and despair. In Book 12 this state is often referred to as "coming close to the Divine", "entering the Divine" and other similar expressions.

How does one get a divine life; how does one enter the Divine? The answer in this book is surprisingly simple and direct. The simple answer is Practice divine behavior, you will attain the Divine, you will attain a divine life. That is the simple thesis.

What are divine behaviors? This book, Book 12, is a prescription of those behaviors. Practicing these behaviors faithfully and sincerely is a "Yoga". The yoga or path to the Divine by performing according to "*bhakti*" or devotion, is "*Bhakti* yoga". That is the theme of this chapter.

The devotee is being asked to express his devotion to the Divine NOT by occasionally or ceremonially performing some rituals, or prayer or sacrifice to a deity or a non-deity. Rather, the seeker is being taught some behavior; willing and regular respectful practice of these behaviors cleanse the mind of the ego-centric and delusional views of the world, which are the root cause of miseries and grief in life. A person whose mind is thus cleansed by such practice (Yoga!) becomes enlightened, enters a divine life, enters the divine. A person thus enlightened is a devotee of the Divine according to BG.

Bhakti is to sincerely behave in life according to the principles laid down here. The path is to behave and conduct yourself with *bhakti*, behave the way a "*bhakta*" (devotee) behaves. That is "*bhakti yoga*".

The reader should NOT assume that the devotee is being asked to express his devotion to the Divine by performing some ritualistic posture or prayer to a deity or a non-deity for those who subscribe only to a non-form-based view of the Divine. The devotee is not being asked to disavow his religious faith! BG's teachings are good for all people irrespective of their own religious faith or dogma.

The key is willing and respectful practice of the prescribed code of behavior in his everyday life and everyday dealings in life. By working according to the prescribed code, by viewing the world according to the code, by understanding the world in terms of formulations according to the code, the mind of the devotee continues to be enlightened; ignorance continues to be burnt away; life attains bliss. To conduct life according to the code is to display "*bhakti*" or devotion to the Divine. The <u>yoga</u> or path to the Divine by performing according to "*bhakti*" or devotion is "*Bhakti yoga*". That is the theme of this chapter.

Looking Ahead:

First half of this chapter (Shlokas 1-9) builds up the question discussed in this Book. The question is which path is more productive for a seeker to follow to build a divine life? Should it be a path of meditation, abandoning actions? Or should it be a path of worship, that is, a path of remaining engaged to and working in material life respectfully and with full sincerity? The answer to this key question is boiled down in the Shlokas of the last half of this chapter (Shlokas 10-20).

By narrating the desired characteristics of the devotee, Lord Krishna is describing what devotion to the Divine is; and what should a person do to continue on the path of devotion and worship to attain a happy, productive, worry free, divine life. This chapter is a condensed version of the behavior code that can be followed by anyone wishing to achieve divinity. Knowing his duties, his responsibilities as a devotee, one can perform them according to the knowledge narrated in this chapter. Faithfully conducting life according to these directives will bring the devotee to a divine life. As in every other chapter, a reader will find that the message is of universal use. The devotee is not being asked to please any specific deity or subscribe to any particular faith. The devotee is being asked to lead his life according to universal laws governing his mind and emotions.

Shlokas 1-5: Which path, the path of meditation or the path of worship, is better and more efficient in attaining <u>yoga</u>, union with the Divine? According to Lord Krishna the path of meditation only, is a lot harder for an average person to attain success in <u>Yoga</u>, because of the unmanifest, unseen, very difficult to describe nature of the Divine. In fact, for an average person, the path of worship, that is the path action, the path of engaging in the material world searching for the nature of the Divine is much easier. As an analogy, one should ask if it would be easier to understand and grasp the laws of physics solely by deliberation and without experimentation with objects in the material world?

BG's unequivocal answer is that the path of experimentation is the better and more productive path. Two millennia of human experience has shown that the path of experimentation, spiritually called the path of worship, is by far the better path. BG provides the same answer (Shlokas 3-5). BG's answer to this question reveals the depth, truth, and beauty of BG's advice that man should earnestly and sincerely adopt the path of worship, that is, adopt the path of working, trying, and figuring out (as in experimentation with objects in the world) as the better means of understanding the nature of his world, understanding the Divine, and to attain a divine life.

Shlokas 6-8: The path of "worship", that is the path of interacting with the material world aka the path of experimentation, is better for comprehending the Divine and being in union with the Divine. Man should relentlessly "worship" respectfully, sincerely focusing on revealing the truths of nature (the Divine), without ever doubting that nature is governed by laws, that is by the Divine.

Shlokas 9-11: BG reasons that working intently, with sincerity and love and by remaining emotionally detached from the results of one's actions (experimentation) is the easiest and best way to understand the nature of the Divine, the laws of nature. BG's activist philosophy of working hard selflessly, renouncing the fruits of work is the key thought here.

Shloka 12: The activist faith of BG is very well expressed here. Rational knowledge founded on material observations and rational logic is much better than ritualistic work and blind faith. Also, sincere actions without being prejudiced by expected results of actions is the most efficient way to be in union with the Divine; that is the best way to arrive at truth and attain peace and success.

Shlokas 13-19 describe the desired qualities of a yogi; qualities that make the yogi a devotee dear to the Divine. Here in an indirect way, BG is outlining the mental qualities a seeker, a devotee ought to cultivate to be able to be one with the divine; that is to realize the truths of nature and one's own life. These are the qualities needed for a devotee to attain a divine life, a life of peace, prosperity, and success.

Shloka 20: It is the concise summary and assurance of the path any desiring seeker can follow to attain a divine life.

Reading Aid - Glossary:

In several places in this translation, the original Sanskrit words have been retained to improve rhythm and to provide a halo of the ancient scripture. In the text all these words have been underlined. They are translated and explained below.

Dharma = Ethics which hold one together for happy living; essential quality or character of a person or a thing.

Samsara = The up and down turmoils of life.

BOOK 12

Bhakti Yoga

Arjuna said...

Ardently do some worship You with faith and devotion;
Some engage the unmanifest You in deep meditation; |

To know <u>Yoga</u> which is the superior of the two;
Please tell me that clearly, oh the Eternal You! || 1

The Holy Lord spoke...

Those who are fixing their minds on Me;
Always with devotion who worship Me; |

Who Worship Me with faith and love supreme;
In My opinion, are the most devoted and serene; ||2

They worship Me knowing,
    I am beyond any destruction,
    I am beyond all expression;
    I am grasped only in realization;
    I pervade all beings static or in motion; |

    No change ever stains me, unthinkable I am;
    Unmanifest immovable forever steady I am. || 3

They worship Me
    With their senses always in their own clout,
    Their intelligence always unbiased and just,
    Doing good to others to them always is a must,
    Crave they do never for any selfish passionate lust;
They also do come to Me. || 4

Whose minds are fixed on the unmanifest;
Effort needed from them is often the greatest; |

Unmanifest unseeable goals are quite more difficult to attain;
One with a material body has to suffer more frustration and pain. || 5

But those with their <u>Yoga</u> unflagging;
To me all their actions are renouncing;
Supreme I am is what they are holding;
Worship Me, on Me who are meditating; || 6

Whose awareness keeps Me in the focus-a;
Before long I shall become their savior-a;
From death and tumults of the ocean of <u>samsar-a</u>. || 7

Contain your mind only in Me,
Let your intellect enter in Me, |
Then you shall always live in Me;
Do never have doubt in this, or in Me. || 8

Bhakti Yoga

If you unable to keep your mind focused on Me,
Then practice yoga steadily aiming to attain Me; |

If can't focus on Me your mind steady and straight;
Then attain Me by practicing yoga in right earnest. || 9

If you are even unable to practice the yoga best;
Be the one who holds My work to be the highest; |

Even if you work for Me faithfully in your mission;
Know without doubt You will attain perfection. || 10

If unable to work taking refuge in My yoga divine;
Then being at peace with yourself your discipline; |

Keeping faith in yourself and with full devotion,
Work, work renouncing fruits of all your action; || 11

Knowledge is by far superior to ritual at every age;
Meditation is lot more distinguished to knowledge; |

Renouncing the fruits of actions is superior to meditation;
Renouncing this fruit yields peace, no delay, no hesitation. || 12

A yogi is who
    For no one does a yogi harbor any hate;
    To all he is friendly and compassionate;
    Free from "me-ness" and "mine-ness";
    He is even toward pains and pleasures; |

He is patient, his endurance is steady;
He is a great yogi, happy and pretty. || 13

Whose peace is jolted not in any situation;
Who is self-disciplined, is of firm resolution; |

Whose mind and intellect is entrusted to Me;
That Me-devoted yogi is very dear to Me. || 14

Who in others does cause no anxiety;
And in whom no one causes any anxiety;
One from whom the world does not shy away;
And who himself does not keep the world away; |

A Yogi free of bondage to lust, indignation and fear;
Also is free of anxiety, to Me that Yogi is very dear. || 15

Who is impartial, unblemished, competent and unattached;
Who has renounced, whose anxieties have all withered; |

Who has relinquished undertakings for his own personal gain;
Is the devotee that is very dear to Me, is devoid of any stain. || 16

Who does not rejoice, nor mourns, does remain natant;
Renounced cravings, for both pleasant and unpleasant; |

One who is full of love and devotion;
Very Dear to Me is that type of person. || 17

Is even to enemy and friend with equal grace;
Who is also even between honor and disgrace;

He remains equal in cold and heat, to pleasure and pain;
Attachment and addiction to him are always in vain. || 18

Is undisturbed by censure, praise or charm;
He is unagitated, his mid is steady and calm;

Is happy and satisfied with anything whatever;
His mind is not fickle, nor does it freely waver;

At-home everywhere and with everything is he;
Fully devoted to Me, that person is very dear to Me. || 19

Practicing the nectar of this <u>dharma</u> as declared by Me;
Who hold faith, who are intent on the Supreme as Me;
Those devotees are indeed very loving very dear to Me; || 20

ঌ   *End of Book 12, Bhakti Yoga*   ঌ

Kshetra Kshetra-Jna Vibhaga Yoga

Attaining Divine Life Following the Path of Distinguishing Between Reality and the Knower of Reality

Kshetra = Manifest reality, field, domain.
Kshetra-jna = One who knows the true nature of manifest reality.
Vibhaga = Distinction, distinguished.
Yoga = A tool, a path, a focused practice to achieve a desired goal.
BG = Shrimad Bhagavad Gita.

What is in Kshetra–Kshetra-Jna Vibhaga Yoga?

"*Kshetra Kshetra-jna Vibhaga Yoga*" is a summary of the *Samkhya Yoga*'s view on the nature of reality. In Book 13, BG narrates this summary in beautiful spiritual poetry in a very logical format. Reality and its knower are deliberated through a dialog on the following basic concepts:

• *Kshetra* = reality, field, domain, material reality.
• *Kshetra-jna* = someone who knows the true nature of reality.
• *Jnanam* = knowledge.
• *Jneyam* = what ought to be known.
• *Prakriti* = material universe.
• *Purusha* = the entity that forces, powers, governs changes in the Prakriti; in non-spiritual terms Purusha could be called the natural laws since it has all attributes of natural laws. In spiritual terms Purusha is also called the Supreme Lord/God. Purusha is the enlivening agent in living beings; it is postulated to be the highest entity in a living body. Purusha controls all transformation in the material universe.

This chapter is about yoga, about a path to achieve a divine life by understanding the nature of the Kshetra, the manifest reality and the nature of the knower of the Kshetra, the Kshetra-jna.

Kshetra is a field. The field here is the reality, the material and emotional universe in which we live. Kshetra-jna is the wise one who knows the true nature of reality. Kshetra-jna or the "knower" of the field is one who knows composition and attributes of reality and laws governing changes in reality.

What is reality? How to go about understanding it? These are fundamental questions in philosophy. These are also the themes of discussion in this chapter.

But why should man strive to know the true nature of reality? It is a fundamental axiom of the "Yoga" schools of Indian Philosophy that man's miseries, grief, and unhappiness are rooted in the ignorance of the true nature of reality. To attain a life of bliss, a man should understand its true nature, and be free of illusion and delusions about reality. BG's opinion of the true knowledge of reality is the knowledge revealed in this chapter.

A basic axiom of Indian Philosophy (Hindu, Buddhist) is that man's grief, miseries, unhappiness all stem from ignorance of the true nature of reality (Kshetra). So, the wise should understand the true nature of reality to attain a happy, stress-free life. In addition to describing the nature of physical reality, this chapter also prescribes a set of mental qualities/habits which are necessary for understanding the true nature of reality. Collectively this set could be called the laws of the emotional universe. Obeying the laws of the physical universe and the laws of the emotional universe, that is, obeying the laws of reality, man would attain a happy and successful life. This is the inner thesis of this chapter.

This chapter is in essence a summary of the "Sankhya" school of Indian Philosophy which for millennia, has been regarded as the pinnacle of rational deliberation of the nature of the world. Here in one chapter BG gives the essence of Samkhya Yoga through really beautiful poetry.

Looking Ahead

Shlokas 5-6: The elements mentioned in these two Shlokas constitute kshetra or reality according to BG. Note that mental qualities and mental states are considered as part of kshetra, that is of material reality. This is a deep insight. The mental states are actually part of the physical body; they do not reside anywhere outside the material body of the feeler. So, it is quite logical that the definition of kshetra includes both physical things and mental characteristics.

Shlokas 7-11 lists qualities which constitute true knowledge (jnan) and mental qualities of those who are jnanee (wise).

Shloka 14-17: Shloka 14 is perhaps talking about the brain as an instance of Supreme (Param) Brahma in living beings. Since the brain of a living being is in command of all functions of the living body, it is quite feasible to think of it in the spiritual language as the Supreme <u>Brahman</u>, the supreme controller of the living being in a living body.

Shlokas 15-17 are a description of the Supreme <u>Brahman</u> in both physical and spiritual symbolism. Equating the attributes of Supreme Brahma as the supreme controller of all events in the world to the laws of nature, readers can get a simple rational description of the notion of the mystical entity, the Supreme (ultimate) Brahman. In the demystified thinking the properties of the supreme <u>brahman</u> maps very neatly to the natural laws of the world.

Shlokas 19-23: These Shlokas address the third of <u>Arjuna</u>'s query; what is <u>PURUSHA</u> and <u>PRAKRITI</u>. The reality is a composite of two main entities – <u>Purusha</u> and <u>Prakriti</u>. <u>Prakriti</u> is the inanimate matter that we see and feel in the universe. But <u>Purusha</u>? It is a bit more subtle but is described very well in these Shlokas.

Shloka 20: This Shloka may be talking about the brain, and consciousness in spiritual language.

Shlokas 24-25: *Paths to realize the True nature of reality.*

The previous Shloka says if one understands reality in the framework of <u>Purusha</u>, <u>Prakriti</u>, and <u>Gunas</u>, then the person will receive liberation from miseries and grief. But how would one understand it? What path should one follow to gain such understanding? The Shlokas 24-25 point out the paths.

There is a spiritual purpose hidden in these Shlokas. It has been told earlier that the Supreme Self or the God (in popular terminology) is residing in everyone in the form of <u>Purusha</u>. One way to realize the Divine, the Supreme Self would thus be to realize the <u>Purusha</u> within us. How would we do so? Shlokas 24-25 indicate the paths.

Shloka 24: "Self" indicates the Divine or the <u>Purusha</u> which makes you living, which makes you what you are. Three ways of understanding the nature of "Self" or the "<u>Purusha</u>" are indicated in these Shlokas:

- Self-effort through meditation; path of serious analytic introspection.
- <u>Samkhya</u>-<u>Yoga</u>: the path of rational deliberation laid out in the <u>Samkhya</u> school of philosophy and following a disciplined life of "<u>yoga</u>" (described in *Patanjali's YogaSutra*).
- <u>Karma yoga</u>: the path of selfless service to others elaborated in the third chapter of this book. This third path is BG's preferred path.

Shlokas 26-30: World view of the "knower" of the nature of reality.

Shlokas 31-34: These Shlokas are a Discussion on the nature of Pu-rusha – once more.

Last five Shlokas (Shloka 26-30) describe the world view of a person who has realized the true nature of reality. In the Shlokas 31–34 the conversation again turns towards description of the *Purusha*, variously called the *Atman*, the *Ishwaram*, the Lord, the Supreme Lord or "*Parameshwaran*". If one believes in a supernatural entity called God the Almighty, then these Shlokas could be understood as Gita's concept of God. These can be interpreted as BG's description of a secular and universal God. In the demystified interpretation these terms are synonyms with universal laws which control every change in the material universe. This interpretation fits perfectly with the descriptions in these Shlokas; that is with the spiritual description of God.

The key is that the laws as also the Purusha, are subtle, not visible to the physical senses; the existence of the laws are known by their effects on the tangible manifest component of reality, that is Prakriti. The existence and nature of the laws are realized through intelligence. Most of the Shlokas in this group describe this subtlety through beautiful poetic expressions.

Shloka 32: A subtle logic is used in this Shloka. To be stained or polluted, a substrate needs a material base. Neither the sky nor Atma has any material base by definition. So, they cannot ever be polluted or stained. Natural laws control changes in forms of tangible prakriti but are not tied to any material form, they have no material body. So, the laws or the Purusha can never be stained or defiled.

Reading Aid - Glossary:

In several places in this translation, the original Sanskrit words have been retained to improve rhythm and to provide a halo of the ancient scripture. In the text all these words have been underlined. They are translated and explained below.

Amruta = Divine potion of immortality.

Bhaaratha = The kingdom of Bharata or Bharatbarsha (current day India). In the epic of Mahaabharatha, Arjuna was a prince of this kingdom.

Brahman = The universe.

Brahma-Sutra = The scripture describing origin and properties of Brahman.

Guna = Attributes of matter or mind. See also Book 14 for detailed discussion

Jnana or Jnanam = Knowledge.

Jneyam = What ought to be known.

Karma yoga = The path of selfless service devoid of greed, lust, or passion. See Book 3 for a fuller deliberation of this subject.

Keshava = Another name of Lord Krishna.

Kshetra = Reality, field, domain.

Kshetra-jna = One who knows truths about kshetra.

Kunti = Name of mother of Arjuna.

Purusha = Entity which controls, governs, forces change in the material world.

Prakriti = Material universe.

Param Aatma = The Supreme Purusha.

Vedas = The Holy Book(s) of Hindus.

Book - 13

Kshetra – Kshetra-Jna Vibhaga Yoga

Arjuna's Questions...

What is kshetra, what is field, what is said to be the reality;
Who is a kshetra-jna, knower of a field, a knower of reality? |

What is jnan; what is jneyam, that we all truly ought to know;
Oh Lord Keshava, these are riddles none of which do I know;
Spell out these mysteries for me, to Thee politely do I bow. ||

The Holy Lord Said...

Oh son of Kunti, kshetra is the body, the reality that is manifest;
Kshetra-jna is that wise who knows the truths of reality the best. || 1

In all kshetra, in all fields, in all domains everywhere;
Know me to be the kshera-jna the supreme knower; |

Insight into reality and awareness of its knower;
Is always the core knowledge, so I declare; || 2

About kshetra, about its form, and its attribute;
About its modification, and what does it contribute; |

And what morphs kshetra, by whose power;
Tell you these all very briefly, hear me with care. || 3

These truths have been sung in many many ways by many sages;
With logic and reasoning clear and irrefutable all through the ages; |

Also in many sacred hymns of the Holy Vedas have these truths been said;
In Aphorisms of Brahman in Brahma-Sutra too these issues are narrated. || 4

The five principal elements "visible" to the five sense organs;
Intelligence, ego and Purusha which are invisible to these organs;
Five sense organs and five organs of action, make up organs ten;
Adding the mind organ to these we get the total organs eleven; || 5

Desires to have, hatred, aversions and jealousy;
Feelings of happiness-joy and of grief and misery; |

Consciousness and steadfastness the ability to endure-a;
And their modifications all together make what is kshetr-aha. || 6

Humility, modesty, and lack of conceit;
Absence of fraud, hypocrisy, and deceit;
Absent from him is any violent tendency and violence;
He is righteous, has rectitude, is clean and has patience; |

Reverent to ability, skill and knowledges;
He adores scholars, scholarship, and wise sages.

With firmness of mind, he remains focused on his goal;
Restrains own feelings and desires, exercising self-control; || 7

Renunciation of sensory passions and pleasures is high in his stature;
In him pride and vanity yields to his modesty, the Knower's core nature; |

He knows birth, death, disease, deprecation are events of nature;
Not being overwhelmed by any these is Knower's noble feature; || 8

Clinging on to son, spouse, house and possession;
Not are signs of true knowledge in any person; |
Remaining even in both a good and a lousy situation;
Are signs of true knowledge in the kshetra-jna person. || 9

Avoiding noisy fracas, a man with true knowledge seeks solitude;
With undistracted yoga, devoted to Me the wise finds rectitude; || 10

Always busy searching the truths of the nature and the Self;
Is the mark of a person with true knowledge, so says the sage. |

True knowledge has the above impression;
Whatever others are they are in contradiction;
Those are not knowledge, they are ignorance, they are delusion; || 11

Now let me you tell what is jneya-a, what ought to be known;
Knowing which the wise attains Amruta the immortality potion; |

Know that The supreme Brahman has no beginning nor any end;
Neither good nor bad it is, nor is it a foe nor is it any one's friend; || 12

It has hands and feet in every direction, at everywhere;
Has eyes, head face in every direction, every so where; |

It hears everything in every world and everywhere;
Everything It does envelop in the world everywhere. || 13

All attributes are reported to It by the senses;
Itself though It has no gunas or nor any senses;

Though not attached to any one thing;
It is the maintainer of every single thing;

Though devoid itself It is of any quality,
But It experiences every reported quality. || 14

"IT" is outside as well as inside of every object;
"IT" is in both stationary and in moving project; objects;

Subtle "IT" is, unknowable "IT" is through the senses;
"IT" appears afar as well as in very close spaces. || 15

Param Brahma!
Though appears to be divided and so differentiated;
"IT" is actually undivided, never IT is ever changed; |

Kshetra Kshetra-Jna Vibhaga Yoga

Ought to be understood that "IT" is the root, the essence;
The sustainer, developer, terminator of every existence; || 16

Param Brahma!
"That" is said to be the Light brightest beyond all darkness;
All other lights of the world are very very dim in its face; |

"That" is The knowledge, reachable only by knowledge;
"That" is what ought to be known by every aspiring sage;
"That" resides in the heart of all, always in every age. || 17

In summary,
I told you of Kshetra, the field, the reality that is in plain vision;
And told you of "JNEYA" that what by everyone ought to be known; |

Told you about true knowledge, "JNANAM" that one should own;
My devotees attain My divine state when to them these are known. || 18

Know that without any beginning are both Purusha and Prakriti;
But that mutability and attributes are realized only in Prakriti. || 19

Causes do always lord over effects, never are they in vain;
*   Know that mutability of Prakriti is the root cause in the end;*
Feelings of experiences are either pleasure or feeling of pain;
*   Know that experiences are enjoyed by the Purusha at the end. || 20*

Residing in the Prakriti, the Purusha enjoys and savors;
*   The "gunas" produced in the Prakriti, in the natural;*
Depending on the "gunas" a person is addicted to
*   The person is born in a womb with good or harsh feature || 21*

Purusha, the supreme entity in the body of the living,
Is the approver, supporter, and experiencer in the being; |

Said to be the Supreme Self, Param Aatmaa the enlivening;
Purusha Is the great Lord living in the body of the living. || 22

One who knows Purusha, Prakriti and the Gunas in this way;
No matter where he is, rebirth walks from him far far away; || 23

Some see "It" by following path of samkhya and rational deliberation;
Many others follow the path of karma yoga,
*   The path of selfless service devoid of greed, lust, or passion. || 24*

Many Many others though not knowing these paths;
Hearing only from others do worship these truths; |

From the grip of death and ignorance they too receive liberation;
Those who hear these truths with respect and with devotion. || 25

Oh Prince of Bhaaratha, you ought to be knowing;
That whatever is born, whatever comes into being; |

Be they in motion or are static, be they stationary or are in motion;
Nothing ever is realized without kshetra-jna and kshetra's interaction; || 26

The Supreme Lord resides evenly in all beings in the creation;
Even when the specific being gets destroyed or face mutation;

The Supreme Lord remains beyond any change or destruction;
One who sees like this is the wise one who sees, has true vision. || 27

On seeing The same Lord is present equally and in everything;
Does not injure himself by himself, nor also is self-deprecating;
That divine highest state such a wise man will soon be attaining. || 28

One who "sees" that all beings in nature;
Act driven by the laws of material nature; |

Therefore, who does not "see" himself as the controller,
Is the one who really "sees" reality in its true feature. || 29

That different beings both moving and non-moving;
Are differentiated forms whether living or nonliving;

That they all are established in the same One immortal root;
So all in the creation are expansions of that same One root;

The wise one who realizes this truth in his own heart and mind;
His intellect has attained the Brahman, nothing else left to grind. || 30

The Supreme Atman is not stained by any guna or by their collection;
Having no beginning, It is inexhaustible, never suffers any mutation; |

Although in the material body "It" does reside,
Though established in matter it is always free and clear;
It neither "does" anything, nor does it have any enmesh-er; || 31

As even though the sky spreads in the world in all corners and crevices;
But being very subtle, it is neither blemished nor stained by any devices;

So does the subtle Atma though existing in the body in all possible way;
Being subtle it never gets blemished, stained or changed along its way. || 32

Oh Arjuna, just as the entire world is revealed by the only One Sun;
So also all the kshetra are revealed by its owner the Supreme Atman. || 33

From the limited view that world is only of living and non-living;
From this limited view who seek, pursue liberation;
With knowledge eye, who realize the distinction;
Between the kshetra and the One who is the kshetra-knowing;

Only They Do Attain the highest state of being! || 34

❧ End of Book 13, Kshetra Kshetra-Jna Vibhaga Yoga ❧

BOOK 14
Guna-Traya Vibhaga Yoga

*Attaining Divine Life by Understanding
the Three Gunas and Their Effect on Quality of Life*

Guna = Mental tendency, mode, attitude, quality, attribute.

Guna Traya = Collection of three gunas or mental tendencies.

Vibhaga = Distinctive features!

Yoga = A tool, a path, a focused practice to achieve a desired goal.

BG = Shrimad Bhagavad Gita.

What is in Guna-Traya Vibhaga Yoga?

This chapter is about the yoga (path and practice) to achieve a divine life by understanding the nature of three gunas and their distinctive characteristics.

Simply speaking "guna" means mental tendency, mental propensity, mental attitude. BG's opinion is that the gunas arise and live in the physical body of a person. BG's thesis is that gunas influence, control a person's behavior. Since the behavior of a person cumulatively determines his actions and achievements (or lack of it), gunas actually determine the quality of a man's life. So, in order to improve his life, it is quite important for an individual to understand the nature of gunas, and how the bondage to the gunas are shaping his life; and how that bondage can be defeated.

BG maintains that depending on the propensity of the dominant guna in him, a person may enjoy a happy, divine life or an average life or a miserable life. BG's first hypothesis is that there are three core or fundamental gunas in a man's physical being. These three are called "Sattva", "Raja-ha" and "Tama-ha". Each guna has its own specific characteristics. BG describes these characteristics in lucid detail. BG also tells us how they affect the behavior of a man (and in turn the quality of his life). In this view, the spirit of a living being is a composite of these three core gunas. And this composition determines the quality of his life. In a sense the gunas have a grip on an individual. A man can attain a happy divine life by breaking the grip of the gunas on him. BG also indicates the path (yoga) following which an individual could achieve freedom from the grip of the gunas; and thus attain a happy prosperous divine (!) life. In Book 14, all these are deliberated in a methodical, analytical way in the medium of superb, beautiful poetry[1].

The mental tendencies or attitudes vary among individuals. In fact, there is a plethora of mental tendencies in humankind. A fundamental question that arises is this. How can the existence of only three gunas explain the manifestation of the plethora of mental tendencies we see in humans? The answer is surprisingly simple. The actual mental tendency of a person is a mixture of the three fundamental gunas. Let us take a physical analogy. We know that there are only three primary colors discernible by our eyes. The primary colors are red, green, and blue. All other colors are mixtures of the three primary colors in various proportions. The eye can see a plethora of colors and hues. But each hue is some mixture of the primary colors. So is the situation with the attitude or mental tendency. There are a plethora of possible attitudes or mental attitudes formed by a composite of only three fundamental gunas. Each of these tendencies in an individual is a mixture of the three primary gunas. This is a basic postulate of the Samkhya philosophy espoused in this Holy Book.

From this point of view the mental tendency of a person can be conceived as his mental color. It can be conceived as the spiritual form of the person or the spiritual engine driving the actions of a person. This metaphor is used throughout the chapter.

In this chapter, like an expert taxonomist, Lord Krishna divides the spectrum of tendencies (gunas) in three core (fundamental) types. He defines them and describes their effects on human behavior. He asks people to overcome the grip and limitations imposed by these natural gunas and advises that people should strive to attain behavior transcending the grip of the gunas. The last few Shlokas describe the behavior and mental qualities of a person who has attained the "guna-free" state. We do find that people in this state are likely to enjoy a divine life; that is, a life of peace, happiness, prosperity free of miseries, agitation, and anxieties.

BG's teachings are of universal application in all ages for all of mankind. Gunas are discussed so that we can have a framework to understand our own mental makeup, no matter what stage of technological or social development we live in. We think that we are all quite capable of understanding others' mentalities. The aim of Geetha, I presume, is that the reader (or devotee) will use this framework to understand his own gunas or his own mental tendencies and through that knowledge would alter the complexion (composition?) of his own mental tenden-

---

1 In the author's opinion, this translation is a poor to mediocre attempt to bring out that beauty.

cies and strive to achieve a divine life. The main purpose of this knowledge is to improve one's own self rather than use the knowledge to be critical of someone else.

Looking Ahead

Shloka 1-4: These Shlokas are a preparation to introduce the subject of the gunas, which are described in Shloka 5 and onwards. These Shlokas also indicate the virtues of having knowledge about gunas.

Shloka 5: Gunas are properties of matter (prakriti), not of the purusha (law). Gunas reside in prakriti.

Shlokas 6-9 describe the three gunas, their fundamental properties, and their hold on a person's behavior.

Shloka 10: At different times, one guna dominates over the other two in the same person.

Shlokas 11-13: How to know which guna is controlling a person (at some time?). This is answered in these three Shlokas (Shlokas 11-13).

Shlokas 14-15: Gunas determine the quality of the future (life) of a person.

Shlokas 22-25 describe the attributes of a person who has transcended the grips of the gunas. That person is not emotional; is without extremes of desire and impulsive propensity. Perhaps it means that the person is rational and thoughtful. This is BG's way of indicating which qualities a person should cultivate to overcome the grips of gunas and enjoy a happy life.

Reading Aid - Glossary:

In several places in this translation, the original Sanskrit words have been retained to improve rhythm and to provide a halo of the ancient scripture. In the text all these words have been underlined. They are translated and explained below.

Amruta = Divine potion of immortality.

Bhaaratha = The kingdom of Bharata or Bharatbarsha (current day India). In the epic of Mahaabharatha, Arjuna was a prince of this kingdom.

Brahman = The universe.

Guna = Attributes of matter or mind; mental tendency, propensity.

Prakriti = Material universe.

Promaada = Craziness, tendency to get into trouble often.

<u>Purusha</u> = Entity which controls, governs, forces change in the material world.

Book - 14

Guna-Traya Vibhaga Yoga

Yoga of the path of understanding the distinction between the three Gunas

The Holy Lord Said ...

Now I shall narrate to that knowledge,
That is robust, sound and never frail;
Knowing which many a wise sage,
Attain their ultimate goal without fail. || 1

Taking refuge in this wisdom and this knowledge,
"My" own attributes are attained by a wise sage; |

They are neither born when a new chapter is in creation,
Nor are they pained at times of chaos and destruction. || 2

Arjuna, the material nature is the great womb of Mine;
I am the One who impregnates it letting life to shine;
That is how all forms and beings come into existence. || 3

All forms and objects and all the living beings;
That are possible in world no matter what their feature;
Are all in the womb of <u>Brahman</u>, the great material nature;
Do know that of all of them I am the seed sowing Father. || 4

"<u>Sattva</u>", "<u>Raja-ha</u>" and "<u>Tama-ha</u>"
Are the three principal <u>guna</u>-ha; |

Born in <u>prakriti</u>, the material body is the <u>guna</u>'s only home ;
They tie down the immutable ageless Atman, a person's inner self,
In the physical body of the person, which is <u>guna</u>'s pleasure dome. || 5

<u>Sattva</u> <u>guna</u> endows Knowledge, happiness, and clarity of vision.
<u>Sattva</u> is sinless, is clear, is unblemished, it expels delusion;
Being transparent make other things visible, brings them to vision;
<u>Sattva</u> gifts knowledge, happiness, and increased comprehension. || 6

With Greed, lust and passion;
<u>Raja-ha</u> ties a man to action; |
<u>Raja-ha</u> powers man to action to gratify his passionate lust,
Believe Oh Arjuna defeating <u>raja-ha</u> is just and is a must. || 7

<u>Tama-ha</u> breeds ignorance and delusion;
It weakens reasoning and discrimination; |
Binds people to charm, silliness, and apathy to action;
Boosts "<u>promaada</u>", laziness,
*   sleepiness and propensity to dereliction. || 8*

Guna-Traya Vibhaga Yoga

Oh Bharata (Arjuna),
"Sattva" gives birth to happiness and peace unending;
Raja spawns actions seeking to gratify lust and craving; |

But by veiling knowledge from the hapless person,
"Tama-ha" hatches in him fantasy and delusion. || 9

Oh Arjuna,
At times in a man sattva becomes his guna dominant;
At other times hold of raja-ha in him is the strongest;
And at other times tama-ha in him is the guna penchant. || 10

When through every door of the body,
Radiates out Knowledge and curiosity,
Ought to know at that time in that body
Sattva guna has become very mighty. || 11

Listen Oh you, the great prince of Bharata,
When Raja-ha guna is the dominant disposition,
Greed and lust of the person leaps past his supervision,
To get the objects of his passion he then initiates action. || 12

Possessed by the tama-ha;
Neither Knowledge, nor curiosity nor clarity;
Brings in the man any surge of joy or activity;
But lethargy, delusion and trouble propensity;
Are what he likes, he gets inclined to inactivity. || 13

Dying in the sattva state, a man reaches that shining place;
Where he lives in the abode with many many enlightened face; || 14

Die with strong "Raja-ha" with unfulfilled lust and passion;
That Man will be Born again with desires for lustful action; |

While those dying with strong "Tama-ha" knowing no better;
Destined to be reborn in the womb of the foolish and inferior. || 15

Well done Sattva effort gifts peace, happiness and clarity;
Grief and frustration are bred from raja-ha propensity;
Ignorance and misery are outcomes of tama-ha activity. || 16

Sattva gifts knowledge; Raja-ha breeds lust and greed;
Frenzy, delusion, and ignorance are Tama-ha's seed. || 17

Sattva powers a man to climb to a higher happier plane;
With raja-ha the person keeps hovering in the middle lane;
Continuing in tama-ha man is destined to ugly, dirty, devilish den; || 18

When a seer "sees" none other than gunas control behavior;
And also comprehends "THAT" is supreme and is superior,
Then he "attains" My divine state then knows the truth better; || 19

Sattva, *raja-ha* and *tama-ha*, these *gunas* transcending;
Amrutam, the eternal bliss is attained by a living being; |
Thence he gets liberated from all griefs of living,
Like birth, death, miseries of sickness and aging; || 20

Arjuna Asked...

Oh Lord, what are the attributes, tone or tenor;
Of those who eschew the three *gunas*' favor; |

How do they act? How do they look?
How do they rip the three *gunas*' grip? || 21

The Holy Lord Krishna Said...

Oh Pandava, he neither strongly desires nor does he feel strong repulsion;
To Enlightenment, nor to lustful actions, nor want to remain in delusion. || 22

Ignoring the *gunas* who sits steady, apathetic without passion;
Knows that *gunas* exist and are active, himself has no delusion;
Knowing this, himself is calm and never itching for lustful action; || 23

To him grief and rejoice are just the same;
Not ever worrying about fame or shame;

Happy and cozy is he with his own self;
Neither cocky nor shy is he about himself; |

Soil, stone or gold to him are all the same;
None of them on him has any special claim;

All things are same to him both dear and un-dear;
Steadfast in flattery or criticism he takes all without fear; || 24

One, who is indifferent to honor and disgrace,
And who impartial to enmity and friendly-ness; |

Ceding ownership of results of own actions without rage;
Is the Mark of a man who is freed from the *guna*-bondage; || 25

Serving "Me" with devotion and without deception;
Crossing the "*gunas*", a devotee becomes ready ;
    To be one with the "*Brahman*", the Creation; || 26

"I" am the foundation of the creation;
And of immortality;
And of inexhaustibility;
And of immutability;
And of dharma;
    The virtuous ethics of happy and prosperous living;
    And of absolute bliss and I am the final abode of every being. || 27

❧ End of Book 14, Guna-Traya Vibhaga Yoga ❧

BOOK 15

Purushottama Yoga

*Attaining Divine Life by Understanding
the Nature of Purushottama, the Supreme Spirit*

Purushottama = The ultimate or the Supreme <u>Purusha</u>, the controlling entity of the world.

Yoga = A tool, a path, a focused practice to achieve a desired goal.

BG = Shrimad Bhagavad Gita.

What is in Purushottama Yoga?

The word "<u>Purushottama</u>" is a combination of two words: "<u>purusha</u>" and "<u>uttama</u>". The meaning of "<u>uttama</u>" is clear and unambiguous. It simply means - the best, the Supreme, the ultimate and such things. So, it would mean that this is the chapter of the best and the Supreme "<u>Purusha</u>". This chapter is about attaining happiness and bliss by the <u>yoga</u> (effort) of understanding the nature of <u>Purushottama</u>, the supreme <u>Purusha</u>, the supreme spirit.

Before proceeding with the rest of this chapter, it is useful to get some sense of what "<u>Purusha</u>" means! See also the discussion in Shlokas 16-18.

In colloquial language, <u>purusha</u> simply means a male person. In ancient Indian philosophies and scriptural literature, "<u>purusha</u>" has an altogether different meaning completely unrelated to gender. In a very simplified form "<u>purusha</u>" is that thing which distinguishes a living from the dead. The universe is assumed to be composed of two things: "<u>purusha</u>" and "<u>Prakriti</u>". "<u>Prakriti</u>" is nature, the material form of nature; and "<u>purusha</u>" is the thing, the essence which puts life or qualities of living in it. Without "<u>purusha</u>" in it, a living being is a mass of inanimate lump. It is the "<u>purusha</u>" which puts life and everything we associate with living inside the otherwise inanimate body. In this sense the notion of "<u>purusha</u>" could be thought of something close to "spirit" - the principle of consciousness and life.

The entire concept of "<u>purusha</u>" is a lot more than this. There is a concise conversation on the nature of the <u>Purusha</u> in the Shlokas 15-17 of this chapter. In BG's teaching <u>Purushottama</u> is that entity which initiates, controls, and governs every change in the material world, every change in <u>Prakriti</u>. Without the <u>Purushottama</u>, there would be no changes in the world; the world would be a dead barren place. In this Book 15, BG introduces the notion, characteristics of <u>Purushottama</u>;

and the personal qualities a person should cultivate to understand the nature of <u>Purushottama</u>.

The discussion starts with the metaphor of a mighty <u>Asvatthwa</u> tree. When this tree represents the universe, its roots are upwards and branches are downwards. Though it appears paradoxical, the analogy is pretty apt when we consider that the whole world draws its sustenance from the Sun; it is as if the world is rooted in the Sun which is far above it. The world itself is the body of this mighty tree being fed from root, the sun far above it.

The mighty tree is also used as a metaphor for a man's life, where its branches represent his actions/relationships; and roots are embedded in community; and that his actions are stimulated by his <u>gunas</u> (Shlokas 1-3).

In either of the tree metaphors, understanding the full nature of the tree is a very complex almost impossible task. BG maintains that a man cannot fathom the complexities of this tree unless he cuts off his own attachments (prejudices, delusions etc.) to the tree (Shlokas 4-6), indirectly hinting man needs to resort to rational thinking to understand the complexities of nature.

Then, in its own inimitable style in Shlokas 7-14, BG describes how the <u>Purusha</u> resides and functions in our own biological machines to make it possible for us to understand the world. It emphasizes and succinctly describes how <u>Purusha</u> supports the living world, by governing necessary changes in the physical world. <u>Purusha</u> makes it possible for all beings to live and prosper in the world. <u>Purusha</u> is neither partial nor inimical to anyone!

The three concluding Shlokas (16-18) succinctly capture Samkhya <u>Yoga</u>'s view of the construction of reality. That view utilizes three terms. These are "<u>Prakriti</u>" and two views of <u>Purusha</u>. "<u>Prakriti</u>" is the mutable, changeable component of reality; in simple terms "<u>Prakriti</u>" is inanimate matter whose form can be changed only by the power of "<u>Purusha</u>". <u>Purusha</u> is nature's laws (in demystified interpretation); the laws themselves are immutable, unchangeable, ever present and everlasting. Examples of such laws are laws of gravity; that every being that has been born will ultimately die; any organized mass in <u>prakriti</u> (e.g., a living body) will become disorganized in time by the power of change wrought on by <u>Purusha</u>. To connect to the last view of <u>Purusha</u>, think of the principles of thermodynamics.

Depending on the context, <u>Purusha</u> is known by different names. When the power of <u>purusha</u> (that is, natural laws) is working through an organized material body of a living being, that power is called "atma" or "jeeva-atma". Otherwise, Purusha is called "param-atma" when it is in the context of controlling the totality of other physical entities. Atma is the name of the Purusha which imparts the property of living in a living entity. The Purusha or the natural laws themselves are invisible; existence of Purusha is visible only by its transformative effect on Prakriti. That is why "Prakriti" can be called as the visible form of Purusha. These ideas are succinctly described in the beautiful poetry in these three Shlokas.

What is the material basis of Purushottama? These Shlokas give a glimpse to the answer. Purusha enlivens a living body; without it the body of a living being is a carcass. It also holds the world together; meaning does not allow it to fall apart. It is eternal, permanent, and ever enduring (Shloka 16). It penetrates everything, every physical matter, everywhere and Lords over everything, every transition. (Shloka 17). In this form of Purushottama it is beyond both permanence and impermanence (Shloka 18). The last Shloka gives the clue of what Purushottama is. Obviously Purushottama is not simply a piece of matter, however esoteric we may imagine it to be. If it would be matter or form of matter, it would be either permanent or impermanent; it could not be beyond both. Also, it controls all transitions in the physical world everywhere. So, what is it? The only sensible interpretation is that Purusha and Purushottama is the spiritual name of the natural laws. Readers will easily find that the description of the Purusha, Param-Atmana or Purushottam are actually names of Physical laws in different contexts/containers in the spiritual language. Taken together these three Shlokas may be the most beautiful poetic description and definition of natural laws in the mystified spiritual language.

The last two Shlokas, 19-20, are a clarion call to people to put faith in the Purushottama, that is to believe that the world is not random; rather it is law bound - in spiritual language, it is controlled by the Purushottama. People should perform their duties with this in mind, complying with Purushottama, the natural laws. Read with this interpretation in mind, the entire chapter will hopefully be totally demystified.

Looking Ahead:

Shlokas 1-3: Two ways the tree metaphor is used to represent the world and also man's life. Also, introduces the complexity of the problem.

Shlokas 4-6: To understand the mysteries in this tree, tree of life, or the world, man should search for the laws which control all aspects of these trees (Shloka 4). However, to get a glimpse of the laws and pro-cesses, the seeker has to overcome his attachments, his prejudices. This can only be done by cultivating certain mental practices (Shloka 5). But understanding the laws will be enlightening and will bring a state of bliss (Shloka 6).

Shlokas 7-12: These Shlokas describe the relationship of the Lord God, the supreme spirit, to the world of the living, that is, to that of the living beings. The nature of the relationship as revealed in these Shlokas is unique.

Shlokas 13-15: Three other facets of the attributes of the Supreme Spirit are described In these Shlokas.

Shloka 13 indicates that food (vegetables) grows in the world by the grace of the Supreme Spirit and that is essential for living. Thus, the Purushottam supports every facet of every creature's life.

Shloka 14: Physiological functions of the living are controlled by the Purusha residing in a living being.

Shloka 15: Mental activities of living beings are also the grace of Pu-rusha.

Shlokas 16-20: The underlying meaning of these Shlokas have been commented on in the previous section.

Reading Aid - Glossary:

In several places in this translation, the original Sanskrit words have been retained to improve rhythm and to provide a halo of the ancient scripture. In the text all these words have been underlined. They are translated and explained below.

Asvatthwa = A type of very large tree in the tropics; it is in the family of fig trees.

Guna = Mental attributes, mental tendencies; mental characteristics. See Book 14 for details.

Maya and Moha = Illusion and delusion.

Paramatman = The spirit governing changes in the world.

Purusha = Spirit which enlivens matter to become living being. Also, it is the entity that forces, governs changes in the material world.

Purushottam(a) = The Supreme Spirit; (natural laws in the author's opinion).

Veda = The Holy Book of the Hindu faith.

Book - 15

Purushottama Yoga

Yoga of understanding the nature of Purushottama - the Supreme Spirit.

Holy Lord (Krishna) Said...

This immutable Asvatthwa tree;
*   High upwards are its root;*
*   Downwards do its branches shoot; |*

The hymns of the Vedas are the leaves of this mighty tree;
Knowing this, true knowers of the Vedas become ignorance free. || 1

Down and up both ways spread its branches;
Sprouting objects "visible" to the senses; |

In this world, nourished by the three gunas;
Its roots spread binding man to action-aas; || 2

Of this big mighty "Asvatthwa" tree;
Its roots and branches spreading free;

Unfathomable is its form, it's beginning or its end;
Nor can it be grasped
*   How it comes into being or how it grows or bend; |*

None can conquer this puzzling bewilderment;
Unless he cuts from it, his own attachment;
With the sharp weapon of firm "detachment". || 3

Therefore, you ought to seek and go to that manor;
Going where no one ever comes back any more; |

Take refuge only in that primal spirit - that eternal Purush-a;
From whom all activities are flowing out from time ancient-a. || 4

Devoid of egotism, pride or vanity, illusion and delusion;
Having conquered vices of attachment, of lust and passion; |

In the Supreme Self who does always reside;
Conflicting duality of happiness or grief;
*   from whom do always hide;*

Unconfused is that soul is among the wise;
Who reaches the eternal abode of peace in paradise. || 5

Neither the sun, nor the moon nor fire;
Can illuminate HIM that Supreme Sire; |

Purushottama Yoga

No one ever returns back having come there;
That place is My final home of joy forever. || 6

A fragment of Me is eternally existing;
As eternal life in the world of the living, |

The six senses the mind including;
Draws material world to itself attracting;
For truths to find It keeps on plowing. || 7

When a new body does the Lord attain;
Or when in a body He ceases to remain; |

He "takes along" these traits in His next course;
Just as wind carries a flower's scent from its source. || 8

Over the five senses and the mind always He is presiding;
Seeing, touching, tasting, smelling and also hearing; |

He enjoys this world of myriad substances,
Brought to It by the organs of all five senses. || 9

Whether He is departing or is in the body residing;
Whether is being adored by gunas or He is enjoying; |

Never is He perceived by those delighting in delusion;
But the knowledge eyed sees Him with clear vision. || 10

Striving hard does the wise yogi can see;
That divine fragment in the mind of his own "sea"; |

Even on striving, the unrefined don't see Him though;
Maya and Moha send their knowledge on furlough. || 11

That brilliance, that light, that splendor coming from the sun,
That brilliance in whose sight darkness is always on the run;

That brilliance which illuminate the world leaving no gap,
That light which is in the moon and always in a fire's trap;

From Me is that brilliance, is that splendor, is that light;
These you should always know; you will be in delight; || 12

When creatures enter this earth, and after they are born;
"I" hold, maintain, support all with My energy, not any scorn; |

"I" nourish them all by being nutrition in the vegetation;
I ripen them taking the form of moonshine and wind's motion; || 13

In the body of everyone living;
I reside as the fire of digesting; |

All the four food groups do I keep digesting;
I balance the breathing exhaling and inhaling; || 14

Sitting in the mind every being,
I grant them memory, knowledge and their retention;
Also, from Me does come their decay and degeneration; |

In all the Vedas, in all disciplines of learning;
In all efforts to gain knowledge and truth searching;
Know that "I" am the One you ought to be knowing; |

"I" am at the end of all knowledge;
"I" am the knower of all knowledge;
So is said by the wise sage. || 15

In world, in two forms is the "Purusha" resting;
Purusha the one makes a body a living being;
The body though never is a permanent thing; |

Outside, Purusha is the core the universe He is holding;
There Purusha is eternal, permanent, and ever enduring. || 16

Exists also in another form The Supreme Purusa-ha;
That form is named to be the "Paramatman-aha";

Enters all the three worlds of whom He is the bearer;
Him is the immutable eternal Lord everywhere. || 17

Because "I" am beyond impermanence;
Also, because I am superior to permanence,
That is why in the world and
In the Vedas, and in the books of knowledges;
I am distinguished as "Purushottama" by all the sages. || 18

One who is unconfused and free of delusion-a;
Knows "Me" this way to be the Purushottam-a;

He worships Me, He loves Me with all his passion-a;
And in every way, Oh Prince oh My dear Arjun-a. || 19

Oh, you the unblemished one, Oh the intelligent one;
I told you this secret doctrine, the most secret knowledge;
Realizing this, perform your duties at life's every page. || 20

☺ *End of Book 15, Purushottama Yoga* ☺

Deva-Asura-Sampada-Vibhaga Yoga

Attaining Divine Life by Understanding the Nature of Divine and Devilish Wealth

Deva = Divine, god, god-like.
Asura = Demon, devil, evil.
Sampada = Wealth, estate, habit, mentality.
Vibhaga = Distinction; distinctive feature.
Yoga = A tool, a path, a focused practice to achieve a desired goal.
BG = Shrimad Bhagavad Gita.

What is in Deva-Asura-Sampada-Vibhaga Yoga?

"Deva" means divine or god. "Asura" means demon, evil, devil and things like that. "Sampada" is wealth – material and spiritual. "Vibhaga" is a distinction.

Yoga is a tool, a path, a focused practice to achieve a desired goal.

Together it would mean the yoga to understand the distinction between the ways of the Divine and the Evil.

Looking ahead

The Yoga of this chapter is the ability to distinguish between the wealth of the gods who enjoy a divine anxiety free life of health, peace, and prosperity; and the wealth of demons or the evil who suffer a life of anxiety, grief, and misery. The wealth here refers to spiritual wealth or mentality which is expressed through behavior, habit, and view of the world. This chapter (Book 16) gives us the knowledge to distinguish between these two types of wealth and behavior. Of course, the implied advice is that by being able to distinguish between these two types, the seeker will choose to cultivate the divine wealth in his spirit and habit; thus, he will enjoy a divine life. Also, this chapter states very clearly the devilish world view and devilish behavior as well. Of course, the intention is that those who want a happy, anxiety free, prosperous life will abhor demonic wealth, that is, will abhor devilish ways.

To understand the distinction and to adopt the correct way requires focused effort. That focused effort is the Yoga described in this chapter. This requires enlightenment to know what is divine and what is devilish; that is, what is good and what is bad. A divine anxiety free life requires focused practice to adopt divine behavior in one's own life and abandon devilish ways. This effort or yoga is the "Deva-Asura-Sampada-Vibhaga Yoga".

One word of caution is useful here. Primary purpose of BG is to improve the quality of our own life using the knowledge in this book. It is very easy for anyone, to use the knowledge in this chapter to criticize other people and categorize them as either divine or evil. The primary intent however is that the reader will use this knowledge to examine his own beliefs, values, world views and most importantly his own behavior. In short, the reader is encouraged to examine his own spiritual wealth ("sampada") and improve himself by integrating deva-sampada in his own life.

Shloka 1-4: These verses embody the crux of this chapter. Shlokas 1-3 is an enumeration of the deva-sampada; that is the type of wealth that the devas (divine people) are endowed with. Shloka 4 enumerates asura-sampada, the type of wealth that asuras (demonic) people are rich in. The implication is that by accumulating deva-sampada, a man attains a divine life, a life of happiness, peace, prosperity, success, freedom from anxiety, tension, and misery. Whereas accumulating the asura-sampada brings the opposite qualities to a man's life.

The original Sanskrit words used to name the divine wealths, have loaded meaning. It is very difficult to provide a one word in-line translation of these words in English without losing or compromising their original meanings. So here liberty is taken to enumerate the meaning of each of these Sanskrit words in a few short sentences below. The deva-sampada or divine qualities enumerated by Gita in these three verses are:

(Shloka 1)

1. "Abhayam" = Fearlessness; (do not do anything which makes you fearful now or in the future).
2. "Sattva-sang-shuddhi" = Purification of heart and mind from which impurities like lust, greed, anger, attachment have been washed away; all characteristics described as demonic in later verses are impurities of heart as well. Practice to keep your heart pure. One way is to continually strive to overcome the temptations of lust, greed; strive to gain control over your impulses of angry behavior; to practice detachment from material possessions. This striving is the process of purification of your heart.

3.   "Jnana-yoga-byabastha" = Focused and sustained pursuit of knowledge; it is the habit of being organized and disciplined in gaining knowledge about the true nature of the world, to understand the laws which control changes in the world including one's own personal world, to understand the mechanisms behind events occurring in the world and in our lives.

4.   "Daanam" = Practice of giving to the extent one can. It is not saying that one should starve to death while giving away his food in charity. Rather, do not be a hoarder; give away as much as you can to the needy. Charity could be in terms of food, money, knowledge, wisdom, or labor to help individuals and communities.

5.   "Dama-ha" = Self-restraint, discipline; the habit of not giving in to impulsive urges (speech, body, thought) are examples of self-restraint or "Damaha".

6.   "Yajna" = Unselfish collaborative work, selfless service; the habit of performing unselfish work for the good of your family, your project team at work, your community, etc. are examples of performing Yajna.

7.   "Swadhyay" = Studying scripture, authoritative books in your discipline of effort.

8.   "Tapaha" = Austerity. It implies the habit of remaining focused on your goal, living within your means, living without showing off, without spending beyond your means; the habit of not being extravagant with your resources (money and time!), not wasting your resources.

9.   "Aarjabam" = The habit of being virtuous and upright as opposed to being dishonest and/or slimy.

(Shloka 2)

10.   "Ahimsa" = Non-violence (physically and mentally).

11.   Satyam = Truthfulness.

12.   "Akrodha" = Anger-less-ness or freedom from anger, i.e., the habit of remaining peaceful and calm. Practice overcoming your anger to anyone. The practice to become free of anger (lingering anger) is a "deva-sampada". It brings happiness and peace.

13.   "Tyaga" = Renunciation; that is, the habit of giving up thirst for material possessions and thirst for sensory pleasure.

14.   "Shanti" = Peacefulness; it is the habit of remaining peaceful, the habit of not itching to engage in fight (physical or verbal) in case of a dispute.

15.   "Apaishunam" = Non-calumny. It is the habit of not uttering or spreading false, slanderous rumors or malicious statements to injure anyone else.

16. "Daya" = Kindness to everyone; universal compassion.
17. "Aloluptavyam" = Freedom from lusting desires; with this habit a man controls urges to get "things", controls desire to satisfy lust and sensory gratification.
18. "Maardabam" = Being gentle and kind as opposed to the habit of being cruel and harsh.
19. "Hrirachaapalam" = The habit of keeping a steady mind; habit of not being fickle minded.

(Shloka 3)

20. "Teja-ha" = Vigorous, energetic, competent; it is the habit of NOT being lazy, apathetic, or indolent. With this quality, a person proactively helps others with his knowledge and skill. It is as if knowledge, skill, compassion are radiating out of this person.
21. "Kshama" = Habit of forgiving; It is the habit of not carrying the burden of anger or vengeance. Practicing forgiving is a divine habit. Ability to forgive cools the mind and enables it to focus on understanding the nature and issues of life. This in turn leads to higher productivity in life and work, and consequently higher reward and riches and a peaceful tension-free life. This is why it is a "deva-sampada" or wealth of the divine people.
22. Dhriti = Fortitude, which is the ability to endure difficult situations with courage, without being disturbed or distracted or breaking down.
23. Shoucham = Cleanliness. Cleanliness implies cleanliness of body, mind, and environment. It implies a clean, dirt-free body; a clean mind not disturbed by lust, greed, anger, illusions, and other irrational thoughts; a clutter free, organized environment. People practicing cleanliness are generally healthier, more efficient, and consequently are more successful in their endeavors. That is why it is a deva-sampada. This is a very important and easily achievable habit to attain a divine life.
24. "Adroha" = Freedom from deep seated meanness or malice to anyone. It is a divine wealth. A person with malice in his heart will invariably make enemies and/or engage in bad deeds, which in turn seeds anxiety, tension, and unhappiness in life. That is why one should practice "Adroha", practice not being mean or malicious to others.
25. "Naatimaanita" = Free of arrogance; free from the feeling of excessive pride or honor; free from feelings like "I am the best, the greatest, etc." Arrogance and lack of humility is regarded as one of the vilest attitudes of the human mind. Why is it a divine wealth? An arrogant mind continuously gets into conflicts (to assert his dominance or assumed correctness), becomes

short-sighted and sinks into ignorance (because he thinks he knows the most, knows the best, etc. and there is no need to learn more). Consequently, lives a life of anxiety and misery (see Shloka 4 of this chapter).

A reader may argue whether the deva-sampada is really a path to reach a divine life or not or if the demonic sampada described in Shloka 4 will really lead to a hellish life. Bhagavad Gita does not get into any argument on either of these issues here. The Holy Book gives Its opinion and guidance; it leaves the reader to make his own choice (Shloka 24).

Each of the sampada or wealth is actually a mental habit. In this narration we have often quoted and underlined the original Sanskrit names for the specific habit (wealth) and attempted to translate them in English. Often the English translation is more verbose (more than one word) since in many cases it has been difficult to find an appropriate one word in English of the original Sanskrit word. Readers knowledgeable in both languages may find a more appropriate translation.

Shloka 4 concisely describes demonic wealths, that is, demonic habits.

Shlokas 5-6 contrasts the life of people of divine habit with those of demonic habits.

Shlokas 7-20 clearly describe the features of demonic habits and the pitiful course of their egotistic bombastic thoughts and lives which always end in grief and misery.

Shloka 18: People of demonic habits hate divine habits and ideas in everyone.

Shloka 21: Here is specific instruction on how to avoid getting succumbed into a demonic womb (environment).

Shloka 22: This is a clear path to redeem oneself to attain a supreme state, a state of happiness, free of anxiety and agitation. The three bad habits in Shloka 21 keep a man tied to an unhappy state in life.

Reading Aid - Glossary:

In several places in this translation, the original Sanskrit words have been retained to improve rhythm and to provide a halo of the ancient scripture. In the text all these words have been underlined. They are translated and explained below.

Asura = Demon, opposed to divine or god.
Deva = God, divine.

<u>Pandava</u> = Son(s) of king Pandu; here it specifically means prince Ar-
   juna.
<u>Sampada</u> = Wealth; here mentality, mental habits.
<u>Scripture</u> = Holy text; authoritative text which stood the test of time.
<u>Yajna</u> = Unselfish collaborative work for the good of the community.

Book - 16

Deva-Asura-Sampad-Vibhaga Yoga

The Holy Lord Krishna said...

Self-restraint, "Yajna", and charity;
Studying scripture, practicing austerity; |

Purification of heart, focused pursuit of knowledge;
Fearlessness, virtuous and upright at every stage; || 1

Non-violence, Truthfulness, and kindness;
Compassion, gentle and steady mindedness;

Renunciation, freedom from lust, anger, and rage
Non-slanderous and peaceful at life's any stage; || 2

Energetic and competent, fortitude and forgiving,
Non-malicious, humble, ego-vanity not bloating; |

Cleanliness of body, mind and environment;
Yields divine life with peace and enjoyment;
All these are divine wealths || 3

Hypocrisy, arrogance, conceit, anger are in Asura always;
Harsh words and actions, also ignorance holding his sway;
These are the wealth of those living in the demonic way. || 4

Divine wealth causes liberation so the sages do say;
Demonic wealth is bondage to misery in every way; |

Oh, Pandava brave, anguish must you not!
Born in divine wealth, grief is not in your lot. || 5

In the world, habits of people have two distinct feature;
Some are divine, while others are of demonic nature; |

About divine nature I did tell you leaving no end;
Now you hear of the nature of the demonic bend. || 6

They do not know when to act, or when to engage;
Nor do they know when to cease or quit the stage; |

Neither clean body or clean mind nor polish nor sophistication;
Not even the truths of the world are in Asura's scope of vision. || 7

Believe they do in no God nor any higher authority;
Nor in any firm base of the world nor in its stability; |

No truths are settled or eternal, nothing is unjust or just;
What else is the world for, they ask other than satisfying lust? || 8

Deva-Asura-Sampada-Vibhaga Yoga

Mesmerized by such views the rotten dim witted one;
They come into being for the purpose of evil to be done;
To the goodness of the world, they do bring erosion. || 9

Grasped by insatiable greed, intoxicated by ego;
Accompanied by hypocrisy unstoppably do they go; |

Swayed by false ideas, and dark delusion as their feed,
To vows and purposes unclean do they merrily proceed; || 10

Convinced are the demons in entirety;
    That enjoying lust is the ultimate goal, |
Stuck thus they remain in deep anxiety
    Till death takes them as its cruel toll. || 11

Myriads of false hopes keep them in trapping;
Indulge do they in anger and desires craving; |

Money and wealth they seek to be amassing;
Even unethically for purposes of lust-enjoying. || 12

Today I obtained this thing the one most charming;
I shall fulfill my other desires too in the days coming; |

This is mine now, that thing will also come to me rolling;
More and more money shall I have as time keeps ticking; || 13

This enemy was killed by me today;
Other enemies also surely will I slay; |

I am the divine lord, I am the great enjoyer,
I am successful, strong, none is happier! || 14

I am the aristocrat, born in high class without any chink;
Who else is there like me? Who dares me? they do think; |

I shall give to charity they think, rejoice in vain exultation;
They remain deeply seeped in their ignorance-fed delusion. || 15

Led astray by wrong thoughts and vision;
Being caught in webs of vain delusion; |

Remaining strongly attached to lust gratification;
Finally, they fall into unclean hell, no redemption. || 16

Self-conceit and stubborn-ness brimming;
Intoxicated by wealth, arrogance unending, |

Participate they do in worship, in yajna but only in name;
With hypocrisy, flouting laws and customs without shame || 17

Taking refuge in egoism, feeling mightier;
They cling to hollow vanity, lust, and anger; |

They do loathe ME, envious of ME they are;
In themselves as also in the person of other; || 18

These worst wretches of this earth;
These hating cruel ones do I cast; |

To the unholy wombs of a demon;
Times again and again on and on. || 19

Getting the demonic womb from birth to birth;
To unholy hellish hearths, there is no dearth;

Without getting ME,
 The deluded ones go from bad to worse with ease;
 Ever voiding their hopes of happiness and peace. || 20

Three types of doors are there to enter the hell;
Doors that destroy the self letting in evil's spell; |

These three doors are the door of lust, anger and greed;
Abandon these three you shall remain happy and freed; || 21

When a man is free of these evils three;
When with gates of darkness he has no spree; |

Then when the man does what is best for his being;
Then that man attains the supreme state of living. || 22

One who abandons <u>scriptures</u> and its injunctions;
But continues merrily with his lusting inclinations; |

Success and happiness are not in his dish;
Nor does he enjoy a life of peace or bliss. || 23

Therefore, study the <u>scriptures</u> and learn a lot;
What you ought to do and what you ought not;

Knowing from the <u>scripture</u> its correct prescription;
In this world you should undertake proper action . || 24

❧ End of Book 16, Deva-Asura-Sampada-Vibhaga Yoga ❧

Shraddha-Traya-Vibhaga Yoga

*Attaining Divine Life by Understanding
the Three Types of Shraddha, Devotion*

Shraddha	=	devotion, respect.
Traya	=	Three, group of three.
Vibhaga	=	distinction; distinctive feature.
Yoga	=	a tool, a path, a focused practice to achieve a desired goal.
BG	=	Shrimad Bhagavad Gita.

Together an appropriate translation of the title of the seventeenth book could be: *The path for union to divine life by understanding the distinction between the three types of "*Shraddha*".* The focused effort to understand is "yoga".

What is Shraddha?
What is Shraddha-Traya-Vibhaga Yoga?

Popular meaning of "shraddha" is devotion, respect, reverence, veneration, etc. BG's thesis is that shraddha itself is of three types: sattvik, rajasik and tamasik. Shraddha itself is invisible; it resides in the mind of the people. A person's behavior flows from the shraddha a man is harboring in mind. Though shraddha is invisible, behavior is visible. A man's behavior is the visible expression of the type of shraddha the man is harboring.

Book 17 builds up a systematic framework through which a person can understand his own inner shraddha and that of another. It describes five different types of behavior which show a person's shraddha to the world (and to one's own self). These are:

- Type of people or personality a person admires; (Shlokas 4-6).
- Type of food a person appreciates; (Shlokas 8-10).
- Type of mindset with which a person engages in yajna, that is collaborative projects for community good; (Shlokas 11-13); the description of tamasik shraddha (Shloka 13) is especially telling. With this type of shraddha a person pays scant attention to the details of his task and has minimal respect for the world and others. With behavior stemming from such shraddha it is easy to see why such a person attains less, ends up in want and grief. Overall, it is easy to see how each type of shraddha determines the quality of a

man's life. In this description lies the therapeutic value of learning about shraddha.

- Preferred type of austerity or discipline in one's lifestyle in body, speech and thinking, (Shlokas 14-16); as also the mindset behind the performance of the austerity (Shlokas 17-19). Both indicate inner shraddha of a person.
- Type of mindset and the manner behind giving, behind charity is an important behavior expressing the inner shraddha of a person. (Shlokas 20-22).

Through these external expressions which are visible as our behavior we can recognize which type of shraddha/respect/devotion we are carrying inside us. BG does not prescribe which type of belief one should/must adopt. By its choice of words, however, it does not hide which type of shraddha BG is encouraging in the seekers. BG defines and shows how, inspired by sattvik shraddha, a person would engage in these five activities to attain a happy divine life (Shlokas 23-28).

BG is imparting the knowledge of reality of shraddha. It is not "telling" which one must be followed. It does not prescribe a specific type nor does it threaten a punishment for not following the prescribed shraddha. It merely states the reality of shraddha as it is; what it is and how to recognize the type of shraddha within our own selves (and in others). This knowledge is important for every man since his behavior (stemming from his shraddha) has far reaching consequences in a man's life. It can make him a happy successful individual by nourishing sattvik shraddha or can lead him to a miserable wretched life by hanging on to tamasika shraddha. With the knowledge in Book 17, a man can get over his confusion and steer himself to a happy fulfilling life.

In this respect BG is hardly a religious doctrine. BG does not invoke any god or any divine edict. Rather the deliberation in BG is almost analytical in nature as if shraddha is a physical thing. BG creates a framework and vocabulary through which we can understand our own beliefs, our own shraddha and those of others. The tone of deliberation throughout this book is NOT "Thou Shall do this ... "; rather it is that "Thou should know this ..."

Looking ahead:

Shlokas 1-3 names the three types of shraddha. It also asserts that a man's behavior flows from his shraddha. So even though shraddha itself is invisible, by seeing the behavior, which is visible, one can understand the inner belief, the type of shraddha in the mind of a man.

Shlokas 4-6: People harboring different types of <u>shraddha</u> admire different types of people.

Shlokas 7-10: Food Preference and type of motive behind engaging in collaborative work indicates the type of <u>shraddha</u> a person has.

Shlokas 11-13: Motive behind Performing Community service is an indication of the type of devotion (<u>shraddha</u>) in a person.

Shloka 12: Note the main motivation is personal gain - not service; the desire is to show off, ego gratification and not humility.

Shloka 13: Lack of <u>shraddha</u> or low intensity of <u>shraddha</u> is the key, behind lack of order and discipline; behind lack of recognition accorded to other participants in terms of recognition, money-gift ("dakshina") and / or eulogy ("mantra"). Overall, such people engage in (public) activities without paying attention to detail of either process or people; they do not appreciate either; just getting it done somehow is their motto.

Shloka 14: People of Enlightened belief do worship divine qualities (i.e., gods), people of knowledge, teachers, and wise people; they keep clean body, mind and hygienic surroundings; they are upright; they are non-violent, have disciplined love life. These behaviors are also known as performing "tapasya" with your body.

Shloka 15: Manner of Speaking is an indication of the type of <u>shraddha</u> within a person.

Shlokas 17-19: Three different types of mindset stem from three different types of devotion or <u>shraddha</u>. Motivation behind "tapasya" or austerity indicates the differences in the three beliefs.

Shloka 20-22: Manner and styles of giving indicate types of underlying <u>shraddha</u>, devotion.

Shlokas 23-28 provide a recommended framework of behavior for the smart and wise. This is done using the holy Indian concepts of "<u>Om</u>", "<u>Tat</u>" and "<u>Sat</u>". Initially the Shlokas appear somewhat mystic; but as we tease through it, we find that there is nothing specifically religious in them. Rather these concepts are being used to describe mode and manner of working for success in everyday (modern) life. These Shlokas will describe the framework of performing "<u>sat</u>-karma", that is honest work for both personal and also for public good without gaming a system for personal profit. It is describing the desired behavior of the smart and wise and leaves a reader to conclude for himself/ herself which of the three beliefs power the behavior of such people.

Shloka 26: Meaning of "<u>sat</u>" - holy, pure, permanent.

Reading Aid - Glossary:

In several places in this translation, the original Sanskrit words have been retained to improve rhythm and to provide a halo of the ancient scripture. In the text all these words have been underlined. They are translated and explained below.

Brahma = A principal deity in Hindu Trinity who created the universe.

Sattva, Rajasa, Tamaha = Names of the three types of shraddha/devotion.

Sattvik, Rajasic and Tamasic = Adjectives indicating the Sattva, Rajasa, Tamaha types of shraddha respectively

Shraddha = Respect, devotion.

Scripture = Holy text; authoritative text which stood the test of time.

"Om", "Tat", "Sat" = Three holy sounds; meaning and use are in Shlokas 23-28.

Veda = Name of the Holy scripture; book of knowledge.

Yajna = Unselfish collaborative work for the good of a community.

Book - 17

Shraddha-Traya-Vibhaga Yoga

Arjuna asked...

Those who forsake rituals of holy text;
But yet do worship with great respect;

Sattva, Rajasa and Tamaha being the three types of devotion;
Which one is dominant in such a devotee's faith and persuasion? || 1

The Holy Lord Said ...

There are three types of shraddha, respect or devotion;
From nature in the mind are all these three types born; |

Sattvik, Rajasic and Tamasic names these three types;
Let me tell you their specific features without any hype. || 2

Enlightenment spawns sattvik-a;
Materialism dominates rajasik-a;
Ignorance do inspire tamaksik-a;
All are born in mind, make no mistake-a. || 2

In everyone the type of his devotion;
Flows from beliefs in his inner sanctum;

The type of devotion a man thus bear;
Truly shows his core beliefs all laid bare. || 3

Sattvika folks worship the divine for divine flavor;
Rajasikas worship those with money and power;

Those tamasikas, those ignorance-inspired wretches;
Worship ghosts, spirits and worse mythical creatures. || 4

Those persisting in great austerities without a scare;
Those defying customs and laws of social welfare; |

Engage in activities they do motivated by vanity and conceit;
Are those whose actions are driven by anger and lust to fit; || 5

Those who emaciate their bodies with efforts spent;
Are also emaciating Me, the body's real occupant;

Those unconscious of lessons and events of past;
Know you for sure are creatures of demonic cast! || 6

Their favorite foods are also of three distinct type;
They prefer community services in different stripe;|

Austerity of different types they do prefer engaging;
Also do differ in their styles of donation and giving. || 7

167

Shraddha-Traya-Vibhaga Yoga

With sattviki devotion one prefers foods nutritious and tasty;
To better life, strength, energy, happiness, and remain healthy; |

They prefer food mostly moist, not very hard mostly smooth;
Opt they not for foods overly dry that might chip a tooth. || 8

With rajasika devotion people desire foods extreme in taste;
Bitter, sour, salty, hot, dry, sharp foods they gulp in a haste; |

Many such foods they know may cause gastro disorder or grief;
But in a greed filled rajasika palette such foods will find no relief. || 9

People of "tamasika" shraddha gladly eat stale food;
Food from previous night which may be dry as wood; |

Food that may be rotten, may be spoiled, may even be cold;
Food part eaten or left unclean,
Gladly does a tamasika palette devour them, feeling quite bold. || 10

With sattviki devotion, a person serves the community;
Following proper customs and methods obeying legality; |

They do so not hankering for personal gain;
They consider it to be a duty and not a pain; || 11

With rajasika devotion, in service for public benefit;
Secretly does a person scheme for his own profit; |

With conceit and to show-off does he serve the public;
Their intention is to boost own ego, that is not quite altruistic. || 12

With tamasik devotion,
    Worship is done with little respect,
    Flouting of customs one can expect;

    Chaos prevails, details starve for attention;
    Missing are proper respect or recognition; || 13

With Sattviki devotion,
They worship divine qualities and knowledge;
Admire teachers, excellence, and wise sage; |

They keep clean body and mind and a healthy environment;
With love life disciplined, upright they are, are non-violent;

Such are the practices that are known as body-austerity;
Done with actions done by those with shraddha-sattviki; || 14

Their talk cause no anxiety in other;
Truthfulness is their happy tether;

Words of love for dear ones they always bring;
Through their chat the truth does always ring; |

Truth is what always they do speak;
Knowledge from chats they always seek;

Such are the practices that are known as speech-austerity;
Done with words uttered by those with shraddha-sattviki; || 15

Mind that is happy, calm and at peace;
Mind self-restrained, laconic with ease; |

Mind that cultivates happy and pure thought;
Is a mind where thought austerity is sought. || 16

Austerity practiced with highest devotion;
By men does also have three distinction; |

If the doer unties his desire from fruits of his austere action;
That austerity is said to be stemming from sattviki devotion. || 17

When austerity is practiced greed-ing for honor;
If done with hypocrisy aiming for power or glamor; |

When he ties thirst for prestige, power to his austere action;
That austerity is said to be stemming from rajasika devotion. || 18

When grasped by ignorance, illusion, or delusion,
If austerity performed subjecting self to affliction; |

When intending to harm others one performs austere action;
That austerity is said to be stemming from tamasika devotion. || 19

When motivated by a sense of duty one is giving;
Not viewing the giving merely as a favor returning; |

Contemplating time, place and quality of the person receiving;
Then the style of that giving is recognized as a sattviki giving; || 20

If the giver desires some reward in return of giving;
Or if grudgingly or unwillingly the giver does the giving,
Then that style of giving is recognized as rajasika giving; || 21

When one gives at wrong time or wrong place;
Or if the recipient is unworthy nonetheless; |

When giver has no respect or has contempt for the one receiving;
Then that style of giving becomes an example of tamasika giving; || 22

Brahma created the knowledge worker, visionary, the Brahman-a;
His edict caused creation of holy texts of "Veda" and of yajn-a Karma; |

The words "Om", "Tat", "Sat" were called up in the scripture;
He prescribed proper use of these holy words for the future. || 23

Therefore, the smart and the wise vouching by Brahma;
Do pray "Om" before engaging in a project or a "yajna"; |

And before performing an act of giving or making a donation;
And before starting an austere program within legal provision; || 24

Uttering "Tat", not scheming for any fruits, they keep on working;
They do keep continuing their charity and their acts of giving, |

Those seeking moksha, those seeking release;
Keep doing austerity and their <u>yajna</u>-sacrifice; || 25

Oh <u>Partha</u>,
"<u>Sat</u>" activities are done with honesty and with attention;
Done in the open they have broad welfare and application; || 26

In worship or in a project, in giving and in related austerity,
Remaining steady and focused is said to be a "<u>Sat</u>" activity; || 27

Dedication, giving, worship and austerity,
Performed without respect and sincerity;

Are all regarded as "<u>a-sat</u>", dishonest;
Never are or were they ever "<u>sat</u>" or honest; |

"<u>A-sat</u>" were not effective in the past;
Nor are they now, nor will they ever last. || 28

ॐ   *End of Book 17, Shraddha-Traya-Vibhaga Yoga*   ॐ

BOOK 18
Moksha Yoga

Attaining Moksha - Divine life by receiving liberation from agitation and sufferings of life.

Moksha = A state of freedom or release, from or oblivion to pain, worry, and the external world. Renunciation; salvation through the union of Atman with *Brahman*.
Yoga = Focused effort to attain a goal.
BG = *Shrimad Bhagavad Gita*

This is the concluding chapter in this Holy Book. This chapter is the final words on the knowledge of reality, the knowledge which can help a man to understand himself and to determine the right course of actions for a happy and successful life.

What is in Book 18 - Moksha Yoga

Together "*Moksha Yoga*" would mean the path to achieve liberation from the miseries and grief of life, the path to attain a blissful life through the practice of renunciation, tyaga. Often "Moksha" is also interpreted as the ultimate, last, or the farthest. That interpretation would also be a fitting title of the last chapter of this Holy Book. What is man's ultimate goal in life and how should he achieve it? Man's ultimate goal is (should be?) to attain Moksha, the blissful prosperous peaceful life free of anxiety and agitation and suffering? What should a man do to achieve such a life? This chapter outlines the path, that is the Yoga, to attain Moksha.

Bhagavad Gita is a very activist philosophy. According to BG, the path to achieve Moksha or bliss in life is through work or *karma*. Performing your *karma*, striving to excel in your *karma* (duty), and renouncing the fruit of the *karma* is Gita's prescribed path to bliss, path to Moksha. Realization that the fruit of an action is determined by the natural laws (spiritually speaking, by the Lord) and not by the desire or ego of the doer is a fundamental axiom (see Shloka 47 in Book 2 "Sankhya Yoga"). Realization of this truth about the nature of reality enables a person to overcome his attachment to the fruit of his action, of his *karma*. Implication? If a man does not perform *karma* in life, does not perform his duty to the best of his ability, he has no path to Moksha.

Bhagavad Gita forcefully dispels the myth that renouncing or abandoning your work/duty leads to Moksha. Rather it recommends forcefully and beautifully that the three *karma*s of "yajna", "daanam" and "tapaha" should never be abandoned. These are obligatory duties of every individual. These activities are necessary to purify the mind and for happy living in society. People should practice Tyaga. But Tyaga is not renouncing *karma* itself; Tyaga is abandoning the fruit of work done with full sincerity and thoroughness. Only sattvika tyaga bestows peace and Moksha to a person.

By Lord Krishna's declaration, *Karma* or Work is the ornament of a person; a man's work is a man's worship to his deity. Therefore, *karma* ought to be performed willingly, respectfully, and with thorough sincerity.

Man's *karma* determines every corner of his life. Though in popular language *Karma* is wrongly equated to destiny, in reality a man's *karma* in life determines his destiny. A man can enjoy a happy life or a broken miserable life, depending on what *karma* (work) a person does and how he does it.

From this point of view, Moksha Yoga is really a treatise on work. It lays out what components are needed to successfully perform a work; what mindset of the doer ("karta") leads to successful work; how work is to be done to create happiness and not end up in anxiety and frustration; why an individual chooses to perform a certain type of work; how/why that choice makes a man happy or unhappy; how society gets spontaneously organized into four classes based on occupational work; and when facing multiple options a man is confused about which path to take or which path to avoid where each option could alter his life in a significant way, BG provides a simple formula to get out of the crisis and choose the path of action to attain success and bliss (Shloka 66).

The purpose of this exhaustive analysis of *karma* is perhaps, that following these as templates, a reader/seeker would easily understand his own mental characteristics and understand why he has succeeded or failed in his life. With the aid of this knowledge, a discriminating reader will be able to solve the puzzle of his own life. And be on the path to Moksha if he so chooses!

This chapter analyzes all aspects of *karma* as if it is an anatomical object. Discussions include what are the components of *karma*; it identifies three main types of *karma*; what inspires an individual to perform a certain type of *karma*; it delineates three different types of intellect and endurance; and shows how intellect and endurance come into play in delivering success or failure in a man's *karma*. Altogether this chapter is a quite extensive treatise of *karma*. This structural decomposition of *karma* and interaction of various agencies (intellect, etc.) impinging on success or failure in *karma* leading to happiness or frustration is universally true.

Understanding this treatise, any man can look at the *karma* he performs (and has performed) in his life; he can figure out what inspired him to perform those *karma*; and he will be able to look into his own psych and see why he failed or succeeded in his *karma*. And he will be able to see that his life is exactly what is predicted by the *karma* he performed. This knowledge shows a man exactly why he performed the *karma* and correlates his *karma* with his present status of life. The detailed knowledge also helps him decide how he could change the course of his life by altering the underlying forces which compel him to perform *karma* of a certain type (desirable or undesirable). Understanding the underlying forces are important because only with the help of this knowledge a man can understand the mechanics of *karma* from its creation by him to its effects (happiness or misery) on him. The knowledge of the underlying forces can help him to choose wisely the habits which bring peace and prosperity; or persist unwisely with habits which prolong his suffering. Being equipped with the knowledge of mechanics of *Karma*, man can transcend the cycle of misery and attain Moksha, the state of bliss.

To attain Moksha, one should recognize and then renounce his own delusions about the nature of reality. Defining delusion as error in judgment, getting rid of delusion would mean removing one's wrong ideas about the nature of reality. The underlying theory (of Sankhya Yoga and *Bhagavad Gita*) is that our miseries and griefs owe their origin in our lack of understanding of the true nature of reality. So, by recognizing our delusions about the nature of reality and renouncing them we would surely attain a happier life, attain a blissful life.

A large part of the analysis in this chapter is based on the guna doctrine of Sankhya Yoga (Book 14). *Bhagavad Gita*'s thesis is that a man is happy when he works in a task (occupation) consistent with his gunas or mental propensities. It elaborates this thesis, which will help a willing reader to recognize his own gunas and engage in guna-appropriate work; that in turn would make him happy.

Further, this chapter shows how Guna-inspired choice of work (occupation) naturally gives rise to four principal classes in every society. Members of a society tend to sort themselves into those four classes according to their own mental propensities or gunas. This insight is true for every society in every age. Gita also comes out hard on the practice of making family/caste as the sole basis to determine occupation and class of a person. According to *Bhagavad Gita*, such practices are a violation of the natural (spiritual) law of guna-based doctrine of Sankhya Yoga. Societies practicing such violations are likely to slide backward in time.

When faced with a crisis, how should a man choose the right path of action if there is more than one path? Depending on his *dharma*, his custom, social rituals and religious injunctions, the man in crisis may face a multitude of paths to follow. But how should he choose the right one? *Bhagavad Gita*'s advice here is clear and unequivocal (Shloka 66).

Faced with such a confusion, a man should forsake all other *dharma*, all other paths and surrender only to rational intelligence and act in compliance with natural laws even if such action is not consistent with whatever path his personal *dharma* prescribes for him. This is the principle one should adhere to. This will remove confusion in his life and show him the right path to follow. Wholehearted adoption of rational intelligence ("Buddhi Yoga" in Gita's language) and acting in compliance with the natural laws of the world, is the right way to find your path no matter how deep the confusion is. In the spiritual language of *Bhagavad Gita*, this is the same as surrendering wholeheartedly to Lord Krishna, the Supreme deity.

What is the final advice in *Bhagavad Gita*? This is very well stated by Sanjay in the last Shloka of this Holy Scripture. Sanjay surmises that when superior knowledge about reality is combined with superior skill of implementation, victory in any project is inevitable. From such victory will follow welfare, prosperity, and peace. This gives the final formula for attaining bliss. Seek excellence in knowledge about reality; seek excellence in skills to implement your task; merge these two to your project and act renouncing attachment to the fruit of your action. You will attain bliss.

Looking ahead:

Shlokas 1-11: Book 18 starts with a deeply philosophical question from Arjuna the disciple. What is the difference between Sannyas and Tyaga? The question is clearly presented in Shloka 1. After defining these two terms BG comes out forcefully in favor of its activist philosophy asserting that "tyaga" that is, renunciation of the fruits of work done sincerely and honestly and never abandoning the work itself is the recommended path. It clearly states that work done to perform "yajna" (= collaborative work for the good of the community), "daanam" (= charity) and "tapaha" (= focused effort to improve knowledge and skill) are obligatory and should never be abandoned (Shloka 5). This paints a clear picture of BG's activist philosophy for a happy successful life. BG further categorizes renunciation (= tyaga) in three different types (Shlokas 7-10) depending on man's motivation for renunciation. It leaves no doubt that sattvic renunciation is the only one which brings unblemished happiness and success.

Shlokas 12–35: Taxonomy of Work

Shlokas 12-18: Here BG provides a beautiful analysis of work. The analysis is thoughtful and universal in application. Each Shloka is worth thinking about in relation to the work we do in our lives. For example, Shloka 12 delineates only three types of results a work can produce. Shlokas 13-14 show that work, no matter what work, depends on five underlying essential components: (1) Seat of the work; that is the environment and physical infrastructure where the work is performed; (2) Karta (=doer); (3) Varieties of tools; (4) Chesta = (efforts); and (5) daivee (= domain knowledge, experience). All these five elements are needed for successful work. To the egoist, to the conceited one, BG gives a clear message, one who thinks that the doer (the karta) is all that matters in the success of effort is a wicked fool (Shloka 16).

Shlokas 18-22: It observes that knowledge, curiosity, what-ought-to-be-known inspires man to work. In a taxonomic analysis, BG characterizes that the knowledge, the doer, the work themselves are each of three different types. By knowing this the reader can easily figure out what kind of worker (s)he has been, what type of knowledge he possesses or possessed and how/why it has influenced/built his/her life. This description is purely analytical and hardly spiritual. One can compare this knowledge with the knowledge we have in the modern time to determine its validity.

Shlokas 23-25 - Three Types/Styles of Work: As long as man is alive, man works; he has to. His work builds a quality life; or destroys the quality of his life. A man's work can fill his life with happiness or engulf it in misery. It is quite important to know how one should work; what kind of work needs to be done; and what should be our motivation in performing the work. How we can attain a happy anxiety free life we desire and we are capable of attaining. In the three Shlokas (Shlokas 23-25) *Bhagavad Gita* divides *Karma*, or more precisely styles of performing actions, into three categories:

- Sattvika *karma*,
- Rajasika *karma*, and

- Tamasika *karma¹*.

Shlokas 26-28 - Three Types of "Karta" (Doer): Karta, the doer, is one of the three prerequisites of *karma* (Shloka 18). The behavior and mindset of the doers are divided in three categories (Shlokas 26-28). Depending on his mindset, a karta has different probabilities to succeed in the work; and either enjoy peace and happiness; or suffer grief and frustration. In these three Shlokas, BG provides the template of the three types of doers. Knowing this, any person can easily figure out the type of mindset he has and thereby understand the reasons behind his level of success or grief in his real life.

Taking together the three types of karta, it appears that:

Sattvika doers are the happiest and most productive. They are not looking for personal gain; they view that their work is service to society (the organization). They are assets to the organization. They have high endurance and therefore are mostly failure proof. They are terrific role models for others. An organization is lucky to have such doers amongst them.

Rajasika doers are mindful about their prestige, power, fame (or lack of it) that can come out of the work, rather than the work itself. They are emotionally insecure; since they need flattery to keep going. That is why they resort to self-flattery ("aham-baadee"). Whatever causes a man to be emotionally insecure is going to make that person a Rajasika doer. He does not care much about the quality of tasks he is pursuing or has been assigned; he cares much more about the flattery he can receive. These people require high maintenance effort from their superiors or co-workers.

Tamasika doers are a drag, a burden to the organization. They are mostly low in productivity and knowledge. They are often failures in life and community.

Can a person transform himself from a tamasic or rajasic doer to sattvik doer? Geeta does not give a direct answer in these Shlokas; but gives a hint after several more Shlokas. Knowing what we already know, it is obvious that transformation can be achieved by awareness, faith in one's own self and by practice.

How to change yourself from wherever you are to become a sattvik karta? Reduce your attachment; learn the truth about the nature of

---

1 A reader naturally may ask: Does the type of belief a person possesses inspire him to choose karma of a certain type? BG does not leave the reader in suspense. From Book 17, it looks like that such is the case. If so, then one should change his belief (inner knowledge/view of the world) to change the type and style of karma he chooses to perform, to improve his life.

the world. Be learned, be wise, be thoughtful and be respectful about the laws which control the world.

Shlokas 29-32 - Three Types of "Buddhi" (Intelligence): To perform *Karma*, especially successful *karma*, man must utilize his Buddhi; that is, his intelligence (See the section on Buddhi Yoga in Book 2). Also, man must have fortitude; that is a man ought to be able to endure in his persistence to task/project in the face of difficulties; that is for success, man ought to have dhruti or fortitude (see Shlokas 33-35).

Shlokas 33-35 - Three Types of "Dhruti" (Fortitude): Dhruti or Fortitude is the mental and emotional strength which enables a person to face difficulty, adversity courageously. When a person fails in his attempt to successfully perform his work, he may feel discouraged. But it is his fortitude that can enable him to spring back to action from the state of sadness of failure. This is why fortitude is also the same thing as the ability to endure in the task with constancy of purpose, with constancy of determination to reach his goal. This mental quality which imparts the ability to spring out of failure and re-engage in the task is dhruti. Dhruti is a mental ability; it is a spiritual characteristic, achievable by understanding reality and by practice (yoga). There is no magic in improving dhruti. In these three Shlokas, BG defines three types of dhruti and their effects on successful works.

Shloka 36-38 - Three Types of "Sukham" (Pleasure): The word "Sukham" can be translated as pleasure or happiness or joy. In the context of the Shlokas (36-38), it appears that "pleasure" is the more appropriate translation of "SUKHAM". Following the guna doctrine of the Sankhya Philosophy, pleasure, that is Sukham, itself is distinguished in three categories.

Shlokas 40-48: Insight Into Social Organization: Based on the guna-doctrine of Sankhya Philosophy, in these Shlokas *Bhagavad Gita* provides deep insight into natural processes of how societies get organized and how people can function in it to achieve happiness and contentment. The insight encompasses the following thoughts.

(a)   Every individual in a society needs to perform some duties. Every society is an interacting machine of duties to be performed by its members. *Bhagavad Gita* classifies these duties into four fundamental types. (Shloka 40). *Bhagavad Gita* is an activist philosophy based on natural laws; no freeloading is encouraged; freeloading and happiness do not go together. Everyone has a duty to function in an organized society.

(b)   The gunas or more precisely the composition of the gunas in a person determines his mental propensity to a certain type of occupation. Based on their own gunas, different people get drawn to one of the four different types of duty, guided by their own mental propensity. In every society, the members of society naturally distribute themselves in four classes of duties or occupations. This is a universal truth. Shlokas 41-44 summarize the mental propensities conducive to each class of duty. (See also the table with Shloka 41).

(c)   Finally, it is asserted that when a person works sincerely in the duty aligned with his gunas, the person achieves happiness and success (Shlokas 45-48).

Together these Shlokas provide us the knowledge needed to understand the dynamism in a human society and also gives us the means to understand ourselves and our own role in it. It also gives us the key to enjoy a happy life which is to serve society by working in duties consistent with your gunas.

Shloka 41: *Bhagavad Gita*'s view is that society is an interacting web of duties of its members (see Book 3- *Karma* Yoga). For a society to function smoothly, different sets/types of functions or duties are to be performed by different members of society. These duties (may also be called functions) are divided into four basic types. These four types of *karma* or duty are named in this verse. These duties and their modern terms are described in the table below.

Bhagavad Gita's terms	Modern Equivalent
Brahma *karma*	Knowledge work - engaged in the exploration and diffusion of knowledge; Occupation involves a heavy dose of knowledge gathering, spreading it in the organization/ society; examples: teachers, researchers.
Kshatriya *karma*	Leadership type role in organizations; enforcement of law and order and defense; protecting the ethical people and punishing the miscreants.
Vaishya *Karma*	Activities to create wealth - entrepreneur, business (agriculture, manufacturing, service, etc.)
Shudra *Karma*	Work to support, serve people in other duties/occupations; followers in organizations;

Readers may note that *Bhagavad Gita* or <u>Sankhya Yoga</u> never says that the occupation a person should choose should/must depend on the occupation of his family or his caste or class. BG's advice is that a person ought to get into an occupation which is aligned with his <u>gunas</u> or mental propensities.

Readers may have also observed that the organization of every society in every age from societies in Europe to the Far East (China, Japan) follow the same mold - the population in each society divides themselves into the four classes defined here in BG. It is another testament of the universal knowledge embedded in BG.

Shlokas 45-48 - A Recipe for a Happy Productive Life: Simply stated BG's recipe is to PERFORM your duty; excel in your duty. Consider your work as worshiping your deity, whomever it may be. Don't ever look down on your duty - no matter how small others may think it to be; no matter how trivial it is claimed by others. Strive to excel in performing your duty. That will bring a man a happy and successful life. It is a simple unequivocal message for everyone.

Shlokas 49-53 - Who Can Excel in the Performance of His Duty?: What mental qualities will help someone to excel in performing his "*dharma*", that is in performing his duty. These Shlokas provide a clear prescription. Much of it has been described in many earlier places in *Bhagavad Gita*, especially in Book 13 (The Field-and-Knower-Of Field <u>Yoga</u>). The Shlokas in 49-53 essentially are a summary of those ideas.

Shlokas 51-53: If one aspires to attain the *<u>Brahman</u>*, that is if one wishes to understand the true nature of reality, one needs to practice some mental disciplines, which are described in these Shlokas. The description is pretty clear though quite succinct. These lessons are spread all through this Holy book and also summarized in Shlokas 7-12 of Book 13 ("The <u>Yoga</u> of the Field-and-the-Knower).

Shloka 54: There is no higher state of existence than being absorbed with the *<u>Brahman</u>, that is, to be one with reality, to understand the true nature of reality; to be free of illusion and delusions*. Money, power, sex, etc. are not the path to a supreme state of happiness. Craving for these ultimately ends in agitation, anxiety, and frustration. They never lead to lasting peace or happiness. Each person has to assess the truth of this statement through his own experience. The supreme state of happiness is to be one with the *<u>Brahman</u>* - to know the true nature of reality, to live by the laws of reality.

Shlokas 55-58 - A Prescription To Achieve a Life of Uninterrupted Bliss: Readers may note how nicely BG is demystified and comes within the grasp of our rational intelligence when we equate "Me" or the Supreme Lord as the deification of the natural laws of the universe; rather than some unknown inaccessible (non-existent?) entity beyond the natural world.

Shlokas 58-60 - An Ego Driven Life Does Not Bring Success or Peace: *Here is a recipe of how to overcome the difficulties in life and enjoy bliss: remove your ego and obey the divine laws. Apply intelligence-yoga in every aspect of life!* (Shloka 58)

One's *Karma*, the physical actions exuded by the body is the result of inner nature ordering the body to perform specific action. Swabhava, or the inner nature, is the commander. The motor function of the physical body merely fulfills them.

Here again Lord Krishna is alerting Arjuna to the futility of attempting to work against his inner nature, his prakriti (described in the previous verse). No matter what you wish to do when time comes to act a man ends up acting according to his swabhava, that is, his material nature (explained in the previous verse). To think that this is not so is a delusion often fueled by one's ego (Shloka 60).

Shlokas 62-72 - Finally – Surrender to the Lord – to the Laws of Reality: When a man is trying to find his path when resolving an issue, he goes through the deliberation of the pros and cons of different solutions. In spite of these deliberations, man can still be unsure of what actions to take. Ultimately, man must decide on an action. How will he choose the action? In this section Lord Krishna lays down the path to choose.

In simple terms the advice is "Surrender to Lord" and do what the Lord says. The next ten beautiful Shlokas are the summation of this advice. As usual in this demystified interpretation the Lord is the deification of natural laws, which control changes in the world. In short, think about your options in a rational way, then finally and wholeheartedly follow the path dictated by natural laws and rational logic. Surrender to the Lord means surrender to the natural laws. One should personally get above his ego and ego-centric view of the world, follow the natural laws to find his path of action.

Bhagavad Gita is not a book of some arbitrary, dogmatic ideology. *Bhagavad Gita*'s path is that of the rational understanding of the world and then making your own decision. It is not a path of unquestioning obedience to some doctrine. *Bhagavad Gita*'s path is not that of a conversion to its teachings by either favor, bribery, or punishment. Gita's path is a path of rational enlightenment about the nature of reality. Gita does not bribe anyone with some rewards in some afterlife; nor does it threaten punishment in a burning hell to convert the non-believer to its path. *Bhagavad Gita* spells out the nature of reality and grants the student (listener) the full freedom to choose his own path. In the world of scriptures of all faiths, *Bhagavad Gita* is quite unique in this respect.

Shloka 62: There is a simple message of hope in this verse. Ultimately man should seek shelter in "Him", his Divine Lord. Only through the grace of the divine Lord does one receive peace.

Who is this Divine Lord? The Divine Lord is the true knowledge of reality. When you have understood the true nature of reality all your pain and suffering is gone; you are enlightened and you are always happy. Ignorance about reality is the cause of pain and suffering. This is a basic doctrine of Sankhya philosophy and is captured in *Bhagavad Gita*. When you seek refuge in the true knowledge of reality with your whole being you are free from emotional attachments and consequently you are in the abode of undisturbed peace. That state of mind is the "abode of supreme peace". It is not a place like heaven or paradise, achievable only in the afterlife. Abode is your emotional abode where your emotions reside. Emotion could reside in sadness, fright, happiness, and joy etc. making you sad, fearful, or happy, etc.

When you have understood the true nature of reality, you know how it works. You have lost fear and anxiety about what may happen in your world. You are emotionally detached from the happenings in the world. Freed of anxiety – you enter the state of happiness, all stemming from the knowledge of the true nature of reality. This true knowledge is the Divine Lord.

Wholeheartedly one should engage himself in the rational understanding of the true nature of reality. That is how one seeks refuge in the Divine Lord. Gaining the true knowledge of reality one discards ego and other irrational myths as a vehicle to conduct his life. The result is that the person enters an abode of permanent peace, free of agitation and anxiety.

Shloka 65: How does one surrender to the Divine unconditionally?

Be devoted to the Divine, worship (act with reverence and sincerity) the divine; sacrifice your own ego and other pleasures for the sake of the divine; and be always respectful to the divine. Equating Divine to the natural laws which control every aspect of the world, the Shloka simply means be respectful of the natural laws; do not attempt to violate the natural laws. This is how one becomes one with the divine himself.

Shloka 66 - The Crescendo...: Literally *"Bhagavad Gita"* means a Divine song, or a song sung by the Divine. If the seven hundred Shlokas of this holy book is considered as one long song, then this Shloka (Shloka 66 of <u>Moksha Yoga</u>) could be considered its crescendo. In this one compact beautiful verse, the final advice is delivered to the truth-seeking devotee.

This Shloka is one of the seven most often quoted Shlokas of this Holy book. It can be interpreted at many levels. It is simple yet deep in spiritual connotation. There are many different interpretations of this Shloka depending on the accepted meaning of "Me", *"dharma"* and "paapa" (= sin). Depending on the context of use, *dharma* has many different meanings which lend to different interpretations. A full analysis and summary of different interpretations of the Shloka is quite beside the scope of this work. Here we will limit our demystified narration based on the demystified meaning of the terms *"dharma"*, "Me" and "paapa".

"Me", that is Lord Krishna, is a symbol of Divine excellence, of Divine knowledge about reality. Krishna is an embodiment of the laws driving the universe and its changes, including the beings living in the universe. The universe is law-driven and Krishna is the deification (embodiment) of the laws and the truths about the universe. The laws driving the universe are ancient, ever present, everlasting, ever immutable, yet unseen! They are not tangible to senses, have no physical form; they are to be realized through intellect! Existence of natural laws are manifest only through changes in the manifest world. This is also the definition of Ishwara, the God, the Divine! Krishna is the embodiment of such laws and truths – and is thus Divine; by this definition He is the Ishwara. When you surrender to Lord Krishna, you are actually surrendering to the laws driving the universe; you are leading your life in compliance with these laws. When you lead a truthful, lawful life – you are never in anxiety, you're never unhappy.

"Dharma" is code of ethical behavior. Following *"dharma"* is not necessarily going to a place of religious worship and singing the praise of some deity on occasions or practicing some specified rituals. *Dharma* is living your life ethically every day. Different faiths, societies may subscribe to different *"dharma"* and can be confusing. A seeker may be confused about which one to follow. Here in this verse such decisions are simplified. Follow only Lord Krishna! That is, follow the path of excellence, complying with the universal laws; forget everything else.

The broad meaning of "paapa" or "dosa" is defect, malformation, deviation from perfection. It is applied to a material object when the object does not look or function the way it ideally should. Commonly, sin is understood to be moral turpitude. In essence, sin is defective moral-ity. It is a "paapa" or "dosa" in the moral space, that is a defect in the functioning of the mind. The underlying assumption is that the mind or spirit is perfect when uncontaminated by ignorance; in perfection it works perfectly according to the universal laws.

So how does one remove defects from a physical object? By striving for excellence in building and maintaining the object? How does one cleanse "*Paapa*" or sinful actions, which are actually defects in the moral or spiritual self-manifested in behavior? *One cleanses himself by pursuing excellence in work according to universal laws!* This is the simple (perhaps the only) way. That is, you absolve yourself of your sins or "*papa*" by surrendering to Lord Krishna. When analyzed ratio-nally, all faiths will be pointing to this same direction.

In a materialistic way "*dharma*" means properties, attributes of an object, like attributes of a man. *Dharma* of a person could be simply thought of as his identifier, the set of properties by which he identi-fies himself. This includes his faith and beliefs (which can nominally be called his religion), his profession, his relationships, his values, his view of the universe, etc. The sum total of these properties consti-tutes the identifier of a person – which is also his "*dharma*". Based on his "*dharma*", man can often be confused in his decision. Should he or should he not perform an action? What if his action contradicts his faith or is detrimental to his attachments to his relationships or is against his own views about his life and his world? What then? Should a man take action or not take action? Which of the possible actions should he take? Such confusions are not rare; rather quite common. Faced with any such confusion what should a man do?

The clear and complete answer is in this verse. The answer is for-getting your own identifier (*dharma*), forget if your *dharma* permits your action or not, simply "seek refuge in Me, take shelter in Me". Now again who is this "Me" or Lord Krishna? Why should people of any faith seek shelter in Him? The answer is simple. In the demystified narration "Me" or Lord Krishna is the embodiment of the natural laws in reality which governs the Universe. He is the embodiment of the "*Brahman*" or the "reality". So, when we are being asked to take "shel-ter in Me", we are being asked to take shelter in the laws governing reality. When we are confused if we should perform an action, we should check with the laws of reality and perform according to the laws of reality or *Brahman*! Once you understand that you are on the right side of these laws, then you will have no other confusion. Actions must be performed according to the laws. Otherwise, misery will fol-low. So, take "refuge in Me", means take shelter in the laws of reality.

This is the only course that will save the doer from the emotional tug of war posed by different attachments.

Since _Brahman_ is reality, and reality is the same for everyone, the path predicted by following "Me" is of universal application. Contrast this to the paths specified by the "_dharma_" or the identifier of a person. These personal "_dharmas_" are very local, very person-specific, very attachment-specific, and often very faith-specific. Hence the path shown by the _dharma_ of different persons or communities can be radically different, causing a serious confusion in the mind of the person whether he is about to do a right thing or wrong thing. In the moment of a crisis, how does he know that he is doing the right thing? In contrast, the path predicted by following the principle "take refuge in Me" is based on knowing the true nature of reality and its laws; this path is free from the confusion generated by an attachment-based view of the world. See it in another way. When you are acting based on an attachment-based view of the world, you are actually working based on emotion and passion. When you are working based on your knowledge of reality (its composition and the natural laws), you are actually dispassionate and rational. Thus, by surrendering to the Lord spiritually, you are actually eliminating the confusions clouding your judgment.

How can following a path based on understanding of reality be free from defect, sin, or "paapam"? The question is what else can it be? Work based on the complete knowledge of reality and done in compliance with laws of reality is always free of defects, since defect is the other name of an incomplete understanding of the nature of reality and a violation of some law of reality.

"_Dharma_" or the personal identifier of a person could probably be the same thing as his ego. In the ego-based model, a person thinks of himself as unique, as different from everyone else, as someone special. Being deluded by ego we think that "we" are the doers of actions; we take credit for or blame ourselves for the results of our actions. However, in truth, the results of any action are predetermined by the natural laws. Always independent of the ego-based view and desire of the doer. By exhorting us to forsake our individual _dharma_ and take refuge in the Lord, the Shloka is actually asking us to overcome our ego-based views and actions and adopt the view and actions which are in accordance with the natural laws controlling the world. Actions in compliance with the natural laws are always the correct ones. That is forgetting your own ego (your personal _dharma_), surrender to "Me", to the natural laws. This is the only way to find the correct path and keep sin away from the doer. Following this prescription, one is destined to enjoy a happy, peaceful life while being active and of service to society.

This Holy Book started with the central question of what Arjuna is supposed to do while a great battle of tremendous consequence is staring him in the face (Chapter 1: "Arjuna-Vishada-yoga" - the yoga of Arjuna's Grief). Should Arjuna engage or not engage in the battle, which inevitably would cause the death of many of his near and dear ones? If he engages in the battle, would he not be responsible for the ensuing destruction? In his confusion he asked for advice from Lord Krishna. In this Shloka (Shloka 66), which is almost the last Shloka of the discourse, Lord Krishna gives the precise, unambiguous answer in the most beautiful spiritual language. The answer is to forget your personal identification and attachment-based attitudes (*dharma*) and emotional feelings. Simply follow the path laid down by the Divine Law, that is follow the path dictated by natural laws of reality. Most of the earlier section of the book actually discusses the nature of reality and the laws governing reality in spiritual language.

Shlokas 67-71 - Spread the Divine Message: These five Shlokas are really the closing section of Lord Krishna's discourse taught to His disciple Arjuna, the mighty warrior. He has taught the fundamental ideas of how to live a happy, prosperous life and how to choose the right path in life through this book, which ended in a crescendo in the previous Shloka (Shloka 66). Now the Lord makes one request to His very dear disciple. The request is: Please spread this divine message to all willing and respectful seekers. That will be a service to the Lord.

But why is Lord Krishna making such a request? It has been obvious throughout this discourse that Lord Krishna is laying down a path not only for the individual listener, but for society as a whole. This is obvious from the teachings in Chapter 3 - "*Karma* Yoga" especially. The reasoning is simple - one should not hoard truth or knowledge and claim monopoly over the knowledge and its source. Hoarding of knowledge is essentially detrimental to progress. Another more personal reason is that a component of a happy life is to associate with good honest people who like you believe in the divine knowledge being delivered here. By spreading the word about divine knowledge, you make it more probable that you will find such people around you.

The core idea is if you have learnt something new or useful, something that improves your life, then it is worthy of being spread to the near ones to help improve their lives as well, and to the society at large. To be surrounded by people respecting the Divine, who holds His teaching dear to their hearts, those who practice the Divine ideas (e.g., performing your duty the best way you can, providing unselfish service, surrendering to "Buddhi Yoga" and rational thinking, etc.), improves your life. In all areas of human activity this is a recommended approach. Give and share your knowledge and skill; do not hoard them. If you do not, you will live with ignorant, lowly productive, quarrelsome people worsening the quality of your life.

In most successful societies successful people often follow this idea in practice, even if they do not articulate it in the same way as was done in the *Bhagavad Gita* several thousand years ago.

We know that after graduation many students go on to teach their subject area to other people. Essentially, they are doing what is in this Shloka that Lord Krishna is asking Arjuna, his favored disciple, to do. Its indirect benefit is living amongst enlightened people of higher productivity. Once a person learns a new or more productive way of doing something, the enterprising ones develop new tools, machines, or services and pushes it to others for use. At the base of it, they are doing what Lord Krishna is asking to do - spread the knowledge! It will make a better society and improve your life.

The pragmatic Lord Krishna also alerts us with a word of caution. Do not waste your effort on the undisciplined disrespectful ones. Such people are unable to learn anything new. Spend your efforts only on those who are respectful, ready, willing to learn.

This is a service to the Lord; This makes you dear to the Lord; This is a service to the society.

Shlokas 67-70: The knowledge and teachings of *Bhagavad Gita* are not meant to be a personal preserve of one specific person or a specific group. Gita's teachings are of universal application and should be spread everywhere. But here Lord Krishna also draws a caution. Preach the knowledge to only those who are ready and willing for such knowledge. Who are they? In the next four Shlokas (Shlokas 67-70) Lord Krishna identifies the characteristics that make someone suitable for learning new knowledge in any discipline including the knowledge of *Bhagavad Gita*. If someone finds that he does not have the needed characteristics, he should strive to develop these qualities; or else his effort to learn the new discipline will be in vain.

This advice is true not only for those who wish to spread the words of BG only, but it is very practical advice in every sphere of life. A disciplined body and mind are a prerequisite for learning anything new. Do not preach to those who do not meet this prerequisite. Do not preach it to those who are not devoted or respectful to learning. Do not preach to those who are not willing to hear the content of what is going to be said; and of course, do not preach it to those who speak evil of the Lord or are indignant to the concept and content of the dis-course.

Note the Holy Lord is not saying that everyone must hear and learn this discourse. He is not saying that people must be converted to His teachings. He is not holding out a threat against those who are unwilling to hear respectfully, or who are not respectful to the teacher or the preacher. He simply says: do not deliver this knowledge to those who are not prepared for it or are unwilling to consider it respectfully. There is no explicit threat of hell or denial of paradise to those unwilling to hear this message. There is no encouragement to gain a "convert"!

Everyone's mind is not prepared for every discourse. Before you bene-fit from a discourse, your mind must be prepared or enriched enough to be able to accept, explore, assess the new material to be taught. If you are not so prepared, then the efforts to enlighten you with the new material will be useless. In academic terms, these conditions are known as "prerequisites". If you are to benefit from a higher level of knowledge, you must have gained proficiency with the lower level of knowledge or the prerequisites. If calculus is to be taught to you, you better have proficiency in its prerequisites like algebra. This is the idea being spelt out here.

Shloka 67: The prerequisites for benefitting from a discourse of new knowledge are spelt out in this Shloka. The prerequisites are:

(a)   People who are willing and able to perform "austerity" with their body and mind. The ill-disciplined ones or who do not believe in austerity to gain a higher goal are not ready to benefit from this teaching.

(b)   People who are not devoted or people who neglect worship are not fit to receive instructions to gain new knowledge. This means people are not willing to practice the teachings in their life. This is a form of lack of austerity. You do not neglect some-thing you love. You do not walk away from worshiping (that is practicing in your behavior) those things you value. If you are one of these people, then Gita will not be beneficial to you. Only those who believe it is valuable to them are the ones who will be benefited and should be told about this. If someone has no respect for the value and usefulness of physics in their life, they are not fit to receive the knowledge of physics, because they will not perform the austerity needed to gain understanding of physics.

(c)   People who are so ignorant or their mind is so unprepared that they are unwilling to even hear about it. Such people are not go-ing to benefit from this discourse. You should save your breath for some other person who is more prepared and is at least willing to hear you patiently on the subject.

(d)   People who are inimical to the content of the discourse, who are hateful and disrespectful to the discourse. These people may not be ignorant or may be performing austerity in their own way, but they may be disrespectful or be sneering at the discourse for a variety of reasons. Some of the reasons may be, they are proud, vain, arrogant and they feel they already know all that has to be known; being in a position of power, they may scoff at messages coming from people whom they consider inherently inferior. There could be a million other reasons. The summary is that if someone is hateful or inimical to the discourse and its contents, then better not waste your effort on deliberating the discourse with such people. One who hates physics (or any science) is never interested in learning or encouraging science.

We see that the four criteria laid down apply to all branches of learning, not only to the abstract, philosophical, or spiritual disciplines. Discipline, respect, devotion, and lack of hatred, that is, love at least to some degree, as evidenced by curiosity and sincere listening, are necessary elements to prepare your mind to be an appropriate receptacle of new knowledge in any discipline. Even an excellent teacher will not help a student who has no preparation in the subject, who hates and has no respect for the subject, and of course who is not disciplined enough to listen patiently and practice his homework and work through the assigned projects. The last criteria are spiritually known as "worship". Those who do not "worship" are the people who do not perform the services – like striving through the assigned projects and homework and other relevant duties. "Worship" does not mean rote-chanting some mantra a number of times or performing unrelated rituals (like praying to a deity, kneeling, or praying on a pew in a church or a mosque or temple).

This Shloka recognizes the need to be prepared in mind before someone can adopt a new and more sophisticated level of knowledge. One should not waste his breath on the unprepared ones. Note this is not an effort to "convert" someone of a different faith to this new faith by following some different rituals (taking a new name, accepting a different god as the supreme, etc.). The effort in Gita is to enlighten the mind to a different level of sophistication through a deeper rational understanding of himself and the world. This is not conversion, rather it is an enlightenment. This is why appropriate mental preparation is a prerequisite.

The preacher should not be upset if the willing listeners are few and far between. After all, in Book 4, it is said that only one in a thousand people are ever willing to pursue the path of sophistication; such is the natural state of the human mind.

Shloka 68: The "Supreme secret" here is the knowledge about reality revealed in Gita. The Supreme secret is truth(s) about reality, only the understanding of which can make man's life happier and more prosperous.

Obviously, to spread the words of this discourse (the knowledge about reality) is a very noble task. Making the effort to spread the divine message is a sign of very high devotion to the message, and through it, is a sign of the highest devotion to the Divine Lord himself. This Shloka is an encouragement to every devotee to spread the word of the Lord, spread the message of the path of happy and prosperous living to everyone, except of course the ones who are disrespectful, hateful, and unwilling to listen (described in the previous verse).

Understanding the message and practicing the message in one's own life is a very good thing. It leads to a happy and prosperous life. It is a personal benefit. The Lord wants you to rise above your narrow personal confines and spread the word to others as well. This would be an act of unselfish giving ultimately leading to a happier and prosperous community.

In any field of knowledge, learning the truths of the domain is a very important personal goal. But to spread the truth, making an effort to enlighten others about the truth is an even higher goal. To enlighten others, to reduce ignorance in others is a higher and nobler goal. The Lord encourages all devotees to do so. Imagine what the world would be like if the people who have discovered truths about nature (say the laws of gravity, medicinal properties of substances, mathematical theorems, etc. for example), would keep it to themselves and not spread it to others. The truths would die with the discoverers and the community would not progress nor prosper. Everyone would have to re-discover the truths, which would be a serious impediment to progress as a whole.

At a personal level, the advice is extremely rewarding. If you have learnt some truth, if you have somehow come to develop a new understanding about some aspect of reality, if you have removed some of your own ignorance in any area through some specific practice, then spread the truth, share the new understanding, share the new knowledge with people around you. This is a noble task. Its practical benefit is that you will be surrounded by more knowledgeable, better-informed people, which will inevitably lead to a better, happier, and prosperous life for you and the others you have shared the knowledge with. If you do not spread the knowledge, you will be living amongst backward ignorant people, which will definitely drag down your progress and prosperity. A knowledgeable person surrounded by hordes of ignorant people is like a fruitful tree standing in a desert. There is no one to share the fruit with. And sooner or later, the desert will erode and weaken the productivity of the tree and the tree will finally decay and perhaps die.

Those who are violating this divine law are actually laying the foundation for a backward, poorer society. This is the reason that societies which made (or makes) education the sacred preserve of a privileged few are bound to become backward and under-productive in time. There is numerous historical evidence in support of this statement. The cause of decay of Brahminical and perhaps Mandarin cultures in India and China, are direct results of a violation of this divine principle.

It is obvious that this principle is equally valid for societies and nations as whole as well. If a progressive nation is in possession of knowledge to better their world, is surrounded by backward nations lacking knowledge and know-how, then it is a recipe for turmoil. Sooner or later the prosperous nation will be balked down dealing with the turmoil rising from the inequity in knowledge and know-how among the nations. It is a much better policy to unselfishly share one's own knowledge for the betterment of all. It avoids conflicts and seeds higher prosperity.

Truth is not a personal possession; truth should not be made into a personal or communal possession. Share your knowledge with others unselfishly. Help relieve the ignorance of people around you. This is a noble task. This is what the Divine Lord exhorts you to do. It makes you very dear to your own God.

Shloka 72: This is the last Shloka spoken by the Holy Lord Krishna in this sacred dialog with his disciple. Just like any other good teacher, Lord Krishna is making sure that his disciple did hear the entire discourse with attention; He is making sure that the student's questions have been answered and the student has understood the content. He wants to make sure that the confusion and delusion in the mind has been cleared.

Shloka 73: "Achyuta" is another name for Lord Krishna. The word itself means "the unfailing one" or "the unchanging one". The Holy Lord is Divine. The Divine is immutable, unchanging throughout time.

The student is confirming that he has heard and understood the discourse. As a result, his confusion and doubts have disappeared.

It is by His grace, we can dispel our doubts and delusions; that is, we get rid of our erroneous thinking and get a view of the true nature of reality, which leads us to the correct path of action.

Shlokas 74-78 - Wise counsel and Conclusion: Sanjaya is the wise minister of the blind King Dhritarashtra, whose sons, the "Kauravas" are waging the great war against their first cousins at Kurukshetra.

The great sage "Vyasa " gifted the power of remote vision to Sanjaya so that he could see what was happening in the battlefield at Kurukshetra and report them to the blind King in real time. The entire discourse of *Bhagavad Gita* started with the King asking Sanjaya to report to him what was happening in the battlefield (*Book 1: Arjuna's Grief*). It seems to be poetically fitting that Vyasa has chosen Sanjaya to narrate the last Shloka of this great scripture and conclude with a wise counsel to the King at the same time.

The gift of remote vision enabled Sanjay to see and hear the divine dialog between Lord Krishna and the mighty warrior Arjuna in its entirety. In Shlokas 74-77, Sanjay first expresses his amazement and thrill at being able to see and hear this divine dialog. In the final Shloka (Shloka 78), the minister gives his wise counsel to the King.

The counsel is: Victory and success is inevitable, when supreme (domain) knowledge guides superb implementation. With such a combination, victory is inevitable; such victory will inevitably be accompanied by virtue, prosperity, and the welfare of all (Shloka 78). This is true for all battles, all challenges, all tasks a man will face in life. This could also be considered as a spiritual law[2].

Shloka 78: This is the final Shloka of this discourse spoken by Sanjay, the wise minister of the king Dhritarashtra.

Where there is "Krishna – the Lord of all yogas" means where there is supreme knowledge, knowledge of the true nature of reality and the laws which govern the behavior of the world.

Arjuna, the great warrior, is the symbol of a highly skilled person who is very competent in implementation of a task in complete compliance of the "yoga", the path dictated by the laws.

Taken together, the Shloka says when superior knowledge and a high-level skill is put together, then success in any effort is inevitable.

2   In this great epic, the story continues to show that the King did not accept the wise counsel of his minister, he did not stop the war; and at the end, the army of the Kauravas got decimated and all his sons were slain in the battle.

If you have the Divine laws (true knowledge of the reality of the domain) on your side and perform your task in accordance with those laws selflessly, dispassionately, without prejudice or attachment, then you will surely attain victory in achieving your goal. And that victory will be beautiful, full of splendor. That victory will come through righteousness. That victory will not be tainted by meanness, by immoral transgressions; and the result will be peaceful prosperous wealthy (body, and mind) living.

In one short Shloka, it prescribes the sure recipe to attain success and prosperity in life (in any project in life). The recipe is: gain as much knowledge of the path and the domain (laws and sequence of actions) as you can, that is Submit yourself to the "Lord of Yogas"; And execute your journey in the path (practice the yoga) unselfishly, relentlessly in compliance of the laws of reality. Victory, success, and splendor will definitely be achieved when superior domain knowledge is married to superb skill of implementation

This seems to be the final advice from this Holy Book. Is this not a very practical recipe for achieving success in any field for a person of any faith/religion at any time in this world?

Reading Aid - Glossary:

In several places in this translation, the original Sanskrit words have been retained to improve rhythm and to provide a halo of the ancient scripture. In the text all these words have been underlined. They are translated and explained below.

Amruta = Name of the divine potion for immortality, health, and happiness. By drinking this potion, gods in heaven have achieved immortality.

Arjuna = Name of the mighty hero; the main character in this dialog with Lord Krishna the Divine.

Bharat = Ancient name of India.

Brahma = A principal deity in the Hindu Trinity who created the universe.

Brahman, Kshatriya, Vaishya, Shudra = Names of four castes in traditional Hindu society.

Buddhi = Intelligence, more appropriately rational intelligence.

Dhananjaya = Conqueror of wealth; a pet name of Arjuna the hero.

Dhruti = Fortitude.

Guna = Mental propensity, attitude; (See *Book 14*).

Jnana-yagna = Deliberation, distribution, and diffusion of knowledge.

Hari = A name of Lord Vishnu, the god in the Hindu trinity; literally Hari means someone who relieves your miseries and grief. If your miseries and grief are relieved, what is left in a man's mind but bliss and happiness?

Hrushikesha = Another name of Lord Krishna.

Karta = Doer.

Kunti = Name of Arjuna's mother.

Madhusudan = Another name of Lord Vishnu.

Mahatma-na = Great soul.

Moksha or Moksa = A state of freedom or release from oblivion, pain, worry, and the external world. Renunciation; salvation through the union of Atman with Brahman.

Partha = Name of Arjuna the hero; it means Pritha's son. Pritha is another name of Kunti, Arjuna's mother.

Sanjaya = Name of the wise minister of the blind king Dhritarashtra. An important figure in the epic Mahabharata.

Sankhya = Sankhya Yoga is one of six schools of ancient Indian Philosophy. Sankhya is rational deliberation of the world of reality.

Sannyasa = Asceticism; monkhood.

Sattva, Rajasa, Tamaha = Names of the three types of guna, or mental propensity.

Sattvik, Rajasic and Tamasic = Adjectives indicating sattva, rajasa, tamaha type of some mental quality respectively

Tamasika = Ignorance, delusion driven actions and mental propensity.

Shraddha = Respect, devotion.

Tyaga = Renunciation.

Varna = Complexion, mental complexion; here means caste in a society.

Vasudeva = Another name of Lord Krishna, who is an incarnation of Lord Vishnu in human form.

Vyasa = Author of the holy epic Mahabharata.

Veda = Name of the Holy scripture; book of knowledge.

Yajna = nselfish collaborative work for the good of a community.

Book - 18

Moksha Yoga

Arjuna said:

I wish to know the truth about Sannyasa;
Also, truth about "Tyaga", Oh Hrushikesha; |
What is the difference between them oh Madhusudan-a;
Please tell me Oh the destroyer of Keshi the demon-a? || 1

The Holy Lord Krishna spoke...

Abandoning work but chasing the fruits of work;
Is Sannyasa! so do the poets hold; |
Renouncing the fruit but chasing dutiful work;
Is Tyaga, the wise men have told. || 2

Work always should be discarded,
Same as any evil ought be dumped;
    Say many many thinkers; |

But work of yajna, of giving and charity;
And also, excellence-seeking-austerity;
Not to be scrapped are these three ever;
Say many many other wise philosophers. || 3

Ok, hear you now carefully, Oh best of the Bharat clan;
Know My own convictions on what truly is renunciation; |

Oh, the tiger amongst men, know this about renunciation;
That Tyaga itself is of three types at its core foundation. || 4

Work of service, charity and giving, as also austerity;
Are never to be abandoned, each one is a holy duty; |

 "Yajna", "daanam" and "tapaha", holy duty are they all;
These three are purifiers of thoughtful mind and the soul. || 5

These tasks ought to be done;
That is in My supreme opinion; |

These ought to be done as if they are dutiful obligations;
Abandoning all attachments to the fruits of such actions. || 6

Renouncing work which really are duties obligate;
Such renunciation is no Sannyas, never appropriate; |

Abandoning obligatory actions on being deluded;
Is tyaga tamasika, so have the wise formally said. || 7

Thinking it to be hard and thus work abandoning;
Or from the fear that it may cause bodily suffering; |

Rajasika renunciation is only what he will meet;
Moksha, real fruit-a of tyaga never will him greet. || 8

When work is done discipline not shun;
Work is taken to be a duty to be done; |

And all desire for its fruit does the doer abandon;
That abandonment, that tyaga, is sattvika renunciation; || 9

Tyagee does not hate work even if it is disagreeable,
Nor is he over elated because the work is agreeable; |

He is filled with goodness and truth; he is the wise;
From him has been chopped away confusion and vice; || 10

No embodied being could abandon work completely, ever;
Never can one abandon work without leaving any remainder; |

Therefore, in whom craving for fruits of work has deserted;
Is the Tyagin who is revered, honored, and truly celebrated; || 11

The fruit of work is one of three in the end;
Desired, undesired, or perhaps it is a blend; |

Always does it happen to the non-tyagi in the end;
Never does it happen to tyagis even at their end. | 12

In Sankhya it has been clearly set;
That five ingredients must be met; |

In every successful action and karma;
Learn them from Me Oh my hero Arjuna. || 13

A Seat for the work, a Doer, as well as an array of Tools;
A range of Efforts, domain Knowledge unknown to the fools; |

Essential is the need of togetherness of these five element;
For the success of any work and for its ensuing predicament. || 14

Man acts with his body, speech or mind;
Actions are either logical or are blind; |

Actions are all caused by the five factors alone;
Nothing else is there on which actions do hone; || 15

That work has five ingredients being the reality;
One thinking that self is the only doer,
That the other four do not matter in actuality; |

Thinks so because to truths in reality he remains blind;
His understanding is imperfect, and he is of wicked mind. || 16

One whose state of mind is free of ego;
In whose intelligence ego is a no go; |

Even on slaying in battle all these braves;
If fame or greed is not what he craves;

Moksha Yoga

In reality does he neither kill anyone in;
Nor does he get shackled by grief or sin. || 17

(Taxonomy of Work: Shlokas 18-25)

Knowledge, curiosity, and the knowledge seeker;
Are three sources of inspirations for the worker; |

Tools, actions, and the doer taken all together;
Karma has these three as its constituent factor. || 18

Based on the Guna doctrine Sankhya makes it clear;
That Each of the three - the Belief, action, and the doer; |

Each of these is also of three different complexion;
Let me make these clear, please hear with attention. || 19

Enlightenment of knowledge spawns;
Sophistication in thinking dawns;

Sees one imperishable entity existing;
In all forms, formations and in all being;|

When sattvika belief shimmers;
A subtle realization then glimmers;

That One unique undivided entity is in eternal action;
Causing birth and death of all forms and differentiation. || 20

With rajasika belief in a person dominating;
The person views and keeps on believing; |
That Different rules apply to different being;
And no single law applies to all different thing; || 21

When by a type of knowledge, a man does get stuck;
To efforts meaningless, trivial but with it he runs amuck; |

That appears to him big and the only thing to be done;
Is declared belief tamasika ought be harbored by none. || 22

Obeying discipline, rules, and laws if Karma is done;
Motivated neither by hate, nor emotion nor by passion; |

Striving without greed for fruits of work, without rage;
Is work said to be "sattvic" karma done by a wise sage. || 23

But work that is done to gratify lust and passion;
When the effort is made after much persuasion; |

When such work is done with ego, vanity, and pride;
Are all examples of karma "rajasika" one cannot hide. || 24

Karma done ignoring fallout or consequence;
Without caring for any loss, injury, or violence; |

Work started one's own competence not considering;
Is said karma tamasika, done in deluded thinking. || 25

(Taxonomy of Doer: Shlokas 26-28)

Is free from staying stuck to results of his action;
Narcissistic self-speaking is not his passion;
Endurance and enthusiasm are his decoration; |
Success or failure in him cause no agitation;
Is said to be a doer, a karta of Sattvika description. || 26

Who is passionate, craving for fruits of his deed;
Who is greedy, violent, or impure in spirit indeed; |

Who is given to wild swings of mood in sorrow and joy;
Is surely known as a rajasika karta, of passionate ploy; || 27

Unengaged is a tamasik doer, crude and often vulgar;
Wicked and deceitful is he and obstinate in his manner; |

He is lazy lethargic often depressed and discouraged;
The tamasik karta will often procrastinate to the end. || 28

(Taxonomy of Intellect: Shlokas 29-32)

Qualities of intelligence and also that of fortitude-o;
Differ in men based on their guna inspired attitude-o; |

Oh Dhananjaya, hear their unique characteristics fully;
I shall explain them to you separately and completely. || 29

Oh Partha,
That type of Intellect which enables one to know;
When to engage and when to renounce or go slow;

What ought to-be-done and what should be shunned;
What is to-be-feared and what is not-to-be-feared; |

What gives bondage and suffering a foundation;
And what brings lasting peace and liberation;
Is truly "Sattvic" intellect in full action. || 30

Oh Partha
That type of intellect with which one gets incorrect feel;
What is ethical, virtuous and what is unethical or evil; |

About what is to-be-done and what ought not-to-be-done;
Is "rajasika" intellect on display, having it is not much fun. || 31

When one thinks an action that is truly non-virtuous;
But in his mind that is no doubt noble and righteous; |

When the mind takes a perverted definition;
To be the essence and correct interpretation;

Moksha Yoga

Know that mind is enveloped by darkness-a;
And that mind is displaying intellect tamasika. || 32

(Taxonomy of Dhruti / Fortitude: Shlokas 33-35)

Oh Partha!
That fortitude by which the mind and the breath;
And sensory and motor organs work together-eth; |

When all these are held firmly in yoga till success is attained;
That unwavering endurance is sattvic dhruti so the wise said. || 33

That type of fortitude, that type of dhruti;
That enables one to firmly hold on to duty;

But motivated only by the desire;
To cling to the fruits the work does sire; |

Only for the purpose of satisfying;
His passion and wealth garnering;
That is how rajasika fortitude is displaying. || 34

That dhruti by which dream, fear, grief, or fret;
Sadness, depression, and also deep conceit; |
Does not wither away from the one dimwit;
Is tamasik fortitude Oh my hero of great might; || 35

(Taxonomy of "Sukham" / Pleasure: Shlokas 36-39)

And now hear from Me Oh hero of the Bharata clan;
Three distinct are the types over which pleasures do span; |

By appropriate practice one enjoys pleasure and well-being;
And happily does he go to the end of misery and suffering. || 36

That pleasure which in the beginning;
Like a poison is bitter or unappealing;

But at the conclusion feels like Amrut-a;
The divine nectar of happiness and health-a; |

That pleasure is said to be "Sattvic" pleasure by the wise,
Born from the blessing of intellect of the self, free of vice. || 37

When contact of some objects cause pleasant sensation;
The pleasure that in the beginning feels like divine potion; |
But at the end feels like nothing but like poison;
That pleasure is recorded as "rajasic" gratification. || 38

That pleasure which in the beginning and in repercussion;
Gives a feeling of pleasure aroused because of delusion; |
That pleasure arising from sleep, laziness or confusion;
That pleasure is pleasure Tamasika, none should have any illusion; || 39

(Insight into Social Organization: Shlokas 40-44)

No one on this earth amongst women or men;
Nor even among gods and goddesses in heaven; |

May exist any one or any god who is guna free;
Born in material nature, gunas are only three. || 40

Oh, Scorcher of the Enemies! the work of the four Varna;
Of Brahman, Kshatriya, Vaishya as well as that of Shudra-na; |

Have been distributed among people in the society;
Based on the inherent nature of their guna derived quality. || 41

A controlled peaceful body and mind;
Leaving agitation and anger all behind;

Purity, cleanliness of body and mind, and also austerity;
Love for knowledge, forgiveness, tolerance, and honesty; |

Faith in wisdom and rational experiential ability;
Are qualities fitting naturally to brahmin's activity. || 42

Firmness, and ability to adhere to purpose and valor;
Not running away from challenge; loving skill and splendor; |

Generosity in charity, the attitude of lordship over one's station;
Are natural propensities of persons fitting "Kshatriya" occupation; || 43

Agriculture, animal husbandry, trade and transaction;
Are natural occupations for persons of Vaisya disposition; |

For people with shudra mental propensity;
Serving others is a natural cozy activity. || 44

(Recipe for a Happy Productive Life: Shlokas 45-48)

Being happily engaged in his own occupation;
A man attains both success and gratification; |

Contented with his own action and occupation;
Hear from Me how one finds success and perfection. || 45

From whom originate every being;
This entire world who is pervading; |

Worshiping Him with work occupation;
Man does find success and perfection. || 46

Superior is one's own duty
  Even though done with some imperfection;
Compared to other's duty
  Done beautifully well and with perfection. |

Performing karma dictated by his own inner nature,
One does not attain sin nor guilt nor any stricture. || 47

Moksha Yoga

Work which is "shahajam", is natural to one;
Even if it has defects should one not abandon; |

All undertakings in the beginning have defects as its cloud;
Just as in the beginning for every fire smoke is its shroud; || 48

(Who can excel in the performance of his duty: Shlokas 49-54)

When not to one single place is his intelligence attached;
Whose intelligence is free to roam and spread;
With conquered self, cravings in whom are dead; |

Actionless-ness is the supreme state;
He crosses through that final gate;
When this wise truly does renunciate; || 49

Oh, son of Kunti, now learn from Me briefly,
How having attained perfection successfully; |

One also attains the awareness of supreme Brahman;
Which is superior even to knowledge, which is wisdom; || 50

Reined in by intelligence clear and pure;
Disciplined by firm self-control to be sure; |

Ignoring persuasions of sound and sensory stuff;
Discarding passion and hatred, not feeling rough; || 51

Who has controlled his speech, body and his mind;
Consumes lightly, in solitude who is not hard to find; |

Always devoted to yoga and to meditation, never is he bleary;
Detachment is whose own happy shelter, his own sanctuary; || 52

Unstuck from egotism, force, and conceit;
Freed from pride, anger, and lusting fit; |

Staying unselfish, remaining calm and at peace;
One is fit to be one with the Brahman with ease; || 53

Who Neither mourns nor craves, nor is lusty;
One Who is peaceful becomes one-with reality;
To all beings who has love and equanimity;
He attains the Supreme, he is My great devotee; || 54

(Prescription to achieve a life of uninterrupted bliss: Shlokas 55-58)

Through devotion to Me, he realizes finally;
How great I truly Am, how great I am really; |

Then having known Me in truth through every pore;
He enters Me without any delay waiting no more. || 55

Moreover, even on performing all actions;
Always taking refuge in Me, in My bastion; |

By My grace and blessing enter they with ease;
That eternal imperishable abode of peace! || 56

Renouncing all your efforts and actions on Me-o;
In your thoughts knowing Me as The Supreme-o;

Taking refuge in the intelligence-yoga-ha,
Always be one with Me in your mind-aha. || 57

(Ego Driven Life Does Not Bring Success or Peace: Shlokas 58-60)

With your mind in Me, and by receiving My grace,
You shall overcome all obstacles leaving no trace; |

But if possessed of ego, Me you shall not listen;
Then surely shall you suffer, always and often; || 58

If or when taking refuge in egotism you delight;
If you resolve in thought that "I shall not fight"; |

That resolve of your will be in vain, will only be slight;
Since your material nature will enjoin you to fight! || 59

Karma is spawned from a man's "swa-bhava" his inner nature;
Everyone performs actions forced by swa-bhava, no mediator; |

If you wish not to battle, since delusion does your mind fill;
You will still end up doing that even against your own will. || 60

The Lord resides in the heart of every one;
Of all beings, Oh Arjuna the mighty one! |
Causing all beings to wander as if each one;
Riding on a machine by the power of illusio-a-n. || 61

Oh mighty hero;
With your whole being go to Him, seek shelter-o! |
By His grace you shall attain-o;
Eternal abode of supreme peace thereafter-o! || 62

This knowledge which is more secret than the secret-est
Has now been explained completely by Me to the best; |

After reflecting on it completely may your mind be set;
Whatever you wish, you do likewise to your very best; || 63

This is the secret-est of all knowledge;
Hear My supreme word for every age;

Very dearly do I love you oh my friend;
So, I say it again for your own good,
before coming to the end. || 64

Moksha Yoga

Be Me-devoted, be Me-worshiping;
   Be Me-sacrificing, Be reverential to Me;
Truly, to Me thus you shall surely come;
   I promise you; you are very dear to Me! || 65

Abandoning all other "dharma";
   Take shelter in Me, in Me alone;
I shall cause you to be released;
   From all sins, you ought never mourn; || 66

(Spread the Divine Message: Shlokas 67-71)

Oh *Arjuna*, do not share this knowledge with those;
Those who loathe discipline in body and or mind,
Those unwilling to perform austerity, leaving lust behind; |

Do not share this with those in whom is missing devotion;
Those unwilling to hear with respect and attention;

Those unwilling to hear, those who are vile;
Not to those who envy Me, or of Me who do speak evil; || 67

Who explains this supreme knowledge hidden and sacred;
Whoever spells out this secret knowledge to the devoted; |

He thus performs acts of highest devotion to Me;
Without any doubt to Me sure does he com-eth; || 68

And not among men there is anyone;
   Who makes me happier;
And there shall not be another one;
   Who to me will be dearer. || 69

And this Sacred dialog between us;
   Whoever studies with love and devotion; |
I shall be worshiped by him;
   Through this *jnana-yagna*, is My opinion! || 70

Even if a person hears this dialog sacred;
   Without jealousy and with devotion; |

Will enjoy happy world, is also liberated;
   Will attain bliss from this pious action. || 71

Oh *Partha*, has it been heard
   By you with undivided attention; |
Oh *Dhananjaya*, has it destroyed;
   Your ignorance and your delusion. || 72

Arjuna said...

Oh *Achyuta*, By your grace to me,